INSIDE APARTHEID

ONE WOMAN'S STRUGGLE IN SOUTH AFRICA

JANET LEVINE

CB
CONTEMPORARY
BOOKS
CHICAGO · NEW YORK

To FSL, RSL, TJL with love

Contents

Foreword

During the winter of 1986, I lived in the "salubrious" Johannesburg suburb of Parktown and traveled throughout South Africa, attempting with my husband to document apartheid in photographs and text. We lived as whites among whites, renting our house from a woman who still called Zimbabwe Rhodesia, billed us for silverware, dishes, and linens used by black guests in our home, and had once threatened a half-blind beggar with a spoon, telling him she would gouge his other eye out if he didn't leave her doorstep at once. She tended her English garden with care and doted on two apricot Lhasa apsos who seemed to her so much like offspring that she tinted her pale hair apricot. On Sunday mornings, Anglican hymns rose from the radio in her carriage house and drifted into our kitchen, scented with the cook smoke of meat grilled by blacks in the alley behind their "houses," which resembled toolsheds in the white backyards. In my diary, I entered my observations under headings having to do with common human needs: shelter, clothing, sleep, food, transport, leisure, and the like.

    On the subject of meat:

18 January 1986: We'd been given the wrong address for the house on Bristol Road in Saxonwold, but the woman welcomed us in to use the phone and offered us tea. "If you should decide to take a house and need someone, I have a man here, father of my houseboy, just in from Zimbabwe. An older man, cooks and does yard work. As he is mature, you would have to pay him 200 rand there 'bouts a month [then $100 U.S.]. And you'd have to buy his sack of mealies and the half pound of meat he gets each day. Be sure now to get the right kind of meat, servants' rations. And cheap tea. They don't like tea bags. And you'd have to provide one of those big metal pots. You mustn't let them take advantage. Don't let them eat from the table. Mustn't let them. They'll show you the right kind of tea for them, the cheap kind, bulk tea. And the mealies. Do let me know if you can use him, won't you? And stop 'round once you get settled."

14 February 1986: By late afternoon the tear gas lifted from Atteridgeville. One woman is dead and thirty wounded. The police have refused to supply the tear gas formula to physicians attempting to treat the women. In today's *Weekly Mail:* "I will never forget what I have seen. They killed my son-in-law in front of me. They cut his throat like a goat's. They stripped his body and left it to rot in the village. I was not allowed to bury him."

Estelle came by to show me the contents of her blood-soaked bundle of butcher paper. "This is the kind of meat the Africans eat. They cook it and cook it until the bones are soft. I'm making it for the dogs. You see, they also love it."

19 February 1986: On the cut stone porch two days ago at dusk, as I tried to build a coal fire in the braai and failed, one of Estelle's workers came over with wadded newspaper and a few kindling sticks, saying "Madam, please, I will help you." With his bare hands he lifted the half-lit coals. I must have reached for him in a gesture of caution. He smiled at this as he stacked the paper and sticks in a lattice of breath and match-light. "These are *kaffir* hands, madam, it is all right, [*Kaffir:* the derogatory name whites give to blacks.] They are not like yours. *Kaffir* hands. Feel no heat."

16 February 1986: While we were washing dishes, Dina said, "We African people, we like the same foods as you, all the same, carrots, apples, vegetables all the same. But white women will tell you to buy us only mealies and meat. That's all I had before, and if I wanted something like this pumpkin, I had to buy it from my salary. So I didn't have it very much. This is how you make the pumpkin: cut it like this, take the rind off, put it with brown sugar and oil on the top of the stove, and eat it when it's soft. The whites don't like us African peoples. That is why they say we will only eat mealies and meat."

By means of such vignettes I had hoped to discover something of the texture of white life under apartheid and of its effects upon the minority whose identity it was intended to secure—"the identity of all four-and-a-half million whites who were complicitly involved in this crime, guilty of the sin of commission," a crime Janet Levine is not afraid to call "genocide." She is also not afraid to point out that the program of "forced removals" in South Africa has "only one precedent . . . the removal of Jews (and others) by the Nazis to the death camps in eastern Europe." If this is true, then those of us who pleaded ignorance during the Holocaust or were born after it occurred are being tested again, and as Janet Levine admonishes, "No one must say, as they did of that other genocide, that they did not know." If our ignorance permits us to bear the unrelieved sufferings of black South Africans, then our intuitive or unconscious recognition of this would compel us to protect our ignorance, as the Germans protected theirs.

Such books as Janet Levine's *Inside Apartheid* do not further such protection. Rather, her work takes a hard look not only at the crime but at its perpetrators (white South Africans) and accomplices (among them, ourselves). It asks the questions we would be compelled to ask ourselves: if we had been Germans, or we were now white South Africans, what would we have done, what would we do, and what would happen if we acted morally and well?

The whites of South Africa have a culture very like our own; among them, white Americans feel, sometimes unnervingly, at home. We share with white South Africa the founding myth of an "unstoried, artless" land, uninhabited and awaiting our ancestors' claim to it, by right of covenant or might. "The land was ours," wrote Robert Frost, "before we were the land's./ She was our land more than a hundred years/Before we were her people." Those who lived on the land before European contact were relegated by white South Africans to servitude, the hinterlands, and, more recently, to resettlement camps. Those who preceded Europeans in North America were annihilated and their survivors confined to reservations (a fact I was reminded of repeatedly by white South Africans attempting to justify the actions of the apartheid regime). Beyond this founding myth, our histories diverge, eroding empire in distinct ways, but sharing always the bond of European whiteness and its assumption of privilege. In the United States, whites became the majority, and in their ascendancy suppressed the founding genocide and built a nation, partly on the backs of enslaved Africans. Abolition, a moral justification for the economic war between the industrial North and the agricultural South, and a by-product of the northern victory, "freed" the slaves and replaced slavery with a segregated system of servitude protected by racial laws resembling those of apartheid. When the civil rights movement successfully challenged those racial laws, the system of economic segregation remained so effective that the majority of American blacks have experienced an actual decline in their standard of living relative to American whites during the last twenty years. How many of us, as whites, have attempted to counteract this decline?

As moral human beings, we deplore South African apartheid. Our children build shantytowns on American campuses to protest economic investment in South Africa (although no one has yet begun protesting the cooperation of the American and South African militaries in defense of the South Atlantic). We are brought to tears during such popular films as *A World Apart* and *Cry Freedom*. How many of us would feel comfortable with the knowledge that in South Africa, among those opposed to the regime, our system is matter-of-factly described as "economic apartheid"? South Africans who have been to the United States refer to our urban ghettos as American "townships" and our Indian reservations as "homelands." The South African government itself invites such comparisons, in an attempt to establish its resemblance to other Western democracies.

South Africa reminds Americans of California, with its gentle climate, its mega-malls, multitheaters, health food shops, skateboarding children, and joggers (as Adam Hoschild has observed). But what are South African whites *like*? They are friendly, polite, reserved, hospitable, and dedicated to family life; they are concerned about pollution and the scarcity of quality day care. Some of them are quite religious, and many have become conscious of the role of fitness in maintaining health. They love their homes, their pets, their sports teams.

They are like us, and we are like them. It follows that we might act as they have acted, given their circumstances, to establish a social system that is the most serious attempt since the Holocaust to control the movements of a race of people and to engineer their lives so as to enslave the useful and destroy the others. (I refer to the "resettlement" program, in which millions of blacks are shipped to remote camps in the wastelands of South Africa, where they are not provided adequate means of survival.) We might, on the other hand, imagine that we would be among those white South Africans opposed to apartheid.

There are such whites in South Africa, an isolated minority of whites, who have declared themselves in opposition, and they are now among the most isolated people in the world. When I made their acquaintance in South Africa, I felt relieved to know that this measure of moral nobility was still possible among those of my race, for despite the realization that they had become superfluous to the cause they espoused, they were willing to risk acrimony, exile, and imprisonment on its behalf. While I had always hoped that I would be of their number, I didn't know anything about their lives. Are such whites *born* opposed to racial injustice, or is moral consciousness acquired, and if so, how? What is life like for them among their own people, and how are they received by South African blacks? What is their role—the role of white liberals—in the struggle?

Janet Levine is a member of this tiny minority within the minority of white South Africans. We hadn't known each other there. I arrived in South Africa a year and a half after she exiled herself to the United States. As it happened, I did meet some of her friends and heard the speeches of her colleagues in the Progressive Federal Party, before and after several of them joined her in abandoning "official" political life, having themselves come to her conclusion that "the days of the white liberal were over." During a few days' respite, I even glimpsed the South Africa she deeply loved: ". . . lost Africa. The fish eagle swooping for bream, the vast sea of floating papyrus grass. . . ." I had passed through the Karoo to the coast and had walked with my husband, picking up beach stones along the Cape of Good Hope, where the Indian Ocean becomes the South Atlantic and the world ends in the subliminal hum of southern hemispheric military surveillance.

"The true story of apartheid," writes Levine, "is not the abrogation of the rule of law by the apartheid regime or the declaration of successive states of emergency. It is the misery and starvation—the genocide—of upward of three million people who were 'resettled,' dumped in the rural hinterland of the country. They are part of the ideological processes of the apartheid regime's grim *social engineering programs*. . . ."

Several times during our stay, we managed to find these resettlement camps—those already inhabited and those still under construction. They are fenced and have single roads and single railroad tracks leading to and from them, maintained for the convenience of labor transport. Potable water is scarce and sanitary facilities rudimentary. The camps are constructed in geologic depressions, so they are often not visible, even from remote stretches of rural highway. Shelter either is temporary or consists of a platform on which to fashion a shack of scrap materials. In the more luxurious camps, the shelter is of breeze-block, and the houses, row upon row, resemble headstones. It is not uncommon for a quarter of a million people to be kept in a single camp, without official permission to leave other than for factory or field labor. The distance from urban areas, the lack of transportation, and the pass book restrictions (whether the controlling document is called a "pass book" or not) effectively curtail other travel. If the twentieth-century agenda was the Nietzschean will to power, that of the twenty-first might be the will for social control; what we are seeing in South Africa might not only be the intransigence of white racial supremacy, but an experiment in labor control by free-market capitalists unfettered by restrictive protections of the civil liberties of the labor force.

It was as a champion of such liberties that Janet Levine

became involved in the antiapartheid struggle, first as a student activist, then as a journalist, and later as an elected councillor. She was a member of Helen Suzman's famous "Houghton group" and a friend to Black Consciousness founder Steven Biko, whose life was celebrated in *Cry Freedom*. She served on the board of the first black-owned business cooperative in Soweto and worked at the side of black trade unionists during the earliest years of black union formation. What she has written is a woman's story of human suffering and moral conscience: a work of witness to poverty, hunger, beatings, detention, bannings, house arrests. It is a work of witness, not only from the white side of the apartheid abyss, but from within the isolated minority of white activists. It is also something of a rare document: possibly the first book by a former elected official from white South Africa, chronicling the development of social consciousness and its ramifications.

I first encountered her writing in *The New York Times Sunday Magazine* a year ago. Titled "Out of South Africa," the brief but eloquent article described her attempt to guide a black South African student to the blessing of an education at Milton Academy, where Janet, in exile, was (and is) now teaching literature. The student had been arrested, held in detention, and physically abused by police before efforts to secure his release and safe passage succeeded. More than sixteen hundred other children remained in detention at that time, most of them under fourteen years of age. Having met with the Detainee's Parents Support Group in Soweto, I read Janet's essay with great interest. Between the lines, I detected the spirit of a woman who might help me clarify my own South African experience.

I left South Africa precipitously, a month to the day before the birth of my first child, taking with me the diary of my life as a white in Johannesburg. As our requests for return visas were denied by the South African government, these notes were all I would ever have of white life under apartheid. They did reveal something of the texture of that life, as I had desired, but they contained nothing to explicate the larger fear that I carried from South Africa with me: the fear that came with the understanding that the antiapartheid movement was not about public toilets; that the struggle was not like our own civil rights movement; that we as Americans were nothing less than fully complicitous. The corporations and industries thriving in South Africa were our own, and the social experiment that succeeded at times in doubling profits was an experiment that could be repeated to some degree wherever bigotry, racism, and greed eroded civil liberties and human rights.

In late 1987 I was invited to speak at Milton Academy. These were (mostly) American children of the Reagan years, and I reminded myself that they were thought to be pragmatists rather than idealists. So as to avoid diversionary arguments, I planned to confine my remarks to events I had actually witnessed, attempting to recount them vividly enough to confound any effort to dismiss them as propaganda. If I had to describe an atrocity, I would try to do so without gratuitous elaboration. Perhaps the assembly hour would afford time to talk about consciousness and the idea that we are responsible for everything we see and everything we hear. In the giving of testimony, the witness begets other witnesses. I would conclude with the prayer of a Sachenhausen survivor: "I have not told you of our experiences to harrow you, but to strengthen you. . . ." My apprehension about this talk was intensified by the knowledge that Janet Levine was in the audience. I worried that she would find my knowledge of her country terribly inadequate, but as I stepped from the podium she took my hand in reassurance, thanking me for lending my voice to hers at Milton. We returned to her home and stayed awake until the early morning hours discussing South Africa, America, apartheid, divestment, activism, exile, and our shared view of the regime's "vast social engineering program." She spoke of a journey she had made to the "dumping grounds" with Len Apfel, a tough activist who rarely took companions on such trips, and never a journalist. *Inside Apartheid* opens with her poignant account of what she found there, and to her unspoken question regarding her work in self-exile, Len Apfel offered: "Someone will have to write about it all, you know." Only a few people in the world can tell this particular story. We are fortunate that Janet Levine has done so with such candor and courage.

Carolyn Forche
Wellesley, Massachusetts
September 1988

Acknowledgements

I would like to convey my thanks, appreciation, and deep feelings to those whose place in my life has made this book happen:

Sandy, who in being himself has been constant and supportive and loving in all of this.

Roger, whose quiet understanding undergirded all my efforts.

Tony, whose enthusiasm and confidence buoyed me over many rough patches.

Eileen Berman, my mother, believed I could from when I was six or seven, and for that alone this book is partly hers too.

And my mother-in-law, Lydia Levine, has been loyally supportive and tireless in my requests for help with material in South Africa.

June Wilson Jones remains "an ever-fixed mark" for me "whose worth's unknown" although her "height be taken."

Annah Kelefetswe, dependable correspondent now, indispensable companion then.

And to Philip and Pam, Irene, Sam, Clive B., Carolyn—believers all—you will never know what your just being there has meant to me.

Florence Ladd, Rose Moss, Alan Sheldon—my deepest thanks for reading the manuscript and giving so unstintingly of your advice and ideas.

Guy Hughes, my department head at Milton Academy, has been encouraging and understanding in so many instances, not only to me but to all my family. My agent, Helmut Meyer, has understood and nurtured me; and my editors at Contemporary, Ilyce Glink and Chris Benton, tried to make me say much of what I wanted to remain unsaid and succeeded in good measure, which has undoubtedly enhanced the book. Their guidance is deeply valued.

This book is a highly subjective (as all autobiographical memoir writing inevitably has to be) expression of memories, events, thoughts, reflections: a pastiche of things South African, as this native South African lived and saw them. For the millions of other South Africans who lived them with me, and for my dearly beloved motherland—we will overcome, we will prevail.

Milton, Massachusetts
1988

Prologue

It is not easy to be a liberal inside apartheid. I came to realize that in fact it is a paradoxical state of being. For although I lived my life in South Africa in resistance to this abhorrent system of racial oppression, by being white I was nonetheless a part of it. Yet the white apartheid regime called me a radical, "a sickly pink humanist," even a danger to the state, while latterly many black activists have called me and other liberals like me irrelevant. It is not enough to hate apartheid, they say. You have to be black to be oppressed, to be a part of the struggle.

The depth of my outrage toward the white racist madmen inside apartheid will not let me accept the black nationalists' argument, but I can see how pallid white liberalism looks from their perspective. For what I believe in and have always believed in, the great humanistic liberal values based on individual rights—human rights, civil rights, justice, equality, habeas corpus, universal franchise—I know to be of little value to those, then and now, black and white, who are driven by a narrow chauvinism.

How does a liberal white South African oppose apartheid?

Or the virulent form of black nationalism apartheid has spawned?

Apartheid is profoundly, deeply unjust; it is corrupt and corrupting; it compromises humanity; it makes life lived within its all-encompassing web a liaison with complicity and contradiction. What does one do if one is a white liberal?

I spent my life in South Africa trying to answer that question, living out my defiance.

For twenty-two years prior to my self-exile to Boston, U.S.A., in August 1984, I lived a life of activism in South Africa, primarily through professional politics and political journalism. For most of those years I concentrated my political energies on the party political process, on the white political arena, on confronting the apartheid regime within its own apartheid structures.

Elected public office gave me a platform and access to a mass audience of South Africans. I strived to use the opportunity well for the liberalism I espoused.

Looking back, I recognize sadly that liberalism began to lose its value in South Africa somewhere around the events of Soweto '76, when the country crossed a great divide, moving from white oppression with sporadic outbursts of black resistance to the rapid growth of a raging black nationalism and a heating up of the ongoing civil war.

I was there when Soweto erupted in June 1976, documenting what with hindsight I see were the seeds of the current civil war. The wounds of Soweto '76 can never heal.

From that time it seemed increasingly obvious to me that the liberal's role—to lead protest and push for change—was becoming less and less effective in opposing apartheid. The tide of black nationalism, cresting in waves of revolutionary activism, challenged apartheid in a way liberalism never could.

These waves shrank the middle ground of liberalism; the opposing forces of white racism and black nationalism eroded it away.

In this context I felt my political role lose its meaning and relevance. But I became increasingly convinced of the validity of my role as a writer, a journalist, a witness bearer. Indeed, I came to realize that bearing witness to apartheid and the civil war it had created was among the most important political acts of all.

But I found I could not write as I wanted to while living in South Africa. I was too involved as an activist, too much a participant in the political drama. I needed distance and space. I needed to be physically inaccessible, unable to respond to requests to engage myself, to be part of the political process—requests I knew I would be unable to deny.

The need to stand back, to see the wood for the trees, was one of my principal motivations for choosing self-exile, for agreeing with Sandy, my American-born husband, that 1984 was a good time for him to take his family "home."

It has been a long road that has brought me to this point. Unencumbered now by the demands of public office and commitment, I feel able to bear witness to what I have seen, to what I am still seeing. I can now write about the demise of liberalism in South Africa caused by the clash of competing nationalisms; I can write about the apartheid that tears asunder my wild, magnificent, seductive motherland.

The true story of apartheid is not the abrogation of the rule of law by the apartheid regime or the declaration of successive states of emergency. It is the misery and starvation—the genocide—of upward of three million people who were "resettled," dumped in the rural hinterland of the country. They are part of the ideological processes of the apartheid regime's grim social engineering programs, programs designed to divide the country into racially separate areas. The true story of apartheid is the story of chilling racial madness.

Thus I begin my story with a journey—a journey into the belly of the apartheid beast.

CHAPTER 1
The Dumping Grounds

My journey began on the verandah of Jean Graham's home in Parktown, Johannesburg. It was a midsummer afternoon in January 1984.

"You should come to see for yourself."

"I'd love to. Could I come with you on a trip? Venda, the far north? I'd like to see the extent of the drought, some of the more remote 'resettlement' areas. And, of course, the work you're doing."

Len Apfel, short, all but bald, with a ruddy complexion and sympathetic blue eyes behind his glasses, pushed his nondescript straw hat to the back of his head. (It was a gesture I was to come to know well.) He scratched his seventy-three-year-old pate.

"It's rough, you know—hot this time of year, no luxuries."

"Suits me fine. I've roughed it before."

"There won't be much room. Mary's coming, and we'll be loaded to the roof with milk powder. There're only two seats in the van. But if you don't mind, we've done it before—made a seat out of a bag of milk powder and some cushions."

"I don't mind at all. Will Mary mind if I come?"

"No, she likes you—heard you speak once, thinks you're brave
. . ."

"Okay, great. When's this trip likely to be?"

"Probably sometime in February—a week?"

Jean Graham, a mutual friend, came back to the verandah
with drinks. "You're honoured," she said to me. "I've been
asking him to take me on a trip for years, but he never has."

Len blushed. I winked at him. Tough as teak she may be
inside, but delicately attractive, English rose Jean Graham in
the Venda bush in February was an image that did not come
easily to mind.

In fact over the years Len had taken only a handful of people
with him—a few carefully chosen fellow travellers. And never
a journalist.

We drank a toast to the trip—an unlikely trio. There has
never been anyone quite like Len or, for that matter, Jean. And
me.

Our departure day arrived, the dawn bright and cloudless. It
was already hot outside at six o'clock in the morning. Len
arrived in the van and shook Sandy's hand. Sandy squeezed my
overnight bag into a crevice among the hundred-pound bags of
milk powder. He had mixed feelings about my going on this
trip.

"Where can I get hold of you?"

"You can't. Len says it's easier for me to phone you. Don't
worry, I'll phone when I can."

Len drove us through the quiet, early Sunday morning
streets to Bryanston, where Mary Hanna lived. The drought
was in its third year, and the usually magnificent Johannesburg suburban gardens were looking brown and dry, despite
the many boreholes drilled in recent months to overcome the
two-year-long municipal watering restrictions.

Mary Hanna and her husband, Tony, were waiting for us.
Tony put a small overnight bag for Mary and a large Styro-
foam cooler box into the van. Mary took over the driver's seat. I
wedged myself back onto my makeshift seat, and Len sat
beside me. I liked Mary instantly. Slightly older than I, with a
short cropped haircut and a lilting Welsh accent, she seemed
down-to-earth and handy.

"Drive carefully." Tony Hanna waved to us as we went through the gateposts. Mary and Len were business partners, and she served as chairman of Save the Children Fund, an international organisation for the welfare of children. Together they ran Imqualife—"a better life"—an enterprise that each month provided high-protein products (mainly milk powder) at subsidised prices to over half a million desperate black people living in the rural areas of South Africa. With Len as my guide, I was going to see the rural "dumping grounds" for myself.

Our route took us through the outskirts of Pretoria, thirty-five miles from Johannesburg, and then through Hamanskraal, another thirty miles north. The farther we went, the hotter it became. The veld had been devastated by the drought, with grass sparse and trees stunted. The miles of mealie (maize) fields, too, showed evidence of the drought: only those areas that had been irrigated were green. I had time for reflection. I was truly apprehensive. In my heart of hearts I did not want to see at first hand the horror of the genocide the dumping grounds meant. I did not want to accept the reality of the direction apartheid racism had taken, to witness this outrage against humanity engineered in the name of "securing white identity." Inadvertently, my identity too, the identity of all four-and-a-half million whites who were complicitly involved in this crime, guilty of the sin of commission.

Already, over the last five years, I had seen several of the camps. Winterveld, an urban slum of about seven hundred thousand people about twenty miles west of Pretoria, was one. Aside from a single tarred road for a bus service that accommodated the labour needs of neighbouring white industries, and a police station, Winterveld has no infrastructure. Water is sold by the bucket, for the water supply is polluted by the pit latrines. Cholera and other waterborne diseases are rife. The people were moved here when black housing development was frozen by the authorities in nearby townships.

I had also seen Crossroads, perhaps the most famous resettlement camp, because of the brave defiance of the residents in resisting the persecution of the police in successive attempts to tear down and destroy their crude makeshift shacks. Despite the efforts of the residents and public support groups in Cape Town, Crossroads remains a festering sore of malnutrition, infant mortality, and dire poverty.

I had seen Rooigrond, in the western Transvaal near Lichtenburg. The people there had been uprooted from their ancestral home in Machaviestad near Potchefstroom in 1971. They were told it was a temporary move. They were given tin toilets, tents, corrugated iron shacks. The area is arid and thorny, the only water supply from one windmill. The people have done little to build homes and improve their living conditions; they still believe the move is temporary. They are apathetic and despairing.

I had seen Dimbaza in the Eastern Cape, Limehill in Natal, Mdantsane near East London—reservoirs of what the government calls "surplus people." And there are hundreds of other resettlement camps. But I had never before had the opportunity to go north, to what Len calls the "real thing."

On our journey that first morning he had told me of what he had seen on one of his most recent trips. "I was in Kwa-Ndebele, another 'homeland,' another reservoir of desperation. At Philadelphia Hospital near Groblersdal I saw appalling evidence of rampant malnutrition. The hospital smelt of rotting flesh—even I couldn't stand it. Forty children in a ward for twelve, lying under cots and on the floor, all emaciated, most with blobs of white flesh where their eyes had been. A shortage of doctors, the administrator said. But when Philadelphia Hospital was run by mission staff, it was excellent. Such government restrictions now . . . no money for staff, for equipment, and with the drought the need is threefold." Len had shaken his head and made a rare political judgement. "Apartheid critics are right, you know. Dumping people in the homelands is genocide."

And now I was to see that genocide for myself. Like Marlow I was journeying to find my own Kurtz deep in South Africa's heart of darkness.

By ten o'clock we made our first stop for a cup of tea at Nylstroom, about a hundred miles north of Johannesburg. Nylstroom was named by the early Trekkers after the great

Nile River in North Africa. A century and a half ago, after months in the wilderness, they had thought they had found the source of the Nile.

The heat beat down on us, and even the grass had given up here. The veld was naked. Raw wisps of last year's grass stalks hung tenaciously to the dusty soil.

At the roadside café parking lot where we stopped (we drank our tea from Mary's thermos flask while standing at our van) we saw a few burly farmers dressed in the customary khaki shirts and shorts, their skin burnt to a ruddy bronze hue. They hurried in and out of the café with *Rapport*, the largest-circulation Afrikaans-language Sunday newspaper. In their "bakkies," small pickup vans, sat their wives in demure floral dresses, some wearing Sunday-best hats for church. A black man desultorily swept the dust from the slate stone entrance to the café; a cluster of black women in the highly coloured traditional dress spoke earnestly while sitting in the dust outside. It was a scene you could have found anywhere in the rural areas of South Africa on any Sunday morning.

Then we were driving north through Naboomspruit (Baobab Spring) in the far north. This is a stronghold of Afrikaner conservatism, the stamping ground of Andries Treurnicht, Jaap Marais, and other reactionary visionaries of the white right wing who during the jolt to the right in the whites-only election of May 1987 had become the official opposition in the whites-only Parliament.

In South Africa's political lexicon, President Pieter Botha's party, which has made up the South African government since 1948, is called the National Party—the Nationalists or Nats. The Nats being conservative in the extreme, it is hard to imagine a political grouping to the right of them, but there is such a group. They—Treurnicht, Marais, and others—call themselves the Conservative Party, and they are currently the fastest-growing political movement among white South Africans. Their ranks include a neo-Nazi cadre, complete with a three-legged swastika emblem and a body of storm troopers. Eugene Terre Blanche (he acquired that surname, which in Afrikaans can be translated as White Earth) is the strident leader of this neo-Nazi grouping, which decries Botha and his party for wanting to "give away South Africa to the blacks." They vow to fight to the death to protect their white "birthright." Botha and his henchmen are watching with apprehension the growth of this far-right movement as it eats into their traditional support—diehard white nationalists. It is interesting to note that in the apartheid regime's crackdown on antiapartheid groups in February 1988 seventeen black organisations were banned, but no white right-wing activists. Yet Terre Blanche's Afrikaner Weerstandbeweging (Afrikaner Resistance Movement) outside of Parliament and Treurnicht's Conservative Party inside of Parliament are avowedly and outspokenly opposed to Botha and what they call his "reform-prone" National Party.

White farmers in the far north use women from the resettlement camps as labour. They pay them about thirty rand ($20) a month and a bag of maize meal. On my journey, I saw in the early mornings several trucks packed tightly with women being transported from the arid "homeland" areas to the irrigated green farms. Sometimes the two were on either side of a road.

About fifty miles past Naboomspruit we swung left, off the highway onto a minor road. We were travelling west into the southwest corner of the "homeland" of Lebowa. A turn onto a pitted sand road took us into the northern Transvaal bushveld. The grass was sparse and dry, but the drought-resistant acacia trees were thriving. The bright green of their tiny leaves on umbrella-shaped branches was in sharp contrast to the browns and greys of the bush.

"St. Brendan's"—the iron letters on the arch over the entrance appeared suddenly. Our second stop, St. Brendan's Mission, Dwarspruit (Lost Spring), was a school and a bush clinic in the dry Lebowa scrub.

The two Irish nuns who ran the clinic were still at Sunday Mass with five hundred black schoolchildren. While waiting for them, Mary and I wandered through the clinic. It was housed in a small, old farmhouse with thick walls, a rusted corrugated-iron roof, and a wide verandah. The building was a weathered grey, in keeping with the surrounding dry bush and the dusty sand.

A black nurse greeted Mary and offered to escort us. The clinic attended to thirty-eight thousand patients a year, the same number as would be attended to in a small city hospital with a full staff and modern equipment. Here there was no doctor, and the staff consisted of two nuns and the local assistants they had trained. The equipment was antiquated and makeshift. The clinic was scrubbed clean, but it was in need of repair—walls, ceilings, windows, paint. In a room crowded with mattresses, about forty women, all in advanced stages of pregnancy, waited, sometimes for days, we were told, for the onset of labour. They stared dully at us, a helplessness in their demeanour, many with small infants pulling at them. In the postnatal room, shining clean, tiny newborn babies slept in cardboard boxes lined with worn blankets.

Outside, in front of an adjoining building, six young children played listlessly in the sand. They were "kwash" patients, their hair tinged red, staring eyes huge and vacant, and limbs stick-thin. Not even my crouching on my knees to photograph them elicited a response. Looking at them, I was reminded of a scene Len had described to me: "I saw my first case of kwashiorkor in a church in the Potgietersrus district. A mother and daughter sat next to me. The child looked all right, with fat, shiny cheeks. She held an orange in her hand. But she just stood there—beautifully dressed for church—stood with her orange, her face expressionless. She was a vegetable. It was such a shock to me. I thought she was about six years old, but her mother told me she was ten."

Kwashiorkor is the name given to malnutrition in South Africa. It is rife in the rural areas; almost every black child suffers from it to some degree. In severe kwash cases the lack of protein retards mental growth, growth that can never be regained—part of the pattern of genocide in the "homelands."

Like much else in the apartheid regime's own brand of double-talk, the "homelands" is an insensitive misnomer. The people who are forcibly removed to the "homelands" are unwilling and impotent victims of a grand apartheid design, made law in the early 1970s. The intent of the design, the "removals," is to divide South Africa into racially separate areas with 80 percent of the land remaining in the hands of 13 percent of the population, the whites. The process of the design, "resettlement," involves a huge bureaucratic network that spans the country. The "homelands" are the most barren and inhospitable areas, the majority of them located in an archipelago stretching across the northern and eastern reaches, islands of blacks in a sea of whites.

Since 1975, upward of three million people have been uprooted in a system of social engineering that has only one precedent on this scale—the removal of Jews (and others) by the Nazis to the death camps in eastern Europe in the late thirties and early forties. The Nazis formulated a short-term solution to their Jewish "problem"; the apartheid regime has designed a scheme of long-term genocide: the slow death by starvation of the people in the "homelands," while they are barely able—and sometimes simply unable—to eke out their own subsistence.

The "homelands" sprawl over a dry, dusty landscape peopled by the old and disabled, the women and small children—emaciated, dispirited, hopeless. They are the "surplus people," all those who serve no purpose in the white economy.

Near St. Brendan's we stopped so that I could speak to an old woman gathering low-growing dry grass stalks about twenty yards from the sand road. I raised my hand in greeting as she straightened up from her task to look at me. She raised her hand back at me. She wore a faded and worn shirt many sizes too big for her and a large piece of cloth wrapped around her emaciated frame. Her long, bony feet were bare, and her arms were spindle-thin.

"Ngogo," I addressed her in the only formal, respectful greeting I knew for an older woman, although I knew it to be a Zulu word and she probably spoke SeSotho. But this greeting brought a smile to her leathery, lined face. She had only a couple of teeth, but her dark brown eyes set deeply in her wrinkled face were not dull. I pointed to the small pile of grasses at her feet.

"What is that? What do you do with that?"

By now Len had joined me, and he translated as she spoke slowly in SeSotho. "She says it is wild spinach. It's her only source of food now. She has to feed her four grandchildren, her

daughter's children. Her daughter is looking for work in Louis
Trichardt but hasn't sent any money yet."

"Ask her how old she is."

Len spoke politely to the old woman while I brushed a worri-
some fly off my face. The heat shimmered around us, bouncing
off the thorn trees and the grey ground.

"Forty-six. She says they were moved here from another part
of Lebowa a year ago. The police came with dogs and batons.
They had to leave their house, which was smashed down by
bulldozers, and their fruit trees. Her family owned fruit trees.
She says there was a lot of water there. Here there is one water
pump for all the families."

Forty-six. Eight years older than I. She could have been
eighty. We eyed one another, a huge gulf yawning between us.
A deep, coursing shame filled me. And a deep, burning anger.

"Ask her where she lives now."

The woman pointed away to the low hills. I heard the words
resettlement and *GGs* (the initials for Government Garage,
which are printed on the plates of the vehicles that take the
people from their homes to the camps). There seemed nothing
else to say. We smiled at each other again, and I proffered my
hand. She clasped it, and we shook hands in the traditional
African way. The feel of her work-toughened hand filled my
eyes with tears—desperate, angry tears. I turned abruptly
away as Len bade our farewells.

"You'll get used to seeing it," he muttered darkly to me, "but
you'll never get used to the idea of it."

After Louis Trichardt at the foot of the Soutpansberg and St.
Brendan's, the road climbed into the mountains. Never before
in all my travels around the country had I seen such mountains,
verdant and lush with foliage.

We drove on in silence until we reached Witvlag (White
Flag). A small settlement on the Venda "border," Witvlag was
not a resettlement area but a "black spot," a freehold patch of
land. The government could not forcibly remove the people, but
it could coerce them to move by buying off the chief and other
leaders, despite the resistance of the people—a tactic that had
worked in other "black spots." The people of Witvlag were
South African citizens, not "foreigners" as the people of the

"homelands" had become. In tiny Witvlag clusters of huts clung to the mountainside amid pawpaw, banana, avocado, maize, and patches of sugar cane. There were fields of lilies on the high slopes and no evidence of the drought: small streams meandered down the mountainside between the groups of huts.

Mary manoeuvred the van a short way along a narrow road pitted by large mud puddles. Len climbed out to open the gate to an even narrower driveway. The leaves of the giant creepers closed behind us, and suddenly we were in another world. A golden shower, a South African vine, cascaded around the van. Terraces had been built around the slope in front of the house. A series of ponds with water lilies and reeds and pumped waterways was the visual focus of the slope. Mrs. Makela, her children, and her grandchildren came out to greet us.

Mrs. Makela had managed to carve out a middle-class life for herself and her family despite the ravages of apartheid. Her activism against the system now took the form of grass-roots community service, specifically in helping to fight malnutrition where she lived.

A big woman in her early sixties, Mrs. Makela seemed to want to clasp Len to her bosom, but she restrained herself and took his outstretched hand instead. She hugged Mary and shook my hand. We entered her house for tea. The house consisted of a series of rooms, one leading into the other in a line, much like adjoining coaches on a train. The floor was earthen with ethnic rugs, and the walls were mud, roughly plastered and daubed an earth-color red. Pretty curtains hung on the windows. From all corners a profusion of plants in handmade Venda pots burst with life.

At tea I expressed my surprise and delight at the garden, and afterward one of Mrs. Makela's children showed me around. There were hidden arbors and benches, and everywhere the birdsong sounded. Her father had laid out the garden, my guide said, and her brother looked after it now.

Mrs. Makela, Len, and Mary were attending to milk powder accounts when I returned. Mrs. Makela's house was the distribution point for subsidised milk in the area. As we left, Mrs. Makela's children and grandchildren sang us a complex rendition of "Amazing Grace." On our way out of the driveway I noticed a signboard in the trees above the house—"Makela Nurseries," it read.

"That was wonderful, Len, so unexpected. What a garden! I felt as if I were in a mountain village above the Italian lakes."

Len laughed. "Yes, Mrs. Makela's husband was a German, a horticulturist. His life was that garden. This was mission property then; that's why they were allowed to live together there. Her son owns the first nursery in Venda—you saw it?

"Mrs. Makela was the matron of Douglas Smith Hospital, you know, near Tzaneen. I'll tell you about it sometime; it's a favorite spot of mine. She always wanted to help the nurses. I used to arrive with all sorts of goods she had asked for to sell to them—linen, kitchen goods, so on. She was a wonderful matron.

"When her husband died of cancer about six years ago, she retired—the Swiss mission sisters left the hospital about then anyway—and came to look after her younger children and grandchildren. They're teachers, nurses, social workers . . . there's even a doctor in her family. The son who's the nursery-man used to be a medical pathologist at Siloam Hospital. You'll see it; we're going there tomorrow."

The road wound higher into the mountains through dense green forests. After about twenty miles we rejoined the one paved road through Venda to Thohoyandou, the "capital" of the Venda "homeland." Once out of the forests, the land was dry again, the subsistence crops standing shrivelled and stunted around the huts.

St. Joseph's Community Centre, about ten miles from Thohoyandou, was a Roman Catholic mission run by elderly Sister Matthews. She was a human dynamo, and the centre hummed with her energy.

After dining alone in the nuns' dining room, Mary and I retired to our room. Out of Mary's small bag came a large bottle of brandy. I laughed in delight.

"None of the mission sisters anywhere want to see alcohol," Mary explained, "so I smuggle it into my bedroom." We started to giggle, then we laughed uproariously. Every time we looked at each other again we burst out laughing. It was a strange chemistry that set us off, for by nature neither of us is a giggler.

Sipping brandy from a tooth mug, leaning back against the thin walls, swatting assorted bugs and moths that came in through the mosquito netting, including some of the largest insects I have ever seen, we chatted quietly before we went to sleep.

At 5:00 A.M. the next day, soft female voices and the muffled crying of children outside the room woke us. It was a misty grey morning. The women had walked many miles to the mission to await the railway bus that might bring the mail. The monthly remittance from their men—migrant workers in the white towns—might be in those bags. A lucky few departed, relieved for another month. Sister Matthews said that the others would return daily until their money came. "It has been coming for fewer and fewer of them," she added, "as the unemployment worsens in the cities."

What if the money never came? I asked silently. I knew the answer. It meant disaster for the women. It meant living on wild spinach. It meant watching your children starving and then dying.

At this early hour a hundred people had already formed a line at the clinic behind the nuns' house. There were old women and some old men, but mainly there were young women with three or more children, usually one at the breast. They were seeking inoculations against childhood diseases, relief from the ailments and pains of old age, remedies for colds, flu, and stomach ailments, dressings for open cuts, treatment for burns. On a busy day they usually had to wait a couple of hours to be seen by one of the hard-pressed clinic staff.

Another long line had formed outside the storeroom. St. Joseph's was a major distribution point for Operation Hunger, the massive private-sector food relief organisation formed in Johannesburg in 1982 to provide aid during this worst drought of the century. Women, followed by small children, wove their way up the hillside, bags of mealie meal on their heads. "Their only food for a month," said Sister Matthews. "The people's crops have failed for the second year, and the rural poor are now destitute."

Mary drove while Len gave directions. He seemed to know every sand road, gully, and path as if they were imprinted on his mind. We were going north toward the Limpopo River, South Africa's border with Zimbabwe, into barren, rocky country where the soil was red.

"Three years ago this was all grass, and the streams ran," said Len, pointing to the horizon. I stared at the red soil and had difficulty imagining it any other way. Now the people walk miles to scattered water pumps, large plastic containers on their heads, for their daily supply of water.

Near the road we came upon a cemetery, a rectangular patch of earth sprouting tiny crosses with large cut-out plywood hearts (love) nailed to them. In the distance we could see the telltale glint of the sun on tin latrines—a resettlement camp, not a large one, perhaps a couple of hundred shacks. Scrambling through the barbed wire, I felt uncomfortable, as if I was desecrating revered ground. But I wanted to see this for myself. On the most recent cross was a name, Mweli Mnegme, and the dates 14 October 1983–21 December 1983. And then my eyes were riveted to a number on the bottom of the cross, 95. Ninety-five children and infants had died here. I walked quickly to the furthest row; the date was 1979. Ninety-five children had died here in four years. I could only shake my head in disbelief.

The sights I saw were beginning to run together. A school here in the bush, a clinic there. Milk powder, peanut butter, fortified biscuits (cookies), milk powder. Children crowding around the van. It was hot, very hot, and windy. A red dust swirled over the valleys. On the sand road through the hills the earth was denuded of vegetation and speckled with huts. The once lovely Venda hills grew a new crop now—mud huts, almost one on top of the other. How were all the people going to fit?

In a valley again, a burning valley under a burnished sky. The red soil was barren. This was Nzelele, one of the most undeveloped regions of Venda. The many huts dotted among the rocks seemed deserted until I spotted the ubiquitous chickens pecking at the dusty ground. There had been no rain for three years. The cattle had died, the goats had died. The rushing rivers and streams of Venda were no more. The women walked miles every day, with plastic containers on their heads, to the boreholes for water.

Dr. Helms greeted us at Siloam Hospital. It was so out of place, a white-painted, white-tiled, shining modern hospital in a devastated corner of northern Venda. Dr. Helms was Dutch as were the five young doctors who worked with him. His wife and their twenty-four-year-old son were doctors too.

There was a laboratory, a pathology staff, an incubator, an x-ray room, a physiotherapy ward. A smiling young Dutch physiotherapist showed us around his ward. "I'm learning a lot here, things you don't see in Holland," he said. Mzikele, a bright-eyed ten-year-old, had been bitten by a hyena. His leg had been amputated, and he was learning to use an artificial limb. Many other children had been lamed and scarred by burns. "They all sleep too near the fire," the doctor told us.

"We have eight outpatient clinics," another doctor told me. "There is poor attendance at the moment. They're going to the witch doctors again. It's the drought, no money from their men, children dying, kwash—it's hard to shake the belief in the evil spirits syndrome under the combination of these circumstances.

There was no grazing, no cattle, for miles. Only bare red soil dotted with large rocks. High on the bald top of a rocky hill we stopped at a newly opened clinic. Two mission sisters lived there in a prefab house, their clinic, a little way off, also a prefab building. Sister Eileen greeted us. She was South African, Catholic, middle-aged, with bright red hair at the edge of her wimple. "I've heard of you," she said to Len. "I would like some milk powder. The babies are dying in this valley, sometimes five a day. I don't know what will happen in the winter. They need this clinic, but they'll take a while to come. They'd rather go to Siloam, which they know, a twenty-mile walk over the hills." She sighed, looking resignedly around her. "I can't get used to how small this clinic is. I used to run a big hospital in the highlands, Rhodesia, you know, Zimbabwe now. Thought I'd retire there, such a beautiful country. But I'm happy to start all over again. They need education here, as well as basic health care. The men send pretty clothes at Christmas instead of food. We have the best-dressed kwash patients in all of Venda in this valley." She laughed. It was a bitter sound in the desolate sunset.

I found myself asking the same question over and over again during this journey: What would have happened in the rural areas without the missionaries? The government certainly does nothing for the people in the "homelands"—out of sight, swept under the carpet, away from whatever conscience there is in South Africa.

We had travelled about four hundred miles, back and forth across the northern and western Transvaal hinterland, a little over half of our journey. Unlike Marlow, I had not had to wait until the end of my odyssey to find Kurtz and the madness he had let loose around him. I had encountered it on my first day, within hours, in every tired, hopeless gesture of that gaunt woman I had spoken to at the edge of the road. The barbarism and cruelty of the grand apartheid design pervaded her being. What could I do in my own way to make the apartheid regime answerable for this massive crime against humanity, against everything I stood for and believed in? At times while driving along the seemingly endless dusty plains, I felt I would burst with anger and frustration.

Once there was a resettlement camp almost alongside the sandy track, instead of in the far distance. I had come here to see all I could, so I climbed through the barbed wire and surprised an old woman at the entrance of her corrugated-iron shack. She was sweeping the dust from her doorway, watching it settle on the dusty ground a couple of feet from where she stood. Within seconds I was surrounded by snotty-nosed, pot-bellied children, their hands thrust out toward me. "Sweets," a bold one kept saying to me, almost as if admonishing me. The old woman gestured toward her shack. I nodded eagerly—yes, I'd like to be able to see inside. It was dark, with bright slivers of light from cracks in the corrugated-iron sheets. There was a lumpy mattress on a plastic sheet on the bare ground, one wooden packing case holding a candlestick, another smaller case, and a five-gallon plastic container bearing the name of a paint company, her precious supply of water. That was all I could see.

There were over a thousand shacks in fifty rows of twenty. But there was no water supply, no shop, no school. We were forty miles from the nearest town, with no means of transport. The old woman must have brought her thatch broom with her, I thought, for there was no grass here. These were the forgotten people, dumped in this aridity like discarded garbage. Three million of them.

We slept again at St. Joseph's, and the next day Sister Matthews told us of a school deep in the bush, on the border of Venda with Gazankulu. The people were starving and dying out there, she'd been told. Mary thought that we could start a feeding scheme for the children, so we set out to find the school.

The drought was so bad here that we could barely see where the road ended and the veld began. Identifiable only by the faint tyre tracks, the road petered out somewhere in the back country. Len had not been in this area before. It was stark, barren—essential Africa in a way—a sandy plain dotted with blasted thorn trees. We found clusters of huts decorated with bold, geometric designs and a store where they sold dried mampari worms (an important source of protein), but no school. With no infrastructure, we were unable to set up a feeding scheme, so we left. I do not know how people survived here—no water, boreholes, crops, or animals.

Then we were in Gazankulu, mile after mile of desolate, sandy plains. We spent the night with a missionary and his wife who lived in Giyani, the "capital" of Gazankulu. There had been no rain here for four years. The temperature was 42 degrees centigrade (102 degrees Fahrenheit), and they offered us coffee when we arrived! She was the local representative of Alcoholics Anonymous. He was translating the Bible into Tsonga, a task that had taken him almost twenty years thus far. Even Mary did not have the temerity to open her bottle of brandy that night.

"She'll smell it," she whispered. Her remark and the heat reduced us to helpless laughter. By now we had only to look at one another and we would burst out laughing. Len thought we had both gone mad. Perhaps I had; perhaps I had just seen too much madness.

The next day we spent in miserable, poverty-stricken clinics.

Everywhere the story was the same—the drought, kwashiorkor, no money from the men, no food. The people were living on
wild spinach, we were told, in those areas where it still grew.
Otherwise they were dying—slowly. The young and middle-
aged were going to the cities. They knew they would be sent
back. But it was better than waiting to die in the "homelands."

In the afternoon we had returned to a part of Venda alongside one of the few water sources, where a river still flowed.
Len stopped at a village where the women made clay pots. The
pots were piled so high around the huts that we could not see
their walls. Len's marketing of these pots, aside from the
occasional tourist's purchase, was the only outlet for the
women. He tried to be fair, buying from each of them.

Within seconds of stopping, the truck was surrounded by
fifty children, the offspring and grandchildren of the eight
middle-aged and elderly women who strolled over. An older
girl in school uniform came with them. She was suckling a
baby. She was eighteen, in her matriculation year, she told me
in English, in reply to my questions. She was going to be a
nurse. Gesturing toward the baby, she said, "It is my love
child." The man she was to marry had been picked for her, but
she did not love him; she loved the father of her child. Did that
worry her? She shrugged her shoulders and grinned. "He's
away in Johannesburg all year, coming home only once a year
for a month." And who would look after her baby while she was
at the nurses' training school? She pointed to her mother,
haggling with Len over the price of pots. "Granny," she said.
But Granny already had eleven children of her own, the youngest not yet five. She laughed. Looking around at the neat
houses, the women and children, I felt the pall of overwhelming
hopelessness.

The van, emptying of milk powder, was filling up with pots.

Saint Scholastica, our next stop, was a surprise. Located on
top of a hill, its architectural style Romanesque, it had a
commanding view of the Venda plains on three sides, stretching away to the northern parts of the Kruger National Park
and the Lebombo Mountains.

Amid the bravery of the school buildings was a small, dilapi-
dated building that housed a remarkable bush clinic, irra-

diated by Sister Lauda. The light of her love of humanity shone
from her. She had a fair complexion and cornflower-blue eyes.
She had spent the three nights before our arrival attending to a
premature baby, as well as doing a full load of medical duties
during the day. There was no electricity in the nursery, no
incubator. Wonderingly, she showed off to us that little fila-
ment of life she had saved.

"Sister Lauda," said Len, "is a legend in this area, a goddess
to the people. Once she found a girl of twelve abandoned,
starving, at the foot of a mountain. They would not send an
ambulance from Elim Hospital—they said she would be dead
by the time they arrived. Sister Lauda nursed her for months,
took her back to her family. She'll matriculate from the school
next year."

Mary and I shared a huge room away from the sisters. The
generator died at nine-thirty at night. So we sipped our brandy
by candlelight this time and spoke of Africa until past
midnight.

Early in the morning we started off for Pietersburg, in the
northwestern Transvaal, and then drove further west, into
western Lebowa. By now I was used to the brown-grey sand,
the monotony of the grassless plains, the numberless thorn
trees. The desert was claiming vast areas in the north of South
Africa.

We were startled in western Lebowa by the sight of rows and
rows of shiny tin pit latrines on a low hill. It looked like a forest
of latrines. "They're getting ready for another removal—and
that's it," said Len, pointing to the side of the road with the
latrines, "the dumping grounds."

One hospital, then another and another. It was pitiful: the
blatant, unnecessary human misery, overcrowded wards, mal-
nourished and dying children, a dulled acceptance in the faces
of the suffering people.

Blouberg Hospital was a small collection of buildings in
western Lebowa. The Rev. Russel Collett, an American Naza-
rene missionary, was energetic, with many schemes for the
people. He showed us the prototype of a chicken farm he had
devised at Blouberg. And he distributed more milk powder
than any other outlet with which Len and Mary dealt. His

mission served a vast area, but Russel Collett refused to be discouraged. Despite his faith, the land was dead—barren, relentless grey sand. There was no doctor at Blouberg, and though the Nazarenes had arranged for two American doctors to come to Blouberg, they were refused visas by the South African government. "South Africa produces enough of its own doctors" was the official reason for the refusal. We certainly saw no evidence of these doctors at Blouberg or at any of the other many health centres I visited in the rural areas. There was no other medical facility for a hundred miles, so the people of western Lebowa had barely any medical care—barely any of anything.

The condition of the patients at Blouberg Hospital was the worst we had seen. Wards and rooms were overcrowded with dying, sick children and hopeless-looking women. Overworked nurses sparingly rationed the few medical supplies, trying desperately to maintain the far from hygienic conditions in the wards. One skeletal three-year-old, who lay too still in a cot, dying of starvation, smiled at me when I leaned over to hold his hand. I cried then. And I could not stop crying until the low hills of those valleys of desperation and dying were behind us. All of this, I thought, in the name of the ideological madness of apartheid. No one must say, as they did of that other genocide, that they did not know.

It was afternoon, over forty degrees centigrade again. We were back in Tzaneen, a narrow strip of land between the "homelands" of Lebowa and Gazankulu. The vegetation was lush here, subtropical. But as we turned off the main road, back into Lebowa, we quickly saw that the drought was here, a few miles into the "homelands."

Lenyene. Home of Dr. Mamphele Ramphele, political activist and physician. I had long been wanting to meet her. The apartheid regime had sent her into political exile in Lenyene in 1977. Yet, without even being able to speak the language, she had built in six short years a health care network that serviced over forty thousand people who lived where she had been banished.

The heat was like a blanket smothering us when the van stopped. The small yard in front of the clinic was fenced in with sagging, diamond wire mesh. A few pawpaw trees, bedraggled rows of mealies, and drooping tomato plants grew in the parched orange sand. Chickens scratched in the dust at the steps of the small modern building. Groups of sleeping people lay sprawled in the scant shade of the pawpaw trees.

Len pushed back his straw hat and mopped his brow with a handkerchief. Mary was already at the back of the van, trying to dislodge our last bags of milk powder without breaking the Venda pots. (We had also acquired baskets and mats, macadamia nuts, small avocado trees, and swaths of wraparound skirts to sell in Johannesburg.) I went to help Mary. But the heat and the weight of the bags reduced us to giggles again and then unstoppable gales of laughter. Len found us collapsed on top of the bags of milk powder, laughing hopelessly.

"Come on, girls, help's here. Mamphele's waiting in her office."

Len was at the door of the van with two young men. He shook his head sadly when he saw us sprawled on the milk powder, but his eyes twinkled. "Been laughing again?" he asked, almost dolefully. The expression on his dear face and the droll tone of his question set us off once more.

Making a stern effort, I was able to compose myself. Mary and I avoided looking at each other. Sheepishly, but soberly now, we climbed the steps with Len.

"Hello, old man." Mamphele stood in a white medical coat in the doorway, her hand outstretched. Len grasped it in both of his. He grinned happily at her.

"How are you, Mamphele?" he asked her fondly.

"Fine, fine." She nodded at us. "Come to my office. I have an electric fan and some iced cold drinks for you."

We followed her tiny figure down the polished corridor. She sat behind her desk, and we arranged chairs in front of her. Len introduced Mary. Mamphele acknowledged having met Mary on another occasion. She looked at me with recognition when Len introduced us. She knew me, as I knew her, through the media. I glanced, almost involuntarily, at the framed photograph of Steve Biko, the martyred black activist, on the instrument cabinet under the window.

Her eyes followed mine to Steve's picture. "That's our son," she said as we turned to the photograph of a chubby six-year-old. Steve Biko's son. Steve's pleasant, open face flashed into my mind. I remembered his eloquence, his sincerity, his incisive political thinking, his maturity, his natural leadership qualities.

Mamphele and Len were telling Mary and me of how they first met. "He wandered in here," Mamphele gestured around her, "before it looked like this. He was looking for me. 'But you're so young,' he said when I introduced myself, 'so small.' And I thought to myself, Who's this old man, lost in Lebowa, in the bush?"

She looked at Len. "Well, old man, I was not wrong to be puzzled. What other white Johannesburg grandfather treks to the rural areas with bags of milk powder? You should be playing in the shade with your grandchildren, not getting heatstroke in Lebowa." We laughed at the self-effacing grin of apology on Len's face.

He spoke gently. "And you, Mamphele, you should be at home tending to your children, not running care groups, adult literacy classes, health clinics, and feeding forty thousand people. You're still too young and too tiny."

A medical assistant in a white jacket and long white trousers brought in a tray of iced drinks. He whispered to Mamphele, who excused herself, then he asked Len to check the order of powdered milk with him. Mary went to the front room to call the Imqualife shop in Johannesburg. Left alone, I wandered around the room. There was another photograph on the cabinet, this one of Mamphele addressing a huge gathering of students. She stood on the podium, her fist raised in the freedom salute, the banner of the Black Consciousness movement above her, and Steve Biko's proud smile beaming among the row of faces behind her on the stage.

On Mamphele's return I deferentially asked her to tell her story. She spoke in measured terms.

"When the government smashed BC [Black Consciousness] in October 1977, Steve had been dead a month. Our son was a few months old. I was working in the Ciskei, a rural hospital. All the organisations I worked for were banned. I was banned too, put under house arrest, exiled here, to Lenyene. It's a thousand miles from my home. I couldn't even speak the language. I knew no one.

"They brought me here under police guard. There were only these few houses you see today and a run-down police station. I was put into an abandoned hut, next to the station. I collapsed then. Until then I had mourned Steve in anger and rage but kept it inside, the rage giving me the strength and courage to work so hard in BC organisations and in my medicine. Once here, I collapsed, mentally, physically. It was just as well that I had my baby to take care of. Otherwise, who knows?" She shrugged.

"When I went out to the general store I had a police escort. If I went for a walk, I had a police escort. The local people were afraid to greet me. They were bewildered too, because, despite the police, I had so many, many visitors." She laughed bitterly. "I was infamous, don't forget. Steve Biko's mistress, mother of his illegitimate child, his activist comrade. Good copy for hungry journalists.

"Under the terms of my banning order I could speak to only one person at a time. My line of visitors dwindled. It was tedious waiting to speak to me here in the bush." We all smiled bitterly, acknowledging how ridiculous was the notion of being restricted to speaking to one person at a time.

"Then they brought a policeman to me. He had been injured in a shooting accident and needed emergency first aid. I laughed at the irony of it. My banning order forbade me to practise medicine, yet I was being asked by the police to break that order and tend to one of the murderers of Steve. A black brother he was, a black policeman. Funny thing, though, I saw the irony only later. At the time I treated him immediately. My Hippocratic Oath will always supersede anything else for me.

"I told my lawyer the story when he visited here. Without asking me, he applied for the restriction on my practising medicine to be lifted." She leaned back, lacing her fingers. "That was the turning point for me.

"Well, after that the police relaxed their absurd and irritating vigilance of me, and the locals began to call. Almost without being aware of it I began to minister to them. A sick baby, a dying old man. I went one night to help with a difficult delivery.

"A woman who had lived in Transkei as a child befriended me and became my translator. I began to look around me. I saw the appalling poverty, the starvation, the deprivation, and the resignation of suffering on faces.

"The police officer was transferred, and the new chief became my friend. He had the hut rebuilt for me. When he got the news of the lifting of my house arrest and the restrictions on my practising medicine, he was wonderful. He gave me a car and a driver, and I was able to see the full extent of the misery in this Lenyene district.

"I wrote to the Council of Churches and other institutions in Johannesburg for drugs and equipment. I was still banned but freely able to move about the district now and see the people. No political activity, of course." She snorted a laugh. "Wasn't what I was doing political? Of course it was, saving people who were supposed to die in poverty, deprivation, and ignorance.

"My visitors now were different from those who had come before—trustees of various funds to which the Council of Churches had applied for assistance for me. Church leaders, social workers, concerned people working in grass-roots, self-help, feeding, and other schemes." She nodded at Len. "Like your Imqualife, Len.

"The drought was in its second year, and the infant mortality rate had climbed even higher than its usual staggering numbers. Kwashiorkor was rife, especially in the two- to five-year age group. It was evident I had to organise some sort of infrastructure to reach the outlying areas of the district. I started care groups along the lines of those developed in Elim Hospital.

"My operation at Lenyene had to grow too, to cope with the flow of equipment, drugs, and money coming from Johannesburg. And to cope with the growing stream of people walking miles over the veld for medical care. The Lebowa government was not given permission from Pretoria to supply me with the nurses and other assistance for which I had applied. So I started training some of the local women and girls who were lucky to have had some mission education. Voluntary workers—students, youth groups—came on weekends from Johannesburg to help with expanding the buildings.

"I was working nonstop, but I thrived on it. The care groups worked wonderfully—one woman in each kraal [cluster of thatched huts] responsible for the distribution of milk powder and other child-feeding. I would hold outpatient clinics in each region at least once a month. In this way we eventually brought rudimentary health care and feeding to about forty thousand people who had never had it before.

"The winters were the worst time—flu epidemics wiped out the children. They were too weak to resist even mild attacks.

"After I had been here for two years my banning order was lifted. I was free to travel to the urban areas to raise funds. Anglo-American Corporation built this new clinic with the classrooms and the communal hall. The old makeshift clinic was taken over by the Lebowa government. There it stands, empty." The abandoned building was visible from the window.

Mamphele had looked down almost shyly to her wedding ring. "I married an old friend, a pharmacist from Port Elizabeth. But I felt compelled to come back here. Although I was pregnant, I couldn't stop working. There was plenty of help now. I concentrated on training nurses, building up the adult literacy classes and the bush care groups. Doctors came, for weeks at a time, to help. There was always someone other than me in charge.

"My second son was born here in Lenyene. Living so close to the clinic, I was able to nurse him and still work. It was the third year of the drought. But because of Operation Hunger and people like you and Mary, Len, we have food for the people."

She leaned back in her chair and smiled in satisfaction. "Now I have a well-trained staff, and I can concentrate on my own medicine again. I've a yearning to travel. I've been invited to New York to receive an award in July. I think I'll go, travel around a bit. It's been six years since I came here to Lenyene, so alone and so broken. My life has changed in six years. I want

to study again—paediatrics. I think I'll take up the residency
I've been offered in Port Elizabeth. I need a break from this
pressure."

Mamphele laughed. "I wouldn't survive another winter here
with everyone's needs pressing down on me. The clinic will go
on. There's a good board of trustees, well-trained people now.
An experienced doctor has been taken on to fill my position.
Joseph, my administrator, is going to Toronto next month for a
course in hospital administration."

At the end of her story no one spoke.

"That's quite a story, Mamphele," Len said into the silence.
Then he turned to me. "You should write it one day."

"I probably will, if that's all right with you, Mamphele?"

Mamphele nodded and shrugged. She laughed, abruptly,
ironically. "Who'll want to read about me?"

Joseph returned, carrying the milk powder accounts. Leaving them all to work on delivery dates and orders, I wandered
into the communal hall, which was set up for literacy classes
and sewing lessons. The walls were lined with cabinets of
books. On the tables were hand-operated Singer sewing ma-
chines. Charts were everywhere—reading charts, health care
charts, nutrition charts. I saw with some surprise many United
Democratic Front (UDF) posters—political posters exhorting
the people to political action. One showed a large picture of
Steve Biko and read, "Martyred, For the People." Surely the
police knew of these posters. Mamphele was courageous to
court again the wrath of the apartheid regime. Any opposition,
white or black, put one in danger of running afoul of the
government. Displaying a poster of a banned person, or wearing a T-shirt with a banned slogan, or even having possession
of a banned book is a serious infraction of the state's security
legislation.

"Come on, Janet," Mary was calling from the entrance hall.
"We've a long way to go."

I clasped Mamphele's hand tightly. "Our freedom is indivisi-
ble, Mamphele."

"Go well," she said, embracing me warmly. "Stay well. We'll
meet again."

Len and Mary were already in the van, Mary trying to back

it out of the narrow gateway without disturbing the prone forms under the pawpaw trees. After wriggling onto my milk powder seat, I joined the others waving to Mamphele and her staff on the steps. The South African flag lay still against the flagpole in front of the police station.

We were subdued and contemplative in the van. Mamphele's story hung over us, both diminishing and uplifting us. Lenyene disappeared from view behind the low, desperate hills.

"Beer?" I asked Mary as I reached behind her to the cooler. She nodded and took the icy can. We smiled at one another. No words, or laughter, were needed. I knew what I had to do now. The heat shimmered around us.

We slept at the Doornspruit Mission that night and returned to Johannesburg late on the next day, Friday, retracing our route from Pietersburg, through Naboomspruit, Nylstroom, and Pretoria. We had travelled a little over seven hundred fifty miles.

In due course, a few months after my journey, we sold our house and made preparations to leave South Africa. I went to the Imqualife shop in Westgate to tell Len and Mary of our pending move.

After the initial shock, Len turned to Mary. "She's right, of course, to leave now. There's a blood bath coming here, the scale of which none of us can imagine. For all the work I've done, for all that I felt I've achieved, for all the understanding I've fostered and the goodwill I've received, all this will come to nothing. For every small cooperative enterprise I've built, I've seen the mountains of oppression, desperation, and hatred that the apartheid government's built. They'll erupt one day—it's coming, you'll see . . ."

Mary and I were both taken aback by the vehemence of Len's words. Ordinarily a mild, soft-spoken person, he had sounded like a biblical prophet. He looked directly at me.

"Someone will have to write about it all, you know."

I knew.

CHAPTER 2
"If You Prick Us, Do We Not Bleed?"

My life inside apartheid began at noon on December 16, 1945, at the Woodside Sanctuary in Yeoville, a suburb of Johannesburg. Family legend has it that the labour ward sister gave my father sitting outside in his car a thumbs-up sign as the church clock nearby struck twelve.

White Afrikaans-speaking South Africans revere the day as a deeply religious holiday. For it was on December 16, 1838, that one of the Great Trek leaders, Andries Pretorius, a man of mythic dimensions in the Afrikaner pantheon, made a covenant with God. Should the Trekkers, beleaguered in their laager of circled wagons, defeat the Zulu impis surrounding them and waiting to attack at dawn, the Boer nation would forever keep the day as a remembrance of the holy covenant.

The Trekkers' guns won the day. The river in the Natal midlands, where the battle was fought, ran red with the blood of Chief Dingaan's warriors and has been known as Blood River ever since. December 16th was ironically called Dingaan's Day and kept as holy for generations. Latterly it was renamed the Day of the Covenant and is currently known as the Day of the Vow. It owes its name change to a rare display of sensitivity by the government, which heeded the angry reaction of black leaders to the name Dingaan's Day.

The National Party came to power in 1948, when I was three years old, sweeping aside the United Party government of General Jan Smuts. During the war years Smuts had played a leading role in the Allied defenses against the Nazis and had neglected his grass-roots political organisation at home. Meanwhile, the Afrikaner nationalists had been organising on a huge scale. Many National Party members were Nazi sympathisers and had formed a fifth column, the Ossewabrandwag (Ox Wagon Brigade), in South Africa to undermine the war effort. Many were arrested for acts of sabotage and for violently breaking up public meetings. They were interned in prisoner-of-war camps. One prisoner later became infamous as a strong-arm leader of the National Party, Prime Minister John Vorster.

The National Party's propaganda, which had proved so effective during the buildup to the whites-only election of 1948, was based on a racist concept called *swaart gevaar* (black danger). The pamphleteering graphically depicted the demise of the white man, and especially Afrikaner identity, that supposedly would ensue should Smuts stay in power and continue to permit the flow of blacks to the cities. It was a strong nationalistic, chauvinistic movement of Afrikaners—a call to the blood, to the loyalty of the "volk." Afrikaner church leaders, educators, and politicians responded in force to the call and embraced the survival of Afrikaner identity as an urgent cause.

To the surprise of most English-speaking whites, the Nationalists won the election from the overwhelming favourite, the popular Smuts, with this blatant racist sledgehammering. It was a lesson the Nats never forgot. After forty years in power, they still fight election after election with racist intent and play on the Afrikaners' greatest fear, the fear of losing their language and "culture" in an overwhelming sea of blackness. It is no longer *swaart gevaar* the volk faces: in the 1980s it has become a "total onslaught." Since 1978 the National Party government has been building a self-fulfilling psychosis of total onslaught among its followers, who are now told the threat is both internal (black and white radicals) and external ("terrorists" and international isolation).

As I was three then, I do not remember my parents' reaction to the National Party victory, but later they told me, and others of their generation confirm this as a popular reaction, that they were terrified of what would happen to them as Jews in South Africa, given the recent history of many of the National Party leaders. There appears to have been little general concern as to the lot of the black population under the new government. Ironically, over the last forty years, the National Party, while its constitution denies membership to anyone not "white" and "Christian," has established strong military and economic ties with Israel, which achieved its statehood in the same momentous year that the Nationalists came to power.

Despite this tie with Israel, almost as if Israelis were not really Jews, anti-Semitism has never been far below the surface of National Party attitudes and pronouncements. This knowledge has kept the South African Jewish population, numbering about 120,000, in a state of perpetual uneasiness. It has helped to foster a natural tendency toward exclusiveness among Jews and a bland "don't rock the boat," blind-eye response to the excesses of the apartheid regime. Most Jews feel frightened when other Jews, activists, run afoul of the state. Most Jews do not want other Jews to take a leading role in political opposition to the government, for fear that it will draw attention to the community as a whole. My mother has told me that fear for me and deep concern about my safety were at the root of my parents' opposition to my political activities.

The fact that we were Jewish (traditional Jews, not religious, practising Jews), that our people had suffered five thousand years of oppression, did not seem to make us particularly sympathetic to the oppression of the millions of people with whom we shared our lives and our (their?) land. I never heard a word of moral outrage from the pulpit of the synagogue that we attended on High Holy Days. (I resisted going to shul, gibing at the fact that women were segregated behind an iron railing from the men, that only the men could participate in the prayers, that the service was in Hebrew, and that I had to wear, a great indignity to my tomboyish soul, a hat!)

Later, when I was married and we joined a Reform Temple, our rabbis were bravely outspoken in condemning apartheid,

and several were founding members of a post-1984 antiapartheid movement, Jews for Justice. But, sadly, members of the
Orthodox rabbinate have over the years on several occasions
even gone as far as telling their congregation to vote for the
National Party.

Despite the political implications, as a child I found it de-
lightful to have a public holiday on my birthday. It meant that
my family and friends were relaxed and at home and happy to
celebrate with me. But from when I was about ten I enjoyed
baiting my parents by admonishing them, as if they were
responsible for the National Party government's spoiling my
birthday with solemn, lugubrious sermons and deathly dull,
funereal music on the state-controlled radio. My parents were
not pleased by my contemptuous comments. My father told me
that such an attitude would lead me into trouble with the
police. This seemed farfetched to me and slightly dishonest.
Why was my father trying to scare me?

From the Woodside Sanctuary I was brought home to 27
Galway Road in Parkview, a quiet, wooded suburb. Our house
was built in the style of the famous Cape Dutch farmhouses of
the winelands of the Cape Province, but on a much smaller
scale. Our house had a gable in front of the roof and a long
verandah that ran around three sides of the house. Wooden
shutters that hooked back onto white painted walls, the roof,
and the verandah were black.

Privilege was not a concept I understood until much later in
my life. I regarded our house, our neighbourhood, not in any
relative sense, but as a norm holding good for everyone. Black
servants lived in rooms in our yard, and as far as I knew, they
had no life beyond the one they led as part of our household. Of
how black people lived in the urban townships and the rural
areas I was to have no knowledge until years later. Indeed, the
vast majority of white South Africans never know how black
South Africans live. They never venture into a black township,
even when, as is the case in many instances, it is adjacent to the
suburb where they live. The white consciousness is filled only
with the images the apartheid regime wants it to see, in clips
shown on the strictly controlled state television system. Of

course, we had no black neighbours. Then and now, residential areas are stringently segregated. And it was not until I became friendly with girls at school who had much more opulent homes than mine, with many more rooms, servants, swimming pools, tennis courts, exotic-looking dogs with strange names, and even horses, that I became aware that social status, wealth, and privilege were indeed relative.

I have searched my memory to determine how and where my burgeoning sense of racial and social justice germinated in the backdrop of my family's bland, white, middle-class lifestyle. The seed certainly was not planted by my parents, who as with so many of their contemporaries were studiedly apolitical. "It was an isolationist way of life," my mother told me, looking back. "Until the war we were a real backwater. And when the Nats came in, there was no future in politics for English-speakers, especially Jews. So we had very little to do with politics." Through disinterest, politics was never discussed in our house. None of my extended family were politically involved; like my parents, they feared the Nationalists, distrusted the blacks, voted for the defeated United Party, and hoped for the best. None of them were racists in the bigoted sense; rather, their racism was an equanimical acceptance of the status quo, a racism implicit in any society built on a white master/black servant relationship. My family's stereotypical responses to blacks were based on their interactions with servants. None of them had ever met a black person in any other circumstance.

The house on Galway Road actually belonged to my paternal grandmother, Bluma Berman, with whom my father had lived for years. She was old, crotchety, and strange to me. I loved my maternal grandfather, Herman Rosenberg, though. He always smelt clean and looked so proper, his love of flowers evident in the rosebud he wore in his lapel. He had been a widower since my aunt Thelma was one year old, and now in his seventies, he split the year among his three children. Among my earliest memories are those of accompanying him for his daily walk on the Parkview Golf Course. We would talk and look at the wildflowers and the birds and sit on the newly mown fairways and smell the grass cuttings in the air.

If any one member of my family planted seeds of social

justice and fairness in me, it was probably my grandfather. He would look at the ten- and twelve-year-old black caddies on the golf course, shake his head, and tell me, "They should be in school. This country is losing generations of talent, of riches. A country's riches are in its people. They should have a chance for education. Everyone should have a chance to be educated."

He was probably thinking of his peers fifty years earlier in the shtetls of eastern Europe, but he made me think (if only in a vague, indistinct way) of my black peers. Was it possible that black children also wanted to go to school?

He would tell me as well, at the family milling business where he still went to work each day, and where I would visit him with my parents on some Saturday mornings, to treat black people with respect: "In this business everyone is given the dignity he has as a person." He would then quote a passage from the Talmud and translate it for me. It was filled with words like *respect* and *dignity*, which acquired rich meaning for me. After all, they had been written in a sacred book thousands of years earlier. I loved to think of the meaning of such adult concepts as respect and dignity, and I was pleased they had been handed down to me from the lofty adult world. But, in honesty, they had little meaning for me then in terms of race relations in my own world.

Though less directly, my father, Solly Berman, also played a role in my developing political and social consciousness. Much older than my mother, Eileen (he was thirty-six when they married and thirty-eight when I was born), my father was fun-loving and energetic. I was never conscious that he was older than my contemporaries' fathers. In fact, he did far more with us when I was a young child than I remember other fathers doing with their children. Among many other things we did together, highlights were the rare occasions on which he took me to the old Bijou Theatre in downtown Johannesburg on Saturday mornings to see Walt Disney movies.

He was close to his family, so I grew up surrounded by many uncles, aunts, and cousins. Year after year, in December, we would go on holiday to Muizenberg, an Atlantic Ocean holiday resort outside of Cape Town, with two of my father's sisters, Aunt Jean and Aunt Golda, and their families.

In my mind, Muizenberg is a collage of hot beach sand,

donkey rides, rows of boxlike wooden huts on stilts at the water's edge, photographers offering to snap the family, the southeast wind, ice cream, yellow cling Cape peaches, the blue-green Hottentots-Hollands mountains, and the sea.

"The most beautiful cape in all the world" is how Sir Francis Drake described the Cape of Good Hope as he rounded it over three hundred years ago on his way from Elizabethan England to the spice-rich subcontinent of India on the (still) all-important strategic trade route to the East.

Three hundred years later the beauty of the Cape landscape remains stunnning—evocative and captivating—even though South Africa's second largest city now sprawls down the flanks of the famous Table Mountain and the suburbs hug the shoreline for miles.

My father used to come into his own on our Cape holidays. He loved being there and sharing his enthusiasm with us. He would take us for spectacularly scenic drives through forests, along mountain paths, over glaring white beaches, where the long lines of Atlantic Ocean breakers would curl relentlessly shoreward in serried row after serried row. But my father's pride was Table Mountain. Every year he took us to see it from every vantage point, by day and by night. We always climbed its formidable height on a small, swaying cable car and saw a tiny ethereal city laid out at our feet, swathed in mists rising from a glittery ocean.

One year, when I was about ten, he had a surprise for us. He had heard of a view of Table Mountain we had not seen before. We drove for about an hour from Muizenberg to a lonely wind-swept beach called Melkbosstrand. Our reward for walking a short distance from the car park was what remains for me the most special view available of Table Mountain. We all exclaimed and basked in the glorious sight of the mountain rising out of the sea.

"What's that island in front of the mountain, Daddy?"

"That's Robben Island."

"Can we go there? It's closer to the mountain; we'll have an even better view." I wanted to share his enthusiasm for the mountain with him. But he became evasive and looked meaningfully at my mother.

"No," she said gently, not wanting to break our mood of communion with the mountain. "It's not for the public. It's a prison."

"A prison!"

I had never heard of such a thing, a beautiful island in the middle of a beautiful bay, in front of the most beautiful mountain in the world—a prison. My shock must have been evident to my parents.

"Don't worry," my father said. "They'll never put you there. It's for political prisoners—blacks, you know; communists, too."

The new knowledge seething in my mind rendered me speechless. Not only had I been confronted with the fact that such a beautiful place could be a prison; I also had learned that there was a category of criminals called political and, I surmised, that they were so dangerous they had to be put to sea on an island off the edge of a continent where no one could rescue them. Table Mountain became to me what the apple from the Tree of Knowledge had been to Eve. But my apple had a worm in it, eating away at its core, transforming its beauty into something overwhelming and evil. And it was not the prisoners on Robben Island.

My father had been born in London, but his parents were Polish. Finding they could not make a living in London, and with two of my grandfather's brothers already living in South Africa, my grandparents left for South Africa in 1909 with six children. My Aunt Golda, the youngest, was a year old. The family lived in Doornfontein, the Jewish ghetto of old Johannesburg, and all the children attended the Jewish Government School there. My father left school when he was twelve as grandfather, a tailor, found earning a living difficult and my father was needed to supplement the family income. He became a trainee salesman at Ackerman's, a chain of department stores. At twenty he was managing a branch of Ackerman's in Vereeniging, a small farming town on the banks of the Vaal River. During the war years he became a clothing sales representative. He was a rep for the rest of his life.

My maternal grandfather, Herman, had come as a young

man to Ramoutsa in the Bechuanaland protectorate to join two of his brothers who had put behind them the pogroms of eastern Europe and were running a trading store. It was cattle-ranching country, and I imagine that the dapper urbanite from Riga in Baltic Latvia must have had a hard time adjusting to the strangeness of rural Africa.

My mother and her siblings were born in Ramoutsa. My Latvian grandmother died under circumstances never really made clear to me. Some of the family say she died of an infection following a poisonous spider bite; others say she bled to death after a self-induced abortion.

The three brothers moved their families to a concession store on the Lichtenburg diamond fields in the western Transvaal. My mother spent her childhood on a farm in Lichtenburg. When she was about thirteen, the brothers were prosperous enough to open a business in Johannesburg, H. Rosenberg & Co., General Merchants. They were grain merchants, and some of my clearest childhood memories are of the times I spent in the murky light of the mill, climbing and jumping off the stacks of neatly piled grain sacks.

Both of my great uncles' wives died in Lichtenburg, and the three brothers bought a large house in Yeoville, where their maiden sister, Ray, kept house and attempted to look after seven motherless children. She was ably assisted by a man servant, John, who came to work for my mother when she set up house in Parkview.

John lived in a room behind the garage. Thick clusters of tall bamboo and an enormous fig tree grew outside of his room. I loathed the sticky, milky sap of that tree, but I loved to sit in the sun outside of John's room and eat luscious overripe figs. Sometimes John would let me share his stiff mealie pap (a ground maize porridge similar to grits) laced with thick meat gravy. The delicious lump would sink to my stomach, and John would tell me of his childhood in a Zulu kraal. I could listen to his stories for hours.

John was also the family cook. He treated my mother as if she were still a child and in his care, openly resenting her presence in the kitchen. The only thing she was allowed to do was to make schmaltz (rendered chicken fat), which was something of a ritual. The fat was stored in large stone jars in our pantry.

John's wife lived in rural Zululand, but once a year at Easter she would visit us with her three children. We always had a school vacation at this time, and I looked forward to this annual event with great pleasure. John's wife was a strange, exotic figure to me. She wore her tribal dress of brightly colored cloth wrapped around her body, wire rings around her ankles, and the traditional beehive headdress of her people. The headdress consisted of thousands of brightly coloured beads, worked into intricate patterns, all of which had some meaning in tribal lore and which she would craft herself. During the days of her visit she would sit in the sun outside of John's room and do her beadwork, creating necklaces, bracelets, and other pieces. She made me a traditional girl's bracelet of red and white beads in a well-ordered cubic design that would be replaced once I reached puberty if I were a Zulu.

Nomsi, John's youngest daughter, was my age, and although she spoke no English and I no Zulu beyond *saki bona* (greetings) and *haai kona* (an exclamation of disbelief), which John had taught me, we played happily together.

We sang Christmas carols and Zulu lullabies to each other. I showed her my books and toys, particularly my dollhouse, a favourite toy, which she would shyly examine for hours, as fascinated by it as I was. My current nanny would bring drinks and biscuits to my room. We climbed the huge jacaranda tree in the back garden, and we ate lunch in the sun outside of John's room. After a week of being together we would both grow bolder, and she would stroke my straight blond hair, exclaiming at the strangeness of it, while I marvelled at the feeling of the tight, knobbly whorls on her head.

"Why can't they live here with you, John?"

"Our home is in the valley with many, many hills. All my people are there. The children can go to the mission school there."

This answer did not satisfy me.

"Why can't they live with John here, Mom?"

"A whole family can't live in John's room. Besides, all his people are there in the Valley of a Thousand Hills. It's their home; there're schools and villages there. There's nothing for the children here in Johannesburg."

At Christmas John would go home for a month with much

ceremony, laden with cardboard boxes full of gifts. My father would drive him to the station, and we would help him pile his goods on the platform crowded with excited men talking volubly. At the other end of the platform—for whites only—the white passengers, mainly holiday makers to Durban, were subdued, staid, even. John would have a good time on the train with his friends, I thought, even if they would be much more crowded than we were when we went on the train.

The Valley of a Thousand Hills had such a magical ring to it that I was sure John would be safe until he was restored to us in January. It never occurred to me that the valleys could be anything but lush and green. I had to see them for myself, years later, denuded of vegetation by overgrazing and overpopulation—dry, dusty, brown, withered. I hoped then that for John and his family, thirty years earlier, they had been as green as my imagination had painted them.

During those childhood years one of my favourite occupations was to ride my tricycle along our wide verandah. Playing with Melanie Oshry, the daughter of one of our neighbours, was another. Between the Oshrys' house and our own was a wire mesh fence covered by a granadilla creeper. Melanie and I made a hole in the fence and used to escape to each other's house.

Our other neighbour was a pilot and used to tell me of the aery splendour of the clouds. Old Mrs. Dunne, his mother, a widow, would vigourously sweep her own porch in the morning, making the dust motes dance in the sun's rays. She had never employed a domestic servant, which made her different from the other people who lived in Galway Road. They had come recently from England, and she did not want "strangers" (maids) in her house.

Across the road from us lived a family from Holland—the van der Sands. Alongside the van der Sands lived a young childless couple. My mother used to chat to Pauline Lipson across the fence. In later years Pauline, a lawyer, founded Legal Aid, a charitable organisation in Johannesburg that provides legal assistance to indigent black people. Years later, when I held public office and handled many requests for help, I often advised people to use the services of Legal Aid.

Next to the Oshrys, on the corner of Galway Road, lived the Papert family. My brother and I used to romp on the Paperts' front lawn with their dogs. When I was about eight, I was aware that there was some concern in the neighbourhood about the fate of one of the Papert sons, then at university. He was "in trouble" with the government for his student political activities. "It's always the Jews," my mother muttered darkly. My father said that he did not know why someone as talented as Seymour would throw his life away "for the schwartzes" (a derogatory Yiddish expression for black people).

These comments created a great ferment in my mind, because I had no family political reference to help me understand them. My father called non-Jews *yoks* and non-Jewish women who married Jewish men *shiksas*. I was unaware of any racial/cultural slur in the terms, if any was intended; they simply established our difference as Jews, so the term *schwartze* did not bother me. But the idea that trying to do something for others could mean throwing your life away disturbed me. Could it be that someone like Seymour Papert could be put into a place like Robben Island *for life* for working with black people? It was not a question I really wanted answered.

Contrary to throwing his life away, Seymour Papert, like so many other activists before and after him, prudently chose the path of self-exile. Among much else that he did, his work with the child development psychologist Jean Piaget in Switzerland motivated his own research into child cognition. A new computer language, LOGO, arose out of that research. Now living in Boston, Seymour Papert is today among the world's foremost educationists.

An annual event that I remember well from those years would bring some of our neighbours together and give us an unusual glimpse into the lives of black South Africans.

Sanitary lanes, narrow roadways for the garbage trucks, run between the houses in Parkview. Because our sanitary lane was considered a "good one," the local chapter of the Jewish Women's Benevolent Committee, of which my mother was a member, would hold its fund-raising jumble sale at our house every year. The sales would take place in winter, in the small plot between the wire fence of the lane and the white brick wall that surrounded our back garden. John planted maize there in the spring. In winter, the plot would lie fallow. Wooden trestle tables would be set up inside our fence and piled high with the outworn clothes of white suburbia, all marked with neatly printed price tags. At the appointed hour the clamouring hordes of mainly black women, many with babies strapped to their backs, would rush to the fence and rummage through the clothes. The committee members controlled the sales, collecting the meagre pennies and shillings thrust at them from the corners of handkerchiefs, where they were tied for safekeeping. Meanwhile John, apparently enjoying this duty, would try to control the women, brandishing his knobkerrie (Zulu fighting stick) and shouting Zulu imprecations at the crowd. Melanie and I would watch the excitement from the vantage of our position in the huge jacaranda tree that grew on her side of the fence but annually showered mauve jacaranda flowers over our back lawn.

I was heartbroken when Melanie moved away. My despair did not last long, though, for our new neighbours proved to be wonderful companions for the tomboy I had become.

Although I knew they were somehow "other," my parents were friendly with their parents—after all, we lived in a "mixed" neighbourhood, and we all went to the same school. Soon, however, I discovered one way in which my new friends were different.

Dennis and Raymond Coole were not Jewish, a fact that was revealed to me after we had built a tree platform high in the jacaranda tree. Dennis and Raymond had a peeing contest from this giddy height, and they warned me not to open my eyes. Girls were tolerated on the tree platform only by special permission, so I promised to heed the warning. Of course I could not help myself and peeked. I also could not help exclaiming at the strange appearance of their uncircumcised penises. (The only other naked male I had seen was my younger brother.) Raymond was so startled by my outburst that he fell out of the tree, suffering a concussion and a broken arm. All four parents accepted the fact of his injuries. What they did not understand was why Raymond had fallen to the ground with his pants and underpants around his ankles. None of us

breathed a word about the peeing competition, and our bond of
secrecy tied us firmly together for years. When my family
moved from Parkview, I lost touch with the Cooles.

In 1948 I began to attend nursery school at Mrs. Marais's.
Her school was three blocks from our house, and each morning
my nanny would walk me there. Anna Marais was a warm,
inspiring teacher, and I never forgot her. She taught me
manners and an early love of African fauna and flora. She read
to us from *Barbar the Elephant* and fed us lumps of sugar as a
reward if we learnt to say in Afrikaans, "Suiker, asseblief"
(Sugar, please). She taught us the names of the garden birds
and how to recognise their calls. We did finger painting and
played on an abandoned Model T Ford. She also had a jacaranda tree with a platform some distance off the ground.
Around the base of the tree was a large sand pit.

I was to learn later that in 1952, four years after I was first
under her tutelage, in grade school by then, courageous Anna
Marais and a few other women became founding members of
the liberal activist movement the Black Sash. The Black Sash
was a women's protest organisation, founded specifically to
protest the actions of Dr. Daniel Malan's recently elected
apartheid government, which disenfranchised those few "coloured" people already on the voters' roll.

Some thirty years later I met Anna Marais at a Black Sash
anniversary celebration. I was a public figure by then and she
over eighty years old but still upright and active. She told me
that she had held a poster in a protest stand some days earlier.
A young white man had thrown a rotten egg at her.

"A plainclothes policeman, of course—no manners. That's
what's wrong with this country: no one has any respect for
anyone else."

When I told her that I had been at her nursery school, she
said she remembered me and recounted some of my recent
political exploits, which she had read about in the newspapers.
I still doubt she remembered individual pupils from among the
hundreds she must have taught over the years, but perhaps I
am wrong.

Professor J.S. Marais, Anna Marais's husband, lectured to

me in history when I was at university. He had a reputation of being different and daring in South Africa in the early 1960s, an Afrikaner who was also a well-known liberal. I learnt that years earlier he had been thrown out of the Afrikaner volk for having demythologised several early-nineteenth-century Afrikaner heroes of the frontier days in the Eastern Cape. His meticulously documented research had revealed the Boer frontiersmen of the Slagtersnek and other incidents to be arrant racist bigots.

After two years under Mrs. Marais's nurturing tutelage, I spent a year at kindergarten. Then, donning my light blue uniform, I began elementary school at Parkview Junior.

At this age, despite Mrs. Marais's inculcation of the gentler pursuits in me, I continued to exhibit the tomboy traits that somewhat distressed my parents. In fact, the scrapes I got into could have more commonly been expected from a boy my age. Ironically, my brother, Roy, and I had little in common, he being younger and a real "mommy's boy." Shy and timid, he felt safest hiding behind my mother's skirts, while I was brash and venturesome. As a result, we did not do many things together. It was I who was pushed off the roundabout at the local playground by some older boys who forbade me to jump on while they were riding it. I had stitches in my knee for that act of defiance. I also once fought the neighbourhood bully at the regular Saturday morning Tarzan or cowboy movie performance we attended at the local cinema. He had stolen some of my comic books, which we all brought to swap with one another. I bit his arm, and he slapped me across the face, making my nose bleed.

At the same time, the curiosity that had been stimulated in me by Mrs. Marais continued to blossom. At Parkview Junior School I discovered that I loved school.

The school was divided into four colour-coded houses. My colour was yellow, and my house was called Lions. It was at Parkview Junior School, on our annual sports day, that I discovered I was fiercely competitive. Winning my potato sack race or the bean bag relay became a matter of the utmost importance to me.

And in the third grade, though I had only a minor role as a

fairy in the school play, I knew every word of everyone else's part. When anyone faltered for even a moment, unconsciously I would blurt out the cues. This brought the house down, much to the consternation of the actors and the teacher-producers. I remember not sleeping for days before the performances, waking up at night with the lines racing through my head.

My mother was proud of my ability to memorize and use words in little plays and stories of my own. "You're going to be a writer someday," she would tell me. I thrilled to that idea and responded enthusiastically when she asked me to read one or another of my creations to my father when he came home in the evening.

By the time the third-grade play was under way we had moved from Galway Road to the Cranbrook Hotel on the border of Doornfontein and Hillbrow. We were waiting for occupancy of an apartment at Kirstenbosch, a building in a garden setting in another part of Parkview. Kirstenbosch was adjacent to Parkview Senior School, where I would be going into the fourth grade.

The family move had come about because there had been a succession of burglaries in our house and in the neighbourhood of Galway Road. Ostensibly, my mother was too frightened to live there any longer. Perhaps, though, it was an excuse for her to leave the house she had always thought of as her mother-in-law's. In any case, there was the unstated assumption between my parents that the burglaries had been "inside" jobs, that somehow our maids had been implicated.

Our maids. One after another, my mother employed a parade of women of different ages, personalities, competencies. They would don a uniform of a pastel-coloured overall, an apron, and a starched scarf, called a *doek*, wrapped turban-style around their heads. Each would come into our home and perform the same monotonous domestic chores as those before her.

One of their chores was walking my brother and me to the playground, to the local shops, to our friends' homes. There would be much laughter and banter along the way with black men, young and old, in languages we did not know. "My cousin, my uncle," was the answer when I asked who the men were. Some of the women were motherly, and I felt warmth from

them, while others were just resignedly doing their duties. It
never occurred to me that they might have had children of
their own or a life beyond our backyard. They simply existed in
a vacuum for me.

Despite my parents' apprehension, I had never felt afraid or
threatened when we were left at night in the care of our maids.
Sometimes men, strangers to me, would join the maid in the
kitchen, and their voices would awaken me. Stumbling sleepily
to the kitchen, I would be rebuffed by a sharp warning not to
tell my parents of the night visitors.

One day on coming home from school I found our current
maid on the verge of leaving. What could have happened? I
wondered. Everything had seemed normal that morning. It
transpired that my mother had accused the maid of stealing a
packet of Marie biscuits (a South African brand of cookies) and
would not accept her protests of innocence. I was mortified. I
had hidden that packet in a drawer in my room, and despite the
wrath of my mother that I knew would follow, I was so consumed with guilt that I hastened to tell my mother of my
crime. She went to the maid to apologise, but the maid had
already packed her belongings in two cardboard boxes tied
with string. She would not stay, she said.

At the gate she told me bitterly, balancing one box on her
head, "Remember that under my skin I have blood the same
colour as your blood. When you white people tell lies about me,
my heart burns with the same anger as yours does."

Those words came back to me about seven years later, when I
was in high school. I had a small part in a production of *The
Merchant of Venice*, and when I heard it for the first time,
Shylock's famous speech to Salarino on the Rialto burnt inside
me with a shock of recognition:

> I am a Jew! Hath not a Jew eyes? hath not a Jew hands, organs,
> dimensions, senses, affections, passions? fed with the same food,
> hurt with the same weapons, subject to the same diseases, healed
> by the same means, warmed and cooled by the same winter and
> summer as a Christian is? If you prick us, do we not bleed? if you
> tickle us, do we not laugh? if you poison us, do we not die? and if
> you wrong us, shall we not revenge? . . .

The anger and anguish of that indignant black woman became even more vivid to me than they had been on that searing day, and Shakespeare became a god for me. If he was able to capture the veracity of her feelings in Shylock's words, other things he wrote must be imbued with the same universality. A glimmering of understanding of the complicity of racism dawned on me then.

But my awakening was a gradual process, not unlike piecing together a complex puzzle over the years of my childhood. And the picture began to emerge from the puzzle when I was in the fourth grade. My teacher that year, Mr. Broderick, was an Englishman who had been a war hero, chosen as a pilot for a mission to bomb strategic German dams, one of the famous Dam Busters later immortalised in book and film. He was our hero, too. And it was he who first opened my eyes to the injustices of apartheid. By then we had moved to Emmarentia. Fortuitously, so had Mr. Broderick, so I was fortunate to have him as my teacher at Emmarentia Primary School for two more years. He imbued me with ambition to write and with a feel for political argument. He simply ignored the official, rigourously worded injunctions against straying from the set syllabus, designed to implement the apartheid indoctrination inherent in the Christian National education that was taught in all state schools.

The format of all state school instruction, black and white, was and is Christian (Calvinist) and National (Afrikaner hegemony). Nowhere was this slant more evident than in the study of history, civic affairs, and social studies. My English-speaking classmates—white education being segregated along language lines—were as deeply suspicious of this blatantly racist material as I was. The interminable account of the Great Trek that our history texts gave us each year was received with healthy scepticism. The compulsory annual pilgrimages by bus to the shrine of Afrikaner nationalism near Pretoria, the Voortrekker Monument, left us with an irreverent, scoffing feeling about Afrikaners and things Afrikaans. It was "their" monument, to "their" battles and killings of black warriors, from whom "they" took the land. We were interlopers. At all times the Afrikaner Nationalist version of history was seen to have little to do with us, the English-speaking white South Africans. If one of the ends of the creation of the Afrikaner political mythology was to inculcate a broad patriotism among whites, it failed lamentably to do so for us. In fact, it reinforced our feeling of alienation from the Afrikaner power bloc. And Mr. Broderick's probing scepticism made that alienation even stronger, at least for me.

"What would happen to South Africa if all black people stopped working for a week?" he would ask us provocatively at the beginning of our history class. Inevitably a most lively discussion would follow, leading us up all sorts of dangerous paths. He would also parody the civics part of our history course, which began with a description of the various tribal groups of South Africa. "The Bantu have krul [tightly curled] hair, flat noses, and thick lips. Coloured people look like the Hottentots and are lazy and cunning. . . ."

Knowing that I had always wanted to be a teacher, Mr. Broderick told me to think of journalism as well. Almost inevitably, I suppose, I did. And it was mainly because of Mr. Broderick's influence that in 1956 I discovered the newspaper headlines I was reading actually reflected what was happening around me. One morning he brought to class a copy of the *Rand Daily Mail*, a liberal Johannesburg daily newspaper. On the front page was a picture of hundreds of black people walking to work in Johannesburg from the township of Alexandra, nine miles along Louis Botha Avenue. The line of walking workers appeared out of the smoky haze hanging like a pall over the township. "White Motorists Banned from Helping Bus Boycotters, Police Take Action," ran the headline. Mr. Broderick said that on the previous day he had been outside of Alex himself to see history in the making.

A few days later I told my mother that I wanted to visit my cousins, who lived in Highlands North, a suburb about three miles from Alexandra, and that afternoon took a bus along Louis Botha Avenue. The sight of hundreds of heavily armed policemen along the road, thousands of black people walking quietly together, and many white motorists in the side streets, driving off with carloads of black passengers, was stunning.

It proved to be a persistent image. Some whites were helping blacks, without being put into prison for it for the rest of their lives. My father had been wrong about that, I concluded. Yet it was obvious to me that what they were doing was daring and confrontational—the belligerent attitude of the police made that clear. Now I could see the Papert saga in perspective and the narrow line white activists trod.

The decade of 1952 to 1962, while I was growing up, was crucial for black resistance in South Africa. It was the decade of the Resistance Campaign called by the African National Congress (ANC). The leaders of the "liberation" movement had structured the campaign along Gandhian lines—absolute non-violence was the injunction of the leadership at mass demonstrations, marches, and mass meetings. Many of the leaders did not want to force the apartheid government to show a ruthlessly violent face to the world, being well aware of the state's potential militancy. At that time South Africa, while not a democratic society, was not yet a police state. The state contained the influence of the black leaders by entwining them in legal ties: prison, lengthy preparation for trial, lengthy trials.

The boycott against using the buses arose originally as a protest against the rise in fares, but it had escalated into a clash of wills between the African National Congress (ANC) and the authorities. The ANC, deeply involved in the Resistance Campaign, was using the boycott to test the will of the white authorities.

A friend of mine whom I met as an adult, Robin Harvey, vividly tells a story of her altercation with the police during the boycott. A young policeman, an adolescent (Robin could not have been much older than eighteen herself then), stopped her at a traffic light near Alex and ordered her to tell her black passengers to disembark so that he could arrest them. "You're lucky I'm not arresting you too, lady!" he shouted rudely at her, wagging his finger near her face. "I saw red," she says. "I rolled up my window as fast as I could, jamming his fingers. At the same time I accelerated away. The policeman pulled his hand out of the window just in time. Otherwise I may have been guilty of manslaughter as well as jumping a red light, insulting a policeman, carrying bus boycotters. . . ."

I must have had a subconscious presentiment of my parents'

later fear of and opposition to my political activities, for I never
told them of what I had seen on Louis Botha Avenue. But I was
pleased that I had made the journey and the connection between the events behind the headlines. Looking back, I can see
that this incident was a turning point for me. My eyes were
opened. In light of what I had already seen and understood, I
could no longer grow up blindly.

As with children everywhere, other exciting new horizons
began to appear in my life. In grade six my mother decided
that I needed to have my elocution polished. My wild tomboy
excesses were disturbing to her, and I think she thought that
elocution lessons would smooth my rough edges. After some
time, my speech teacher suggested to my mother that I might
enjoy joining a drama group. And so I came into the life of June
Wilson, who became my mentor and my friend. As Mr. Broderick had led me to political awareness, June shared her knowledge and enthusiasm for literature and her love of the Eastern
Cape coast with me. I loved her for that and for much else over
the years.

As well as my drama classes, I went to "mixed" (boys and
girls) parties where we rocked to Little Richard and Elvis
Presley. "Blue Suede Shoes" became the signature tune of my
friends and classmates. But we also sang "If I Had a Hammer"
along with Pete Seeger.

And a little later, when Joan Baez asked her audience at a
concert if she might take off her shoes, she opened up vistas of a
new freedom for me: the blowing away of old social prohibi-
tions, the dawning of new social mores. For me, "the times they
were a-changin' " more than I could have known.

CHAPTER 3
Alpheus's Legacy

While I was ending my years at primary school and beginning high school in 1959, the Resistance Campaign of the African National Congress was reaching its climax. In the early days of 1960, Robert Sobukwe, one of the leaders of an offshoot of the ANC called the Pan African Congress (PAC), burned his pass book on a bonfire in protest of the government's racial dog-collaring scheme. In the early 1950s the new government had passed a law requiring all "nonwhite" males initially, and later all nonwhite females, to carry identification documents stating their racial classification. Sobukwe was promptly arrested for his act of defiance, but his courage had not gone unnoticed by his peers, and the pass-burning campaign was ignited around the country. Tensions were high, even in remote areas.

One such area was Sharpeville, a township near Vereeniging, a small Transvaal town on the Vaal River. Residents marched to the local police station to stage an antipass demonstration. A crowd of several thousand ringed the wire fence around the station and peacefully sang traditional songs, while hundreds of people tossed their pass books onto a huge fire. The crowd grew. The heavily armed white and black policemen

51

inside the compound grew increasingly nervous, although eyewitness accounts emphasize the peaceful nature of the demonstration. Then, without warning, the nervous police opened fire on the unarmed crowd. Sixty-eight people were killed and over a hundred injured. An inquiry into the shooting months later revealed that the vast majority of the deaths and injuries had been caused by bullet wounds in the back; the police had shot into the panicked and fleeing crowd. This massacre on March 21, 1960, had created new martyrs for the resistance struggle and shocked the apartheid leadership, which now began to fear severe mass uprisings.

On March 30, 1960, nine days after Sharpeville and eleven days into the antipass campaign called by Robert Sobukwe, Philip Kgosana, a twenty-three-year-old student and lieutenant of the dissident PAC, riding on the crest of the wave of black anger, led a march of between fifteen thousand and thirty thousand migrant workers almost to the gates of police headquarters in Cape Town. There they intended to demand arrest for a massive demonstration of pass burning. Sobukwe wanted to break down the prison system by flooding its jails.

Political analysts and historians agree that Kgosana's march was a turning point in South Africa, despite the fact that the Bastille was not stormed that day, nor did the Winter Palace fall. For in the aftermath of that march, those black leaders who spoke for the struggle no longer advocated nonviolence, but rather a course of violent resistance, which they now saw as the only alternative to the violence of the state.

The march was the culmination of weeks of strikes in Cape Town, the first of the current Resistance Campaign, and all over South Africa mass black resistance was growing. Inevitably, the historical record shows, the state was resolving to strike back. By March 30th mass raids and arrests had already been conducted in other parts of the country. In Cape Town, Kgosana, in the press of events, was unaware of the changed mood of the authorities. He stuck to Sobukwe's dictum of absolute nonviolence, and his fellow marchers heeded him.

Within blocks of their headquarters, the police ordered the marchers to disperse. Kgosana demanded to see the minister of justice. After a conference between the police chief and Kgosana, Kgosana was promised that he could see the minister in a few hours if he would tell the marchers to disperse. Cape Town—all of South Africa—held its breath, although at the time the full significance of the moment was not marked. Kgosana agreed, and the men dispersed. A few hours later, realising too late that he had been duped, Kgosana was arrested and thrown into jail. A state of emergency was declared in the country. The police moved quickly, using their sweeping emergency powers to smash the front of black resistance. Effectively, this state of emergency became a permanent way of life in South Africa, for the white regime has maintained its power only by using the fusillade of quasi-legal, arbitrary repressive legislation it assembled and then expanded after Sharpeville and Kgosana's march. Today no such march could take place, for military camps cordon off most black townships, and any black leader likely to stir the masses, as Kgosana did, is preemptively thrown into detention.

In 1960, the ANC and the PAC were outlawed, and the leaders who had not managed to escape to exile were sentenced to life imprisonment for charges of treason. In exile both movements have grown and now seek to overthrow the apartheid state by infiltrating "freedom fighters" into the country. However, internal state repression and effectiveness in dealing with "terrorists" have also increased. Despite its seeming ineffectiveness over its seventy years of resistance, which make it the oldest liberation movement in the world, the ANC retains the loyalty of the majority of black South Africans.

Until that day in 1960, white South Africa had lived a golden, blessed life in Eden. But the government's iron-fist response to black resistance at Sharpeville and elsewhere brought a dawning chill of reality to the white consciousness. "How long do we have?" whites asked each other. "Five years" was the usual reply. For the white man, the clock ticking away the seconds to mass racial violence has been stuck at five years to midnight since 1960.

And for those who considered themselves liberals, participating in antiapartheid activities became a prohibitively risky business. Through their lone representative in Parliament, Helen Suzman, as well as in the press, in public meetings, and in peaceful street demonstrations, white liberals had shown their solidarity with the Resistance Campaign. But Sharpeville and the subsequent police crackdown, as well as the state of emergency, broke the impetus of their opposition.

Somewhere in the political matrix of those years my nascent political awareness came to life. Avidly, every day I would read the *Rand Daily Mail*, which was the only newspaper in South Africa attempting to inject serious political analysis into its coverage of the Resistance Campaign and which became essential reading for anyone involved in South African politics. There were many stories of Afrikaner public servants in Pretoria who hid the *Rand Daily Mail* inside their progovernment Afrikaans-language newspapers to read surreptitiously. By reading the paper and listening to adult conversation about politics, I naively felt that I was very much a part of the political events sweeping South Africa.

In September 1961 I began my political career by pushing my bicycle along the Emmarentia sidewalks and dropping election pamphlets into the neighbourhood mailboxes. I was helping Jack Cope, whose daughter was a friend of mine, in his bid for reelection to Parliament.

Jack Cope had been one of nine other members of Parliament who, in 1958, had broken away from the moribund white opposition party, the United Party, and lost their seats. Those ten members had stood for the fledgling Progressive Party, whose platform was an amalgam of a progressive commitment to human rights and the rule of law and a more conservative commitment to black voting rights. The Progressive Party adopted a nonracial, qualified franchise as its key political platform, the right to enfranchisement resting on educational and property qualifications for all South Africans, irrespective of race. This was a long way from the universal adult franchise that some of its members thought it should espouse, but it was heresy to most white voters in South Africa.

Jack Cope failed to win reelection, and he and his family left South Africa for England shortly thereafter. But one member of the 1958 breakaway group was reelected to Parliament. Her name was Helen Suzman, and with this election she began thirteen years of brave but lonely defence in Parliament of human rights and civil liberties in South Africa. It was a defence conducted in an atmosphere of general hostility and personal vindictiveness and vilification from white politicians both inside and outside the Houses of Parliament—unlike her international reputation, which has been so positive.

Born in 1917, Helen Suzman grew up in Johannesburg. In 1934, barely sixteen, she enrolled in the liberal University of the Witwatersrand, eventually earning an honours degree in economics. She began lecturing there in economic history in 1945, when she was twenty-eight. In 1953 Helen gave up her career in academia when she was elected to Parliament as an antiapartheid member for the constituency of Houghton. As this book goes to press, she is still serving in Parliament, an unbroken run of thirty-five years in the House, thirteen of those years (1961–1974) as the sole antiapartheid liberal member.

Nominated three times for the Nobel Peace Prize, Helen was the recipient in 1978 of the once-a-decade honour the United Nations Award for Human Rights. She has received honourary fellowships and degrees from Oxford University and the London School of Economics, as well as Harvard, Brandeis, Columbia, Smith, her alma mater, and universities in Europe. Her many invitations to lecture mark her widespread international reputation for her courageous stand and unswerving opposition in and out of Parliament to the racial policies of the National Party's apartheid government. A champion of justice and habeas corpus, she has earned the respect and admiration of long-term political prisoners for her concern. Those on Robben Island, in Pollsmoor, and Pretoria Central Prison call her "Our Lady of the Prisoners." Helen's political career is synonymous with the struggle for liberal values in South Africa.

Ironically, in the same year that I took my first firm steps toward political activism, South Africa became a republic. Prime Minister Hendrik Verwoerd, after a confrontation with British Prime Minister Harold Macmillan and other Commonwealth prime ministers over the apartheid ideology of his government and its agenda of repression against black people, walked out of the annual prime ministers' conference. He took

South Africa's membership in the Commonwealth with him.

Shortly thereafter a referendum was held among South Africa's all-white voters on whether South Africa should declare itself a republic. The answer was positive, but by only a slender majority of 60,000-odd votes out of more than 1.5 million.

The great day of independence was announced. All schools would hold assemblies at which "Die Stem" ("The Voice"), the national anthem, would be sung. Schools would then close for the rest of the day.

I was attending the well-known Parktown Girls' High School, a fine school with a tradition of scholarship, fair play, and good behaviour. Many of the faculty were teachers trained in Britain, with a strong allegiance to the queen and the Commonwealth. Despite the fact that teachers were subject to stringent restrictions against using the classroom to further the political aims of any organisation other than the National Party, we students were made aware of the heightened emotion among the faculty as Republic Day drew near.

Miss Paynter, then the senior history mistress and singing coach, later to become headmistress, had a red face and a look of steely determination as she seated herself behind the piano on the assembly stage. Our current headmistress, Miss MacGregor ("the Grog"), and the other faculty members stood firmly at attention on the stage, looking serious and grim. There was an atmosphere of mourning in the hall, not, as one would have expected, of happy jubilation. We were losing our place in the civilised world, being led to isolation and the entrenchment of Afrikaner Nationalist hegemony.

We ran through the usual format of prayers and readings. Then our headmistress told us that we were gathered together to witness the birth of a republic in South Africa. We took out the piece of paper on which "Die Stem" had been typed and prepared to sing it as we had been taught to do over the last few weeks. But instead of the solemn tones of "Die Stem" rolling around us, we heard the familiar chords of "God Save the Queen." We snuffled and giggled while the faculty began singing. Rebellion and dissent, political defiance in the hallowed, panelled hall of Parktown Girls' High School? Yes. It took seconds for us to recover; then we lustily joined in with the faculty. We left the hall in high excitement. Miss Paynter and several other faculty members were crying. I felt as if I were on the verge of a great precipice. The earth would open, and all of us would plunge over into the vortex of an encounter with the Nationalists.

To my knowledge there were no repercussions among the faculty for their rebellion. The Nationalists were too busy with their own celebrations and too preoccupied with ruthlessly smashing the ANC and black resistance. They were also too embroiled in amending the statute book, wiping away any remaining vestiges of civil liberties and habeas corpus. There was, for example, the Public Safety Act (Proclamation 91), which provided for declaration of states of emergency. There was the Extension of University Education Amendment Act, which banned black students from white universities. There was the Population Registration Amendment Act, which streamlined the work of the Racial Classification Bureaux. And more. The repressive legislation that replaced the old statutes gave quasi-legal form to the Nationalists' oppression. It was a cynical abuse of parliamentary procedure, an abuse that the Nationalist government has used extensively during its more than forty years in power.

At the same time it did not occur to me that these excesses of the Nationalist Party government might impinge directly on my life. Not being politically active, the people I knew were in little danger of running afoul of the repressive legislation that was appearing almost daily on the statute book. Yet in some vague way all that repressive legislation made me feel uncomfortable. Slowly I realised that the loss of civil liberties in South Africa diminished the quality of life of us all.

For many years it had been common practise for the police to conduct pass raids in the white suburbs. By law, employers were permitted to have sleeping on their premises only those employees who were legally working for them. In order for an employer and employee to be acting legally, a contract between them had to be entered into at the local Pass Office.

Pass Offices, or Labour Bureaux, were run by government bureaucrats with the authority to either approve a work contract or order a black work seeker to return to his "homeland" within seventy-two hours. As the pass law regulations changed frequently, both employer and employee, by going to the Pass Office, were playing Russian roulette with the work seeker's pass book and, therefore, his ability to earn a livelihood in a white area.

The police had and still have the right of entry into any backyard servants' quarters, at any time of day or night. The rationale given by the authorities was that the police were protecting the white suburbs from "vagrants" and "illegals"— black men and women who were in an area "illegally" in that their pass books did not carry the official stamp allowing them to be there.

The pass raids—often violent, with many people hurt—always netted a fair catch of "illegals." Husbands, wives, and even children found in the room of the legal employee, but without official permission to be there, were subjected to jail sentences for trespassing. Later, in a further effort by the authorities to control the burgeoning mass of people entering the cities from the impoverished rural areas, employers were also made subject to a court appearance and the choice of a fine or a jail term for harbouring such "illegals." Concurrently it was made more difficult for black persons seeking work in the cities to register themselves as workers at the Pass Office.

Most of the people my mother, other family members, and friends employed had some irregularity in their passes. My parents and other employers were consciously breaking the law by employing these people and by turning a blind eye to whatever "illegals" were sleeping in their backyards. They knew they were breaking the law, the employees knew they were breaking the law, and the police knew every second house in every suburb "harboured illegals."

One night in 1960, when I was fourteen, a police whistle tore through the air in quiet Emmarentia, waking me. Hurried footsteps sounded on the grass outside my window, then I heard more footsteps, a gunshot, and a thump as someone fell over the six-foot wall between our house and our neighbour's. My father went to the kitchen door to answer the insistent knocking. Martha, our maid, was wailing outside. Creeping down the hallway, I listened to my father and the policeman.

"Your Bantu had a boy in her room," the white policeman said accusingly, in guttural English cluttered with an overlay of Afrikaans-sounding vowels.

"I don't know anything about that." My father was noncommittal. He was telling the truth.

"It's the law that no illegals can be on your property."

My father made no comment. Martha, wrapped in a blanket, looking woeful and sobbing quietly, had appeared behind the policeman. Two black policemen were behind her.

"The buck Bantu tried to run away, so I shot the bugger. He's lying there by the wall. He's not dead, so we'll take him with us, but you'll have to appear in court, man."

After taking some details from my father, the policemen disappeared into the dark. Martha was left standing in the pool of light cast by the outside floodlight. My father spoke quietly to her.

"Are you okay, Martha?" She nodded her head. "Who is that boy, Martha?" We could hear the police vehicle engine being revved in the street. "He's my son, master," she said equally quietly.

"Call your mother," my father said to me. I did not know that he knew I was standing behind him. "I'm here," my mother said behind me. "Come in, Martha. I'll make us a pot of tea."

For the first and only time, I saw my mother serve a black person and sit at the table with her, while we all drank tea. "The government does a lot of terrible things," my mother said.

"Yes, life is heavy for us," Martha replied.

Martha was given the next day off to try to find her son at the Non-European Hospital in Hillbrow, where he had been taken the previous night. My father had elicited this information on the telephone from the charge officer at the Parkview Police Station.

Martha's son recovered from his bullet wound. On his release from hospital he was immediately charged with trespassing and sentenced to three months of farm labour on a potato farm in Delmas in the Transvaal. As soon as he could, he returned to Johannesburg, staying with Martha and looking for work—"odd jobs" since he could not "fix" his pass. Martha told me that he had livid scars on his back where he had been whipped by the farmer.

The theme of domestic servants, pass laws, and arrogant policemen acting with the impunity the Nationalist legal system gives them is as familiar to white South Africans as the suikerbosch (an indigenous shrub) and the piet-my-vrou (an African garden sparrow). But to me the sudden intrusion into our lives of police brutality, court appearances, Martha's pain, and her son's inhuman treatment came as a brutal shock.

Ten years later a similar incident had even more significance for me. By then I was aware of my complicity, but I was still not able to translate my burning anger at the police into political action.

My father had died, and my mother was living in Roxdale, an apartment building on the Louis Botha Avenue side of Houghton. Apartment occupants were allowed to employ one domestic servant. The women lived in bleak, Dickensian conditions on the roof of the building. Segregated from them, on another part of the roof, lived the male cleaners, the "flat boys." No men were allowed to be in the women's section of the roof after ten o'clock at night, and no women in the men's. This rule was largely ignored, but the rooftop dwellers knew each night that they were playing a dangerous game with the police.

At about eleven o'clock on Friday night when Sandy and I were visiting my mother, we heard a commotion in the vicinity of the elevator and stairwell. We rushed out of my mother's apartment to the scene. Nothing was happening on her floor, the fifth, so we peered over the balcony. We saw the crumpled form of a man lying on the concrete paving outside the glass wall of the staircase. Shards of glass and a crowd of black onlookers surrounded him. Some of the women were keening. The flashing blue light of a police van cast an eerie pallor over the scene. Two policemen were lounging against the side of the van. Elizabeth, my mother's maid, was among the onlookers.

A black woman I knew came slowly up the stairs. "Aw, Missy Janet, it's bad, bad. The policee he chase Alpheus across the roof. Alpheus, he a little drunk. He very frightened. He run through the glass at the stairs. He fall. Dead." She shook her head. "The policee still catch many others there tonight." She gestured with her head in the direction of the roof. "Aw, how can we live like this?"

Alpheus had been the cleaner assigned to my mother's apartment. Every day he would come in at the appointed hour, and on his hands and knees he would polish the parquet floors and clean the bath and toilet. Once a week he would come to spend the afternoon cleaning the windows, inside and outside—five stories up, with no safety precautions. Alpheus was a middle-aged migrant worker. Once a year he would return for a month to see his family in rural Zululand. For almost thirty years he had lived in single-sex quarters on the rooftop and worked in Roxdale. Now he was dead.

I wish I could say that I rushed down to the policemen, took their numbers, and laid charges of manslaughter against them. I wish I had made the effort to find a way to send a message of condolence to Alpheus's family in far-off Zululand, telling them that someone had appreciated his work and his kindly demeanour. I wish that I had done then the things I would have done once I achieved public office and was more aware of access, communication, and channels that were open to me.

We returned resignedly to my mother's apartment, Sandy and I. While ranting and raving against the system that allows such excesses, I still felt that trying to do anything about it was futile. The story of Alpheus and the policemen was being repeated with hundreds of variations around the country that very Friday night, as it was every night of every year—our very special brand of South African roulette.

By then I was an active member of the Houghton Progressive Party, and I mentioned the incident to Helen Suzman. She did take it up with the minister of police, and Alpheus's widow was paid some compensation by the police. Helen also made sure that the widow received the pension due Alpheus.

But it was not enough. It would never be enough to pay for the life of Alpheus—of all the Alpheuses of South Africa.

CHAPTER 4

"For Some of Us,
Politics in South Africa
Is a Deadly,
Serious Matter"

It was 1961, my sophomore year in high school. My classmates and I were waiting for our history teacher to come into the classroom. I had been thrilled that morning to read of Helen Suzman's quixotic election victory the previous day. As a schoolgirl I was a highly imaginative romantic (my patient husband says on occasions I still am), and I responded eagerly to the appeal of this dauntless woman, this passionate spokesperson for liberal values. She spoke of things like respect and dignity with the same reverence that my grandfather had. She was the only member of her party, the Progressive Party, to be returned to Parliament. I exclaimed to the class in general, "Did you see Helen Suzman retained her seat for the Progs?"

Odette Mostert, an Afrikaans-speaking girl who was at Parktown Girls' High only because there was no Afrikaans-language high school in the area where she lived and whose father was a National Party official, frowned at me. Her seat was alongside mine in an adjoining row. Behind her the blue sky was a bright plane of colour through the window.

"She's a commie. All her party love kaffirs [a derogatory term for blacks]. She's a danger to South Africa."

Odette's voice was cold and intense, a tone I had never heard before. An unusual still silence fell over the room, and I stared at her in surprise. We were good friends, had won many tennis matches together, and played on the same hockey team. I retorted quickly.

"Come on now, she's not a danger—all she wants is equal opportunities for all South Africans."

The Progressive Party slogan—"Equal opportunity for all South Africans"—flashed into my mind. I had seen it so often, plastered on trees and walls around the suburbs where I lived and rode my bicycle to school. Odette was really angry.

"The blacks will swamp us. There'll be nothing for the whites if she has her way. You English-speakers, you know nothing of politics, nothing of the dangers in this country."

Now I too was angry. A school debater, I hated being bettered in an argument.

"It's not her or the Progs, you know. It's your bloody government. If you don't give the blacks a chance, you'll drive them to hate us. Then there'll be a war here, you know—and your government will have made it."

A few nods of agreement around the room emboldened me, and I delivered another thrust. "It was their country first, you know. You took it away from them. If you don't share it with them, sooner or later they'll take it back from you—and kill all of us doing it."

I was pleased I had said it, although I knew I had probably gone too far for most of my classmates. A few girls spoke at the same time. Faith Hope said, "My father says if there weren't blacks to push around, your government would be after the Jews." And Deirdre Cunningham added, "Janet's right in a lot of what she says, but it's our country, too; we helped to build it."

On exploited black labour, I wanted to retort (Deirdre's father was an industrialist). But Odette's words brushed mine aside. With eyes blazing and face red, she spat, "That's because all the commies are Jews anyway. And we'll fight to the death to keep this land!"

At this point Miss Paynter entered the room. If she felt the tension, she ignored it, and we began our lesson on Sarajevo in 1914. European history was so remote. I longed to have a discussion led by an adult on South African politics, but such a discussion was not part of National Party doctrine, not integral to the greater good of the narrow Christian National path they had chosen for us. I did, however, learn a few lessons from that brief exchange. One was that we were five Jewish girls among twenty-eight "others"; another was that we were twenty-seven English-speaking girls to Odette's lone Afrikaans voice. But perhaps the most significant revelation was that for me political arguments were heady stuff. I had loved the feeling of danger that overcame me as I said brave things. I loved being out on a limb.

Aside from my gibing at the doctrinaire curbs on what I was learning, school was a milieu in which I thrived. I enjoyed wearing a uniform, being in academic and sporting contests, upholding tradition, being a prefect.

Of my many friends at school, Brenda Yule was inadvertently responsible for opening my eyes wide to what living inside apartheid means. Brenda's mother, Hazel, like Anna Marais, was an active Black Sash worker. The Sash helped to support a crèche (day nursery) in Alexandra, the black township near Johannesburg where the bus boycott had taken place in 1956. Mrs. Yule was the Sash liaison with the crèche personnel. I was fifteen when one afternoon I accompanied Brenda and her mother to the crèche. I had never before been inside a black township, and looking back now, I recognise that visit as an important step on the road of my transformation from a naive white middle-class Jewish girl into someone who was really beginning to see the ravages of apartheid.

As we drove through Alex, the dismal makeshift shacks, the narrow dusty unlit roads, and the grimy, half-naked children appeared to me through a miasma of shock and disbelief. How could these people live in these conditions in a city as big and as modern as Johannesburg?

The crèche was a cold brick room with a stone floor, and though it had no heating and paneless windows, it was as clean and well cared for as it could be, as were the many small children there. In contrast to those children in the streets, these were dressed in neat smocks, happily drinking mugs of milk when we entered.

I was introduced to the supervisor, and we shook hands. It was the first time I had encountered a black person on any basis other than that of master to servant.

Mrs. Nthuli was telling Brenda's mother that the only faucet at the crèche had stopped working. A city council official a few days earlier had said that the water had been cut off because the crèche had not paid its water bill. Mrs. Nthuli produced the receipt for us. The bill had been paid, but the official would not look at the receipt, she said. On the day that we paid a visit, an official from the city Health Department had called to tell Mrs. Nthuli that the city council would close down the crèche in twenty-four hours unless they had running water on the premises. "So, what do I do now, Mrs. Yule? These children have nowhere else to go; we must stay open for them." She spoke with resignation and defeat.

"Don't worry, Alice. I'll do what I can."

Brenda's mother seethed all the way home. She called the chief medical officer of the Johannesburg City Council and told him off in no uncertain terms as to the misdeeds of his staff. She also threatened to tell the *Rand Daily Mail* of the incident. He promised to look into the matter. Water was restored the next day.

My visit to Alexandra seared me. Nothing in my life had prepared me for this first encounter with the South African reality I saw that day. I contrasted my home, my school, my life, with that of the children of Alex.

My home had many rooms and a garden with fruit trees in the backyard. We had electricity and hot and cold running water. No one had ever come to us to deny us services that I accepted as essentials of daily life—water, sewerage, power. The homes in Alex were uniformly tiny boxlike structures or corrugated-iron and wooden shacks. The streets were rutted sand tracks with piles of rotting garbage and pools of stagnant water. There was no electricity.

My school was huge—several buildings together, many classrooms, a panelled library, science laboratories, gymnasiums, a huge swimming pool, and several playing fields. Alexandra High School, the sole high school for over a hundred thousand people, was a converted Catholic mission with a few classrooms and no facilities. Students learnt in two sessions, 8:00 to 12:00 and 12:00 to 4:00, in classes of up to eighty students.

We wore our school uniforms proudly, whereas in Alex the minority of children who attended school wore cast-off shorts and shirts. In winter only a few had sweaters, and fewer still had shoes. School for whites today is compulsory for ten years; for blacks, for four. I had three meals a day—meat, fish, fruit, whatever I wanted—and when I would not eat, my parents would admonish me to "think of the starving children in *China!*" The children of Alex were fortunate to eat meat once a week.

The inequality, the injustice, the immorality, the inhumanity of the South African way of life had become clearly etched for me. For the first time I looked into the faces of the black people around me and saw their resignation and surrender. I saw the oppression in the drawn lines of their faces and in the suffering in their eyes.

The long lines of black people waiting for their twice-daily bus trip to and from work said to me that no black people owned cars. The groups of black people idling and chatting on the city's pavements said to me that black people had nowhere else to go.

Diffidently I approached the domestic staff we employed and asked them about their families and the conditions of their lives. But the information I sought was not forthcoming. It was impossible for me to come to terms with the inequities of the world I saw around me.

I tried to speak to my parents about my discoveries. "There's nothing we can do about it," they said. "It's dangerous to get involved. Of course the government is wrong to do things the way they do, but the blacks are not ready for government themselves. They'll kill each other first and then us, like all the other tribes have done in Africa. They're different from us— savages deep down, still."

My father's earlier warning that being critical of the government put me in danger was echoing hollower and hollower. What real danger could I be facing compared to the ultimately dangerous lives—the health hazards, the living hazards—that black people were forced to lead just because they were black?

I could never be in the same life danger as blacks. Political danger was artificial, contrived (but the thought of being imprisoned on an island in the sea *was* scary to me). Although my view of danger did broaden later, at that time the concept of danger that appalled me was the threat that blacks faced every day, every moment.

As for being different from us, I did not buy that argument either. Nomsi was not different from me; John was not different from me. And Mrs. Nthuli seemed to be able to run her crèche efficiently and well.

I tried to speak to June, my drama teacher, whose opinion I valued above all others, about my new perceptions.

"It's a waste of time to try to do anything," she said. "All politicians—black and white—are self-serving egoists. The blacks are generations behind us in terms of education and living a modern life with all the new technology. Don't waste your time with politics!"

We were standing in the driveway of her home. It was a bright, sunny day, and I remember reeling inwardly from the brunt of her words. This was June, my beloved teacher and mentor, who had been so lovingly supportive of my intellectual forays over the years, who had shown me the realm of mountain and sea and fabulous birds in the Eastern Cape. How strange that we had never spoken of politics before.

I felt uneasy, insecure about my inclination to involve myself in politics, to try somehow to redress the inequality and injustice I could now see all around me, all the time. It became a lonely, defiant commitment without my parents' support and June's interest and concern.

I spent much of my spare time with Brenda, whose family helped fill the void. Besides having a mother who would listen to me, Brenda had a brother, Brian, at university, and he took me to a public meeting to hear Helen Suzman report back to her constituents. The Houghton Primary School hall was packed with people overflowing into the corridors and courtyard. Helen, impeccably dressed, small in stature, seemed to fill the stage with the fierce intensity, the passion with which she spoke of the ideals of human rights and justice. Incisively she cut through the parliamentary, legislative cant that had

further entrenched apartheid during that session in the name
of state security. I was spellbound by both her speech and the
fervour and enthusiasm of her supporters. At the end of the
meeting I signed a membership form to join the Young Progressive movement. I had taken a decisive step, and I knew
that my parents would be furious. They were.

"Don't sign anything!"

"Don't you read the newspapers? Don't you know the government's cracking down on students? Look at all the young people
who are in jail, banned, exiled. Do you want to be arrested?"

No, I never wanted to be arrested. I did not know what would
become of me in jail. But it was a risk I took and grew used to
living with. I wanted to be involved, to be active, to oppose the
apartheid government that had created such misery and turmoil for us all.

Being too diffident to go to any of the functions alone, at
school I tried to interest some of my contemporaries at school in
joining the Young Progs. I also tried again to engender political
debate in the classroom. Most of the girls shied away from the
subject. Politics was a dirty word and a dangerous business in
South Africa. But politics, even for me, was not of primary
significance. School and schoolwork, sport and competition,
boys and parties, plays and debates, vacations—these were the
grist of our days.

In my matriculation year I was duly appointed to the ranks
of Parktown Girls' High School prefectship and anointed the
Head of my House. As a matter of course, along with many of
my classmates (there is no competitive entrance procedure for
white students to white universities), I gained admittance to
the University of the Witwatersrand, where I enrolled for a
liberal arts degree in teaching.

Looking back, it seems to me that then I was more politically
aware than my contemporaries at school. Yet it was more the
play of personalities in politics that fascinated the romantic in
me than the significance of the patterning of the political
events of the time.

Helen Joseph was one such personality. I read of her in the
newspapers and admired her from afar. Then in her mid-
fifties, she had been an activist for years. In 1958, for example,

she had been a treason trialist along with Nelson Mandela and 180 others. As perennial secretary, she was deeply involved in the multiracial Federation of South African Women and was caught up in the government's crackdown on the ANC and other activities in 1962. During that fateful year she became the first person in South Africa to be served with a house arrest order, and over the next twenty years she would be served with several others. This order was served on her a brief few months after her first five-year banning order had expired in July.

When I first learnt of the terms of her banning order, I was horrified. I did not know then that hundreds of others would become the victims of the same repression:

(a) She must remain in her home from 6:30 P.M. until 6:30 A.M. every weekday and from 2:30 P.M. on Saturday until Monday morning and on all public holidays.

(b) She may have no visitors there except her doctor (unless the doctor is a listed person [one who cannot be published or address the public]), and her attorney may also visit her only under the same conditions.

(c) She must report to police headquarters between 12:00 (noon) and 2:00 P.M. every day except Sundays and public holidays.

(d) She may not attend any gathering, including gatherings at which the persons present have social intercourse with one another (her writings and statements may not be published).

(e) She may not communicate in any way whatsoever with anyone whose name has been listed or who has been served with a banning order.

(f) She may not leave the magisterial district of Johannesburg, nor may she enter any African township, compound or hostel, or any factory premises.

Helen Joseph was house-arrested for an undisclosed offence, without trial and without any opportunity to defend herself. It was illegal to publish any statement by her. It still is.

For many years she lived in a small house in Norwood, around the corner from the house my husband and I lived in when our children were young. I used to visit her when she was allowed visitors, between her banning orders and house arrest edicts. It was the late 1970s, and she was in her seventies then;

she was of medium height, with a slim build and with her grey hair swept back into a neat chignon. By this time Helen had been ill with heart problems and cancer for almost fifteen years.

One night at about ten-thirty Sandy and I heard gunshots nearby.

"Helen's house again," I remarked.

"Probably," answered Sandy.

The complicity of living in South Africa struck home to me again. An unknown gunman (I attributed the shots to right-wing reactionary violence) had aimed his weapon at the house of a friend, and I—a supposedly aware, concerned, and involved South African—was complacently commenting on the incident as if it were as unremarkable as a Sunday braai (barbecue).

I went to see Helen the next morning and found her a little shaken but still resolute. Before I had arrived, a BBC-TV crew had come to interview her about the shooting, and we noted the irony that she was being shown and quoted in Britain while in South Africa no one was allowed to hear what she said or read what she wrote. Helen thanked me for caring and sympathising, for being her friend and city councillor—another bit of irony, for as soon as she was named a banned person she was removed from the voters' roll and had never been allowed to vote for me or anyone else.

Had she reported the incident to the police? Major Olckers, the chief officer at the Norwood Police Station, was a caring man—at least he tried to be just in his execution of his unjust duties. No, she shrugged; she had not bothered this time. Major Olckers would read of the incident in the press. Besides, if the police had not uncovered any traces of the perpetrators of all the other assaults on her over the years, why did I think they would do any better this time? It was my turn to shrug.

We had a cup of tea and chatted in Helen's small, neat living room. The two bullet holes and the shattered glass around them in the window facing the street stared mutely at me. I could interpret them any way I wanted to. "She got what she was looking for," some would say. "It's a violent society," others would rationalize. "She's a martyr, living alone," would be the response of still others. I chose to be reminded that for some of us politics in South Africa is a deadly, serious matter.

That morning Helen wanted to reminisce about the 1956 march to Pretoria by twenty thousand black and a handful of white women to protest the application of the pass laws to black women. Led by Lilian Ngoyi and Helen Joseph, the women had braved the very seat of government, the Union Buildings. I had read elsewhere of the march, an event of high emotion, courage, triumph. I had also heard Helen tell her story before, but I could listen to it again and again.

Another incident that captivated me was the story of how Arthur Goldreich and Harold Wolpe, political prisoners, escaped to England. It was not so much their personalities that drew me, but the high drama of their situation. Goldreich and Wolpe, together with two other "politicals," Mosie Moolla and Ahmed Jasset, escaped from political detention in Johannesburg in August 1963. They had been arrested at Rivonia, a suburb of Johannesburg, along with several other alleged members of the High Command of the African National Congress's military wing.

At that time my parents were friends with a couple named Marie and Ben Langley, who owned a weekend cottage in the village of Kosmos (named for an indigenous South African daisy) on the Hartebeestpoort Dam in the Magaliesberg. It was about a two-hour drive from Johannesburg, and we often spent Sundays there. The Langleys were childless, and my brother and I were made to feel especially welcome by them. As I loved being near the water and being able to climb in the unspoilt, wooded kloofs and rocky cliffs behind their cottage, I often availed myself of their invitation to spend weekends there.

Marie was a broad-shouldered, big-boned woman, with tremendous energy and an ability to make things happen. Almost single-handedly she had built her curtain business from a garage operation to one of the largest curtain contractors in South Africa. Ben, a tall, robust man with a wide-stepping, rolling gait, was her front man, dealing with clients and the company's public relations. The cottage they bought at Kosmos was an unfinished eyesore when they acquired it. Three years later it was a weekend luxury home with a garden of unparal-

leled richness of colour, scents, textures, and shapes. It was a
terraced wonder of the deep colours of the bougainvillea and
the mingled scents of honeysuckle and wild roses.

Marie was from an Afrikaans-speaking family known in the
South African political lexicon as *bloedsappe* (pronounced
"blud /supper") Afrikaners, who were loyal to the South African Party of General Jan Smuts even when it formed a coalition with the English and became the United Party.

Ben, whose family had first come to South Africa in the
1820s with the settlers from England, was a charming, well-
spoken man, with many old world mannerisms. He was also a
supporter of the United Party, but he was not usually as outspoken in his political views as Marie.

Marie hated Helen Suzman and the Progressive Party with a
passion that was exceeded only by her generic hatred of "the
blacks" and "the communists"—anyone who had fallen afoul of
the government's repressive measures. It was a mark of her
affection for me that she tolerated me, even after I had joined
the ranks of the Progressives.

Often at night we would sit on the terrace, nursing our
drinks and watching the moon rising over the water. The night
air would be alive with the sounds of the African veld. Most of
the dinner guests would be sitting quietly, replete with their
dinner and alcohol, with the natural surroundings wrapping
them in a sumptuous, sensuous cloak.

But Marie's loud voice, with a full-bellied laugh never far
below the surface, would intrude with stories laced with an
offensive racism. Why was she like this? Was it some deep-
seated matrix of unthinking prejudice, historical precedent,
four hundred years of inbred racism? Perhaps. Her stories and
comments, like the stories and comments of all the other racist
South Africans, would make me cringe. Later, I recognized
and accepted the simple truth: blacks were not people to them.

Invariably someone would respond to Marie with equally
bellicose and affrontive anecdotes. Too young to make my
views known, I would sit as far away as possible from the group
and pretend to be thoroughly starstruck by the natural beauty
of the scene, which indeed I was. But Marie's words and attitudes hurt me. I felt isolated and alienated, as if I were a black

person being forced to listen to the conversation. In every other aspect of her life Marie was a warm, generous, good-humoured, and supportive person. When I asked my parents how they could sit by in silence—indeed, how they could remain friends with the Langleys—it was to these traits they pointed.

One visit to the Langleys began with a discussion of the daring escape of four of the "ANC leadership" from their police cell in Johannesburg during the previous week, a month after their arrest in Rivonia on July 11th. Details of the escape were unknown, but the police had offered a large reward for information on Goldreich and Wolpe and had also arrested Moolla's and Wolpe's wives and Wolpe's brother-in-law for questioning.

"An inside job," said Ben. "Makes the police look like fools."

"Maybe they let them go," reflected Marie. "Sometimes it's better that the public doesn't hear what they say in court."

"Never," replied Ben. "Why arrest them in the first place? What's the point of leaving them loose to incite the kaffirs, spread communist filth everywhere?"

"Jislaaik man," Marie swore in Afrikaans, then switched to English. "If I saw those buggers, I'd tell the police. Making fools of us . . . from a prison cell inside police headquarters!" Marie sounded fierce.

As usual I pretended to be struck dumb by political conversation. Marie was not in a forgiving mood that afternoon. She turned to me and taunted, "And your Helen Suzman—what did she say? She loves those commie buggers, you know?" I was blushing but must have looked sceptical. It was so unfair. I did not know Helen Suzman at all, having seen her deliver a speech only once.

"You're too young now," Marie continued, "impressionable, but you'll see what a commie lover she is." End of conversation.

The next day I awoke at six-thirty as usual for my walk before breakfast. The sun had just risen, and the water, lying still below the cottage, was shrouded in grey-white mist. No one else was stirring except the Langleys' retainer, an elderly black man called Boy, who was chopping wood in his kiya (hut) above the cottage.

Striking a footpath behind the Langleys' cottage, I walked off to the left, where there were no houses. Basking in the feeling of renewal I always experienced on my first walk in natural surroundings after having been in the city for some time, I sat on a favourite rock high above the dam and cottages and ate an apple while the sun poured warm and blinding fingers of light over my face. Later I descended by forging my way through the tall grasses, not bothering to find the path but still on the lookout for snakes.

I was far to the left of the Langleys' cottage and even far to the left of the sole cottage below theirs when I saw smoke rising from the chimney of the lower cottage as well as the circular driveway and the creeper-covered stone house. Because I had never on my many previous visits seen anyone enter or leave the driveway, I was curious when I spotted a car driving in. Two priests clambered from the car and, after taking their hand luggage from the trunk, waved to the driver, who drove off quickly. The priests entered the house. The sun was high enough now to remind me that if I lingered I would miss breakfast. Straightening up. I started back up the slope to find the footpath.

"Hey, you," a man's voice floated toward me from the driveway. "Get off my land! You're trespassing!"

Waving to the small, distant figure, I shouted as loudly as I could, "Sorry!" Consciously I forced myself not to look down at him for some time. When I did, he was still watching me, this time through binoculars. I found that intriguing enough to mention it at breakfast.

"Oh, he's a mean old man," said Ben, "but he does have trouble with climbers and walkers befouling his stream. They kick stones and sand into it, sometimes closing it up. He's not on the village water system. They use their own springwater. He does hate trespassers, though. I'd be careful next time. He's been known to take a few potshots with his shotgun before— kaffirs and so on."

Nodding my acquiescence, I relaxed in the sun. Other houseguests arrived, and Marie went for a walk to the water with them.

"Saw two priests walking," she said later. "Except they didn't look like priests. Something not quite right about them— the one kept on falling over his skirt."

"I saw them too," I said, "early this morning when they

arrived at that cottage." I pointed to the trees below us and above the cottage.

"Now wait a minute," Ben said softly, leaning forward, a tin of beer in his hand. "Doesn't that old bastard have something to do with those commies who escaped this week?"

Marie chortled, her face growing red. "Yes, yes, one of them's married to his wife's daughter from her first marriage . . ."

"I wonder . . ." Ben mused aloud. "No, they wouldn't dare. It's too close to Jo'burg—broad daylight. They're probably in Europe by now."

"They didn't look like priests, but they didn't look like escaped prisoners, either," Gerry, one of the houseguests, laughed. "They even greeted us. No, I think they looked more like foreigners. Perhaps they're here for a visit. They're tired after a long journey. I don't know." He shrugged his shoulders.

"I think I'll phone the police anyway," Marie said. "I'd never forgive myself if it was them and I hadn't done anything about it."

By now I was in terror. I just knew that the priests were two of the escaped prisoners. And I had identified the place where they were staying.

"Don't!" I leapt to my feet, placing a restraining hand on her arm. "What if they aren't, if it's a mistake? He'll never forgive you. He's a bit nuts already, shooting at people on his property and so on. He's here all alone all week while everyone else is in Jo'burg. There's no telling what he could take into his head to do to the cottage, the garden. You know these queer, eccentric, old people . . ."

"Perhaps she's right," Ben said. "No good causing trouble. We'd be bloody mad if someone set the police on us to examine our guests. And priests too. Leave it for the moment. I'll ask some questions later."

There the subject rested. We did not see the priests again, nor did anyone call the police.

The following week we learnt in the press that Arthur Goldreich and Harold Wolpe had fled across the border to Swaziland, dressed as priests. They were flown to Bechuanaland (later Botswana), then to Tanganyika (later Tanzania), and eventually to London.

Marie was agog at the news. She dined out for months on how

stupid the police were, on how they had allowed two wanted men to walk around Kosmos in broad daylight without knowing that they were there.

"Must we do their business, their snooping and informing, for them? What do they get paid for? First they let them escape, and then they can't find them. Jislaaik man, this would never have happened if Oom Jannie [General Jan Smuts] was in power."

I felt smugly pleased that the two men had escaped from South Africa. Goldreich certainly, who had been one of the high command, had narrowly avoided a life sentence with Mandela on Robben Island. I hugged my secret to myself, feeling enormously implicated in the whole escape episode and happy about its outcome.

Another adolescent memory that stands out as pivotal was seeing Athol Fugard and Zakes Mokae in the very first production of Fugard's *The Blood Knot*. Playwright Fugard may not have been a political personality, per se, but his early plays were packed with incisive political commentary, and his impact on me was a political bombshell. In *The Blood Knot* the protagonists are two "mixed-blood" brothers, one light-skinned, the other dark. They live in a small Cape town. The former "tries for white" and obtains legal documents at the Racial Classification Bureau that proclaim him to be of the white race. Meanwhile, the dark-skinned brother, left alone in the small dorp (village), answers, has a response from and then a correspondence with a lonely white girl who places an ad in the personal column of the local newspaper. The denouement comes when the girl wants to meet her correspondent.

The play was produced in the Intimate Theatre, a small venue attached to the YMCA in Braamfontein, Johannesburg. I was sixteen at the time, and even the minor nosebleed I had to contend with during the performance did not detract from its impact on me. I was riveted. It was as if the words and images on the stage struck open a layer of my life beneath the one on which I was living. When I walked out of the theatre on that rainy evening, my life was changed. It occurred to me for the first time that I could fall in love with a black person. And it made me explore in my imagination the horror of that situation within the nightmare of South Africa's racial labyrinth. I simply could not view South Africa and South Africans as I had done only hours previously.

Fugard grew up and still maintains a home in Port Elizabeth. I know that area well. Often I had tea and scones at Skoenmakerskop there, in a seaside café a few yards from the cottage where Fugard spent most of his adult life while in South Africa. (More recently he has been a resident dramatist at Yale University.)

Skoenmakerskop is a collection of fishing shacks and cottages housing a few elderly residents. From his cottage Fugard could look out over the vast reaches of the Indian Ocean. Across a sand path from his cottage are rocky coves where paths crisscross the beach scrub. On any day of the year people who could be models for his famous Boesman and Lena characters appear on those paths, sacks over their shoulders, carrying their worldly belongings as they shuffle from one temporary shelter to another, up and down the Port Elizabeth coastline. One needs only to read the Boesman and Lena dialogue to taste the salty Indian Ocean breezes, to feel the sting of the beach sand, and to hear the waves as they surge against the rocks of Fugard's Skoenmakerskop.

It seems that few South African expatriates can easily loosen the ties that bind us to our tragic motherland.

CHAPTER 5
Driver, Robertson, Kennedy, and King

In 1964, my first year at "Wits," the University of the Witwatersrand (Ridge of White Waters), student politics was in a state of turmoil. Conservative student bodies (backed by government funds) on the English-language campuses were running well-organised smear campaigns against the liberal student union to which by dint of my student registration I belonged—the National Union of South African Students (NUSAS). This campaign included issuing fliers alleging that the aim of NUSAS was to hand over the control of the organisation to nonwhites and to participate in the freedom struggle aimed at revolution, sabotage, and the invasion of South Africa. In the ensuing clash it was a heady time to be a political activist on campus.

The NUSAS president that year, Jonty Driver, toured the campuses to reassure the student bodies that NUSAS was not planning insurrection as alleged and that it had no intention of being intimidated by government front organisations on campus.

Driver was tall, dark-haired, and charismatic. Feeling shy and nervous in my first weeks at university, I nonetheless forced myself to attend a lunch-hour meeting that he was addressing.

He passionately presented his vision of NUSAS, a vision of students upholding liberal values under siege in our society and fighting for justice and equality—a vision to which I could relate. And I was swept away by his presence. He was the first political leader other than Helen whom I had heard speak, and he was young, attractive, male.

Looking around the lecture theatre, I recognised only a few faces I had seen at Young Prog meetings; all the others were strangers. A number of Indian students were present, as well as a sprinkling of young black people, but the audience was mainly white and male. The racial mix was representative of the student body as a whole, although there were proportionately many more white girls on campus than the sample few at the meeting.

Driver's speech prompted me to sign up as a NUSAS worker. A work party was to be held that very evening. With my newly acquired sense of campus geography, I located the NUSAS offices in a run-down prefab building adjoining the student cafeteria. But my parents would not agree to let me ride the bus home after dark, and my father refused to fetch me. (Having just turned eighteen, I did not yet have my driver's licence.)

"Wasting your time with politics again," they both said on the telephone, sounding angry but resigned. Our clashes over my political activities were dying down by this time. They knew I was determined to be involved, so they accepted but never approved of my activism.

My reticence kept me from attending that work party, and I never saw Jonty Driver again. At a NUSAS congress soon after in May 1964 he was censured for having during his term of office as president "expressed personal opinions which would inevitably be associated with NUSAS policy." Driver's comments had been the focus of another nasty smear campaign. NUSAS, aware of the government's hand in this adverse propaganda, sensed the real political danger of an imminent banning order and so felt forced to defend itself against the smears. Driver became a scapegoat.

One crisis followed another, for almost immediately after

that congress the student leadership was embroiled in the
"Leftwich affair." Adrian Leftwich, a recent past president of
NUSAS, had been arrested for security reasons. He turned
state witness and said that he was one of the leaders of the
African Resistance Movement, an organisation alleged by the
head of the Security Police to be plotting the overthrow of the
government. Leftwich implicated other past NUSAS office
bearers. Although he was not named, Jonty Driver was arrested for twenty-eight days under the Ninety-Day Law, Section 17 of the General Law Amendment Act No. 37 of 1963,
which provided that a commissioned officer of the police could
without warrant arrest any person who he suspected had committed or intended to commit sabotage or any offence under
the Suppression of Communism or Unlawful Organizations
Acts or who in the police officer's opinion was in possession of
any information relating to such an offence. Persons arrested
under this law could be held without trial and without habeas
corpus. Two years later a 180-day clause was added to the
legislation. In the final analysis, this legislation allowed the
police to keep detainees incommunicado without ever having to
bring them to court, for as long as they pleased. No charges
were ever laid against Jonty Driver. He left South Africa for
England shortly after his release.

John Vorster, then the minister of justice, said in Parliament
in June 1965 that "thanks to the past executive leaders of
NUSAS, who had been involved in subversive activities, the
organisation was an obnoxious and reprehensible one." NUSAS
repeatedly asked him to appoint a judicial commission to en-
quire into its affairs. He never did.

Campus political activities took up a good deal of my spare
time. We seemed to be always organising mass rallies, as
government spokesmen, one after another, cast doubt in the
public mind as to the nature of NUSAS activities. Looking
back, I see that we allowed ourselves to be caught in the trap
the government set for us. We were always on the defensive,
reacting to unsubstantiated government allegations. Our public image was effectively being tarnished. The white English-
speaking public to whom we looked for support were mainly
conservative, reactionary, and suspicious anyway, and they

began to label all English-speaking students "communists"—
the generic tag for those South Africans who choose political
activism outside of the parliamentary system in protest of
apartheid ideology and practise.

In fact, NUSAS worked mainly on community projects in the
deprived black urban areas of the country, offering voluntary
assistance at township medical clinics and schools, and in the
rural communities, helping to build simple schools and clinics.
NUSAS also worked for member benefits, raising funds for
grants and scholarships and for overseas study opportunities,
as well as helping students with vacation jobs and other employment options.

NUSAS saw its political role as primarily a defence of academic freedom. Dialogue among racial groups having been
denied to students on campuses by the government, NUSAS
sought and forged links with similar student bodies on black
campuses. (Afrikaans-speaking students refused to be associated in any way with NUSAS. They had their own national
student body, the Studentebond.) And on the broader South
African political stage, NUSAS aligned itself within the spectrum of the liberal protest movement in the country.

As part of that protest movement NUSAS invited Dr. Martin
Luther King, Jr., to deliver the annual Day of Affirmation
lecture, in 1966, intended to commemorate the passing of the
Extension of University Education Amendment Act in 1960.
(The Day of Affirmation is commemorated at English-speaking campuses around South Africa and reaffirms the universities' stand on the principle of academic freedom.) Dr. King was
denied a visa. The students were downcast but undaunted, so
they invited Robert Kennedy instead. Kennedy's host for his
June visit was to be the newly elected NUSAS president, Ian
Robertson.

Ian was of medium height, with slightly curly light brown
hair and an honest, open face. He was not an inspiring speaker,
but he was a dedicated and determined opponent of apartheid
and a good student organiser.

In May 1966, two months prior to Kennedy's arrival, a letter
to new students was published on NUSAS campuses purport-
ing to describe the aims of NUSAS and bearing the false

signature of Robertson. The letter stated that NUSAS had pledged its support to various "leftist, liberal movements," including the controversial and banned Liberation Movement of South Africa. NUSAS and Robertson denied the authenticity of the document and asked the police to investigate its authorship.

On May 11, 1966, the government served on Robertson a five-year banning order. Under its terms he was confined to Cape Town and prohibited from speaking to more than one person at a time, from entering any educational institution except to attend lectures for which he was already registered, from entering NUSAS offices and in any way participating in the activities of the organisation, and from assisting in any way with the preparation of any matter for publication.

It was at this time that the iron in my political soul was forged, for the banning order provoked mass student protests almost on the eve of Kennedy's visit. The government was challenged, "Charge or Release Ian Robertson" at mass rallies and at continuous silent poster demonstrations on main roads off campus. Symbolic flames of freedom were lit on campuses around the country. The public, numbering in the thousands, signed "Charge or Release" petitions, and thousands of cars carried the message on bumper stickers. The student protests received public support from university faculty, prominent public figures, churches, and other organisations, as well as student bodies in other countries. Students took to the streets in mass protest marches. In Johannesburg I was one of four thousand student marchers.

We formed our column on the grounds of the Wits campus. We were asked to wear our academic gowns, to carry posters, to walk eight abreast. Under a banner that read "Charge or Release Ian Robertson" at each column's head were national NUSAS office bearers. They were joined by leading members of the Progressive Party and the Liberal Party, ex-NUSAS office bearers, the Anglican bishop of Johannesburg, and other church leaders. Behind them, with me, were current local NUSAS committee members, followed by faculty members and the student body. Student marshalls kept control of the long line.

It was midmorning on a bright, crisp day in early winter, the sky a cerulean blue, a color only a highveld winter sky can be. The clear light etched with silver the silhouette of the Braamfontein skyline, and the last few red and russet leaves fluttered on the campus trees. We were a gravely determined, sombre body of marchers that morning. The lines began to move slowly into the streets.

As we walked through the campus gates I could see the plainclothes policemen take photographs of each student rank. I smiled grimly at the sight of these very serious photographers, each with his dark glasses and Adolf Hitler moustache. The plainclothes security police had their own uniform, just as if they were wearing the khaki official dress of their uniformed counterparts, who watched us from various vantage points along the way. They must have quite a file of photographs of me by now, I mused, for I had been photographed every day for the past week: with my poster, on Jan Smuts Avenue, and at the allnight vigil on Wits campus when we lit the flame of freedom. A file of honour, I acknowledged, and so bolstered, I reflected on my feelings of sadness for Ian Robertson, his young life destroyed at the moment of his greatest achievement, and for the loss of human rights and civil liberties in South Africa. Sadness, too, for South Africa herself.

We walked in silence along main roads that had been closed to traffic, between sidewalks lined with spectators. And we walked without incident until we crossed the Queen Elizabeth Bridge into the domain of government offices around the Johannesburg Railway Station. Government workers had gathered on the sidewalks and leaned out of windows overhead. We began to hear abusive epithets in Afrikaans from among the crowd. Someone's spit landed on my head, but I made no move to remove it; it was a badge of honour. I held my head higher and fixed my eyes more steadfastly on the student leaders ahead of me. And the policemen watched as flowerpots, water bombs, and the contents of bedroom chamber pots were thrown at us as we marched between the city buildings. The mood of the onlookers became uglier, with scuffles breaking out among burly white men and black passersby.

And the policemen watched.

The march ended at the steps of the city hall. There had been no serious injuries. The event had been recorded by a slew of local and foreign reporters and overseas TV crews.

Ours was the last legal protest march in Johannesburg. Two years later, students attempted to make an illegal march along the same route. It was broken up by uniformed policemen, who brutally smashed into the students with batons and snarling police dogs.

Re-creating my thoughts and reflections of the march makes me aware of how dramatic we all were, of how important we all felt, of what an impact we thought we were having. Then it seemed so vital to make a stand, to be counted. Looking back now, I am pleased I felt that way, that I was so earnest, that I had an opportunity to express my opposition to the government, that I was one who took a stand. And I see that the government, unable to brook any protest, took us seriously, too—at least seriously enough to imprison, ban, or exile many of our leaders.

The consequences of being a student leader at that time made me examine myself. I did not want to be imprisoned, banned, or exiled. I wanted to be able to be actively involved, to be doing something. One did not have to be more radical than I was to run afoul of the state; one simply had to put oneself on the line, take on a leadership position. I made a fundamental decision then. I chose to be active in grass-roots involvement rather than in leadership roles. I put my energies into African Night School, into teaching English to black adults, rather than into bearing office in NUSAS.

After the march, many student leaders gathered in a tea-room café outside the bus terminal in Loveday Street, half a block from the city hall. We were eating sundaes and sharing our elation over how well the march had gone, marvelling at the discipline and determination of the student body, even under such verbal and physical provocation from sections of the public and risk of injury from missiles hurled from above. We were happy, almost joyous, to be sharing this moment of triumph, a shaft of light in the overall gloom cast by the government's actions against the student movement. But we all carried deep within ourselves the image of Ian Robertson, his dreams, and ours too, although many of us did not know it yet, which were shattered by his banning order.

Lyn Murray, a NUSAS office bearer and a friend who lived near me, gave me a ride home from the university that day. She was nervous because she was driving her mother's car. A tall, dark-haired girl, vivacious and energetic, with dark-rimmed glasses over her peering, nearsighted eyes, Lyn always seemed to be leaning forward, as if she could see better that way. She was outspoken and often shocked me with her profanities and curses. She had been to a convent school and found she hated not only religious conformity, but conformity of any kind. I felt braver, more alive, more capable of morally courageous acts when I was with Lyn.

We were animated and exuberant after the march, and this mood, coupled with Lyn's nervous driving, induced a kind of hysteria in us. We shrieked with laughter and tried to outdo one another in stringing together the most insultingly profane descriptions of government ministers and government actions.

We turned off Empire Road into the quiet, wooded streets of suburban Emmarentia. As we rounded a corner we saw a grey police van at the side of the road, black police constables herding subdued, passive black people into the back of the van, and a queue of black people waiting for the young white policeman to look through their pass books. This was an everyday sight in white suburbia.

"A pass raid!" Lyn slowed the car, and we crawled by the scene. A young black man, dressed in the ubiquitous dark blue boiler suit of the male domestic servant, was protesting to the policeman while holding up his palms in a conciliatory gesture. In a flash the policeman had his gun out of its holster and had struck the black man across the face with it, the force of his blow throwing the gardener to the ground.

I do not remember Lyn moving the car to the kerb, but she did so, while almost instantaneously leaping from it and rushing over to the white policeman. Fearing for her impetuosity, I followed quickly behind.

Her rage giving her unusual strength, Lyn had the young policeman by the collar and was holding him against a sidewalk tree trunk.

"You little Nazi shit," she was screaming at him. "We saw you hit him. We're going to lay charges of assault against you! We'll see you prosecuted and in prison!"

By now most of the line of black people, making use of this unexpected interruption of the hated proceedings, had melted away behind the surrounding garden walls. The pale young policeman looked bewildered and amazed at this female dervish who had pinned him against a tree. His light blue eyes stared bemusedly at Lyn. He was shorter than she, only about seventeen, with just a fuzz of fair hair on his upper lip.

We all turned at the sound of consternation in the black constables' loud exclamations. Lyn's mother's car was rolling down the slight incline toward the police van. Lyn released the policeman and covered her face. I watched, mesmerised. An older black man, in custody for a pass offence, leapt from the police van, flung open the door of the slowly moving car, and pulled on the brake. The car stopped inches from the van. In the general commotion that followed he made good his escape, together with a number of other pass raid victims, who simply jumped from the van and disappeared.

"Dame," said the policeman, now at Lyn's side with his notebook out, "wat is u van?" (Lady, what is your surname?) Lyn looked at him in astonishment. Then she leaned back against the tree and began to laugh. I, too, could not stop the hysterical giggles from clawing at my throat, despite (or maybe because of) my knowledge of our predicament. We had obstructed the police in carrying out their duty, physically assaulted one of their members, been instrumental in assisting pass law offenders to escape, and almost rammed a police vehicle. A small crowd of black onlookers stood stoically by, perhaps not quite comprehending this white man's farce. For even the fallen, stricken, and bleeding gardener had vanished.

"*You* want *my* name? You, you . . . scum!" Lyn had closed in on the policeman again and was wagging her finger under his nose. "Well, you'll have to wait 'til we're in court to hear it. But don't worry, I've got *your* name, Van Rensburg"—she pointed to the metal name tag pinned over his left breast pocket—"and your number!"

The policeman pushed his hat off his head and scratched at his almost shaven skull.

"Jislaaik lady, give me a break. I didn't mean to hurt the kaffir . . ."

But we were back in the car, quickly driving away. Lyn stopped the car again after we'd gone a few blocks. Her hands were shaking now. I hugged her.

"You were incredible, so brave! He was going to arrest you, and now he's shit scared you're going to lay charges."

We laughed together.

"Are you really going to take him to court?"

"Don't be an idiot! Christ, you really are naive sometimes. We were lucky he was so young. We'll be really lucky if they don't trace my old lady's car. My God, what if I'd smashed it into the back of a police van?"

Lyn looked at me with a startled expression of near panic, and then we both started laughing again.

"Don't breathe a word to anyone, especially my folks." I nodded my agreement. "Nor you to mine." She nodded solemnly at me.

Police officialdom never bothered Lyn over that incident, but she had many other brushes with the Security Police, the guardians of law and order in the country. The incident served to highlight for me once again the parameters of the two worlds of South Africa. We could laugh at the absurdity of Lyn's highly dramatic gesture, but for a black man such a gesture would have been an act of suicidal stupidity. That day remains vividly memorable to me.

John Vorster's reaction to the unprecedented mass student protest was not unexpected and was in itself highly provocative, fueling student protest activism through Robert Kennedy's visit. Vorster told a delegation of student leaders that he would not charge Robertson because he need not have been a communist to have been banned. Robertson had been banned in his personal capacity, he said, and his banning had nothing to do with NUSAS. Yet at the meeting Vorster repeatedly told the delegation of his repugnance toward NUSAS, that its principles were diametrically opposed to his own.

In the ensuing two years, further acts of intimidation were taken against prominent NUSAS members. Inevitably, as the liberal NUSAS leadership was incarcerated or banned or chose self-exile, a more conservative NUSAS leadership was elected. Without having to actually ban NUSAS, the government had succeeded in smashing organised white liberal student activism in the country.

But in 1966 I did not see the writing on the wall. I was riding on the crest of the wave of activism, of making a difference. And I was inspired by the example set by Helen Suzman.

The first time I spoke to Helen was outside the Johannesburg City Hall. She had addressed a lunchtime rally organised by the Progressive Party in support of our banned NUSAS leader, Ian Robertson. Her speech had moved me to tears. As she left the stage and the huge crowd filed out of the city hall I dashed after her small, bustling figure on the sidewalk. Her husband, Moisie, a small older man, an internationally famous physician, his characteristic cigar in his mouth and a tape recorder in his left hand (Moisie recorded every speech of Helen's that he feasibly could), held open the door of their car for her.

"Mrs. Suzman, thank you, thank you so much!"

Helen turned toward the sound of my panting voice. She looked a little taken aback, no doubt at the intensity of my tone.

"It's a pleasure, my dear." The frank interest in her startling blue eyes struck me dumb.

"For Ian, for all of us . . ." I managed to stumble through a few inane words. She smiled at me and seated herself in the car. "It's a pleasure," she repeated, "not that I think it's going to mean a damn thing." She waved at me as I stood, feeling foolish, on the sidewalk.

Nineteen sixty-six was a heady year for me. Not only did I have my first real contact with Helen Suzman and the Houghton political force, but I was closely exposed to a man who made an indelible impression on me—indeed, on my whole country.

On July 9th, the day after Robert Kennedy's unforgettable speech, an editorial in the *Rand Daily Mail* hailed his four-day visit:

> . . . the impact of it all has been immense—far beyond anything that its enterprising NUSAS sponsors had dreamed of. This younger Kennedy, so like his illustrious brother in so many ways,

has taken the youth of the country by storm, or a substantial part
of it. He has done it not so much through the youthful zest of his
own personality, although there is an immediate rapport between him and young people, nor even through the sheer profes-
sionalism of his handling of people and audiences. What is really
important is that he has done it through his message of confident,
unashamed idealism. A clear and unequivocal endorsement that
the hopes and ideals that all decent youngsters feel are indeed
part and parcel of the great traditions of the contemporary
Western world and not, as they are told so often, something alien,
unwholesome, or worse . . . the effects of Senator Kennedy's visit
will be felt for a long time to come. He has stirred up ideas long
in disuse. He has started up new, livelier controversies among us
and about us.

Many Kennedy historians regard his Day of Affirmation
speech, presented at the University of Cape Town, as the best
speech he made in his career. In it he said:

> We must recognise the full human equality of all people—before
> God, before the law, and in the councils of government. We must
> do this not because it is economically advantageous—although it
> is; not because the laws of God and man command it—although
> they do command it; not because people in other lands wish it so.
> We must do it for the single and fundamental reason that it is the
> right thing to do.

A ticket to the Great Hall of the University of the Witwatersrand to hear Robert Kennedy's address (he would speak at four
university campuses in four days) on that cold winter's night,
July 8, 1966, became a highly prized possession. Tickets were
allocated to Wits NUSAS committee members, and as I was on
the African Night School Committee, I had my ticket. Philip,
my steady boyfriend, had not been prepared to queue all night
some weeks earlier to ensure his ticket from the public pool, so
he did not accompany me. But my friend and classmate, Barbara, and her fiancé, Aubrey, had queued all night. I sat with
them.

They had been at Jan Smuts International Airport to greet
the Kennedys, too, along with thousands of other students and

well-wishers on that Saturday night, four days before the Wits meeting. Philip, tall, lanky, good-looking, earnest, preferred to see a movie. He was studying accountancy, working as a clerk during the day and attending lectures at night. We could see each other only briefly, on weekends. Our time together seemed so precious that I did not think twice about forgoing the excitement of the Kennedys' arrival to be with Philip.

Barbara and Aubrey arrived at my house at six o'clock on Sunday morning. It was barely light, and a soft rain fell. The low grey clouds matched the drabness of the winter garden. We spoke in whispers through the burglar proofing over my bedroom window so as not to awaken my parents. Barbara and Aubrey had been up all night and had come to invite me to join them for breakfast at a downtown hotel. They were exhausted but exhilarated, especially Barbara, who was a politics major and a Kennedy admirer. They explained that after the Kennedys had left the airport many students, themselves among them, had gravitated to the campus, where impromptu partying had gone on through the night. The whirlwind Kennedy visit was off and running.

As the three previous days had been, July 8th was a day of triumph for Robert Kennedy. At dawn he was flown in a helicopter from Durban to Johannesburg. In Durban he had addressed thousands of people the day before and met Nobel Peace Prize winner and former leader of the banned African National Congress, Chief Albert Luthuli, at his home in Groutville.

July 8th had been a memorable day in my life, too. Together with several other NUSAS committee members, I had gone into Soweto to greet the Kennedys at Regina Mundi Cathedral in Moroko, a church that had been the site of many earlier major political meetings and rallies. The plan was that the Kennedys would enter the church briefly, meet the ministers, shake a few hands, and continue on their tour.

By early morning, thousands of people stood waiting for the Kennedys in the dust outside the church. Buses unloaded schoolchildren; shuffling old men and matronly women arrived on foot from the neighbouring streets. Press photographers arrived. White nuns from Johannesburg parishes joined their black sisters and brothers. The air was vibrant with excite-ment, and the mob shoved, sang, and swayed in the dust.

My colleagues expressed concern for the safety of the Kennedys. Security personnel tried to keep the crowd off the road, but it was only when the first car was sighted that the crowd moved back. The singing reached a crescendo of stirring tribal songs and joyous hymns whose words I did not under-stand but whose chanting choral melodies stirred my blood, too.

Standing on the steps of the church, I could see Robert Kennedy being helped to clamber onto the roof of the car. He stood there, a lock of his light brown hair flopped characteristi-cally over the left side of his forehead, his right hand fiddling with the cufflink on his left wrist, as he anxiously watched many hands help Ethel, dressed in a pastel tweed suit and white gloves, to his side. A sea of black faces, hundreds deep, swarmed around the car. It would be impossible for the Kennedys to enter the church.

Robert spoke briefly from the car roof, his words inter-spersed with the high-pitched ululations of hundreds of women. It was a fervid, emotional scene. I was caught in the crush of people as the crowd tried to move closer to the Kennedy car.

What was Robert Kennedy really thinking? I wondered as he stood on the car roof gazing over so many bobbing heads awash in full-throated song. The squalid, depressing uniformity of the rows of dingy houses stretched away on all sides and faded into the winter smog. Overhead a weak sun broke through the grey mass. And at the edges of the crowd the many buses and ubiquitous Soweto taxis parked in long lines. Two solitary high-mast lights perched in the street outside the church, as well as several bedraggled eucalyptus trees, their leaves cov-ered in dust, their mottled white and grey trunks left uncov-ered by large strips of peeling bark. What associations did this scene trigger in that Kennedy mind? Or was this glimpse of urban Africa something new to him?

After he had spoken, and Ethel was safely ensconced in the car again, Robert Kennedy waved to the crowd characteristi-cally, almost hesitantly, with his right arm, his left arm held

close to his body. He glanced at us, an island of earnest young
white faces, cheering madly and waving back from the steps of
Regina Mundi. His famous boyish grin crossed his face, and he
waved harder. We could see his triumph and excitement. I
savoured that smile, that almost intimate look, for a long
time—it was a rare glimpse of the man behind a faraway
public face.

Barbara and Aubrey fetched me early for the eight o'clock
meeting that night. Those who had not been able to obtain seats
in the Great Hall stood in the vestibule and overflowed into
adjacent lecture rooms where public address systems had been
placed to relay Kennedy's speech. I have never before, nor
since, seen such a huge crowd in the Great Hall. We jostled our
way through a milling throng of well-dressed people to our
seats. It was a bitterly cold night, but people spilled down the
imposing Great Hall stone steps simply to be a part of the
excitement.

Inside the packed hall the feeling of anticipation was palpable. Executive members of the convocation and preeminent
faculty members were seated on the stage, together with Wits
University NUSAS leaders. Kennedy was late, and with each
passing moment the excitement mounted a notch.

Then he was there in the hall, being escorted down the aisle
by a tightly knit phalanx of NUSAS members, through the
tumultuous applause of an audience already on its feet. Afterward I learnt that the crowd was wedged so tightly outside the
hall that a glass panel had to be smashed so Kennedy could
enter. He spoke, stirringly and well, echoing reassurances that
we young people of South Africa were not alone in our struggle,
that others like ourselves struggled for freedom, too, in the
United States, across Europe, in South America, and elsewhere in Africa. The applause soared to the high ceiling. It
amused me that Barbara was trying to record the moment on a
tiny tape recorder.

Merton Shill, a NUSAS vice president, rose to speak. Merton
was a mesmerising speaker, and he used the occasion well.
Some, including me, felt he spoke even better than Robert
Kennedy had done on that night: "You leave us with the lights of

freedom being snuffed out all around us, but you have lit a tiny flame of hope in our hearts . . . a flame that will grow into a raging fire that will free us all."

Manoeuvring myself into the wave of people flowing to the stage, I lost Barbara and Aubrey. I wanted to congratulate Merton, to somehow prolong the excitement and the sense of mainstream involvement the occasion had generated for me. Lyn Murray grabbed my arm.

"I want to speak to Merton," I shouted at her, gesturing to the stage.

"It's hopeless here," she replied. "You'll never get to him. Come with me to the Menells—drinks and whatnot . . ." Her words were barely audible above the noise of the crowd.

Nodding agreement, I held on to the back of her coat and followed her out of the hall through a quieter side entrance.

The Menells lived in Parktown, sharing a quiet cul-de-sac in this salubrious suburb with Harry Oppenheimer, the international gold and diamond magnate. Clive Menell was the scion of another family involved in the gold mining industry of South Africa. The Menells were the Kennedys' hosts in Johannesburg.

When we arrived, a crowd had already assembled in the elegant front hall of their home. A long table to the left of the room held wineglasses and teacups. The dining room table in another well-appointed room to the right of the hall was laden with cakes and savouries. Clive, tall and elegantly handsome, was surrounded by excited people speaking volubly. Irene, his polished, poised, dark-haired wife, was pointed out to me. She was animated and radiant holding court, leaning up against a doorjamb of the room, brandishing a cigarette. I had no idea then of the close ties we were to share later. Helen Suzman was there, as were legendary sociologist Ellen Hellman; Laurie Gandar, the liberal editor of the *Rand Daily Mail*; and Benjy Pogrund, a crusading journalist of the paper. The Kennedys were sitting in the subtly wrought luxury of the Menell sitting room, talking, still talking.

Merton Shill appeared in the front doorway and was mobbed with acclamation. Other students I knew wandered in—Margie Marshall, the tall, blond acting president of NUSAS; Robin

Margo, dark-haired and mercurial; and many more; also Young Progressive leaders I knew, including Johnny Fedler and Steven Suzman (Helen's nephew).

White-jacketed, white-gloved, and red-sashed waiters took away empty glasses, brought fresh drinks, and passed around dishes of food.

I sat spellbound at Robert Kennedy's feet as he told us stories of his brother, Martin Luther King, and the civil rights movement. Eventually, after many people had drifted off, those who were left at around two in the morning gathered in the front hall and sang freedom songs, and then the Kennedys retired to bed.

Finding myself shy and strangely reluctant, I went up to Irene Menell to thank her. Although I was unknown to her, and she was obviously exhausted herself, she was polite and warm to me. My head swam with the glittering, strange hours I had spent in her home. Until that night I had no idea that the world of liberal politics could have so many wonders in it.

Merton Shill married one of my best friends. They left South Africa in 1969 and live in Ann Arbor, Michigan.

Margie Marshall became NUSAS president in 1967. She left South Africa a year later and now lives in Boston.

Robin Margo, a brilliantly gifted student and a born leader, became chairman of the Wits Student Representative Council (SRC), a NUSAS vice president, and a Rhodes scholar. He left South Africa in the early seventies and lives in Australia.

Ian Robertson, the banned NUSAS president at the time of the Kennedy visit, also lives in Australia.

Johnny Fedler lives in London.

Steven Suzman lives in San Francisco.

And so on. The cream of the young white English-speaking leadership of South Africa has been scattered for over thirty years to the farthest corners of the English-speaking world. A tragedy for South Africa, a tragic loss of talent, commitment, promise.

CHAPTER 6

The Knysna Loerie
Dies in Captivity

"But your country is beautiful."

Many people who visit South Africa make this comment about the striking landscapes; it is almost as if they utter these words in compensation for having been condemnatory of the racial policies of the apartheid regime. Indeed, it is a magnificently beautiful country, and the physical beauty of the land resonates somewhere deep within me, striking at the core of my being. If I dig deeply enough, it is to something essential, powerfully meaningful, beneath and beyond the sensory perceptions. And if I can never consummately describe that essential beauty, I know that for me its qualities are manifest in an indigenous South African bird, the Knysna loerie (pronounced "Neyesna lur'ee").

If I never see the Knysna loerie again, at least I have deeply embedded in my memory its emblematic beauty; it remains a source and symbol for me of a thousand evocations of my intimate love for the land of my birth, a yearning for the deep, mysterious coastal mountain forests of the Eastern Cape along with other South African mountains and dry bushveld landscapes.

I think I know why this is so. It is because of the confluence of emotions and unconscious instincts found in the treasure house of my subconscious mind, where my love and admiration for June Wilson, mentor and guide to me, is linked to my personal mythology of my love for the silent, deep coastal forests of the Tsitsikama and Outeniqua mountain ranges. The Knysna loerie is my personal emblem for these strong currents of love and affinity that lie deep in my being.

The fabulous Knysna loerie inhabits the indigenous forests of the eastern South African seaboard. It is still fairly common in at least one of these forest areas, the wooded slopes of the Tsitsikama Forest and Coastal National Park, which stretches from the Stormsrivier mouth in the north to Nature's Valley, a remote cluster of beach cottages forty miles north of Plettenberg Bay, in the south. It is an area I know well.

The Knysna loerie is heard more often than seen, and that characteristic "kok, kok, kok" sound, uttered with the head thrown right back onto the shoulders, lures the serious bird-watcher and the casual hiker alike, again and again, deep into the indigenous forests.

The bird is akin to the Guatemalan quetzal in size and spectacular colouring. Both birds have crested heads. While the quetzal has crimson, white, and brilliant green plumage with an elongated tail, the Knysna loerie is a dazzlingly bejewelled phenomenon in green, purple, and red. In flight the beautiful red wings are seen to best advantage.

Jewels of the forests, both—the mythic quetzal, now an endangered species in the high cloud forests of its native land, and the Knysna loerie, less well known internationally but as fabulous as its South American cousin. The quetzal is the national emblem of Guatemala. The Knysna loerie is a highly evocative, personal emblem for me.

Four times in my life I have seen the Knysna loerie. The first occasion was when I was sixteen and on holiday with the Joneses—June Wilson, my drama teacher; her husband, Dave Jones; their daughter and my friend, Diane; and young Michael.

June, Diane, and I were on the precipitous cliff walk above the foaming Indian Ocean, a part of the Krantzhoek Forest

Reserve near Knysna. Behind and around us quietly breathed the tall yellowwoods, blackwoods, ironwoods, and other trees. The ground cover, known as *fynbos*, was an intertwining maze of varieties of protea, erica and other heath, and forest ferns. Around the many tiny streams, beds of bright green moss grew strong and tough. Ahead of us and slightly to our right we could hear the roar of the waterfall as the water dropped three hundred feet through a chasm to a narrow riverbed a quarter of a mile from its mouth. The mouth itself was guarded by the jagged orange-tinted rocks of this part of the coast.

June waved to us to follow her along a faint path to the right, which cut the corner to the waterfall and the parking lot. None of us spoke; we were each lost in the natural beauty around us. A few steps into the forest, and it seemed to close in on us, shutting off the incessant roar of the sea. It was still in the forest, the occasional birdcall breaking the heavy, hot silence.

June stopped suddenly. In front of us, across a clearing, was a bank of queen proteas in bloom, their delicately pink-tipped white blooms spectacularly massed against the variegated green background. We were about to move on when a flash of red burst across the clearing. Scarcely breathing, I looked, imprinting on my mind every detail of the almost unreal beauty of the Knysna loerie.

It alighted on a branch of a wild fig tree and began to preen itself. One leg and then another was pulled taut to help stretch out a wing. The sheen of the brilliant red wing feathers shimmered in the sunlight, dazzling and enslaving me. Then the bird twisted its green-crested head around to reach to its shoulders. The light played on the green feathers where they merged into purple. It looked at us, standing frozen at the edge of the clearing, with eyes that seemed not to see us. Then it hopped with agile grace through the branches and leaves of the tree to emerge near the top, where after raising its tail it proceeded to eat a wild fig. It threw its head back onto its shoulders and uttered its "kok, kok, kok" sound. After a moment, another loerie answered from deeper in the forest. It called again and, with a prodigious hop to a branch of a nearby keurboom, disappeared from view.

"Well," breathed June. "Well, well, well. And they say you

only see them at dawn or dusk, and then only fleeting glimpses through the leaves. Well, wasn't that something?"

Diane and I nodded our agreement, still caught in the thrall of seeing, after having heard them so often, our first loerie.

Many years passed before I saw a Knysna loerie again. In between I often saw its savannah cousin, the grey loerie, in the low-lying bush country of the inland animal reserves. And once, when I was staying at Stuart and Jean Graham's seaside home, Seaward, at Ramsgate on the south coast of Natal, I saw another cousin, the perhaps even more spectacular purple-crested loerie.

This loerie came early in the morning and at sunset to drink from the stone birdbath set at the edge of the lawn in the subtropical coastal scrub. Watching intently from the deck, I would see it bob its head into the birdbath and then tilt its head back to swallow, its noble purple crest outlined against the blue-grey of the sea below.

The sight of any loerie is an enriching experience, and the next time I saw a Knysna loerie I was fortunate to be able to share it with my family. It was April 1983, and my husband, sons Roger and Tony, and I (joined later by my mother-in-law, Lydia) were spending six weeks at Nature's Valley. It was the last time I was to visit my dearly beloved haunts before we left South Africa. I did not know then that we would be leaving in the following year, so our holiday was not so significantly nostalgic.

We stayed in the Perlmans' cottage. Short, dark-haired, chain-smoking Ina Perlman worked for the Institute of Race Relations in Johannesburg and had the most widespread network of contacts among the region's black, "coloured," and Indian communities of anyone I knew. She was told before anyone else, including the press, of the presence of the Security Police, or of the army in the townships, or of impending unrest, strikes, or boycotts. During the time we were in her family's holiday home, she was stoutly heading up Operation Hunger, whose work I had seen on my January 1984 trip to the "homelands."

Nature's Valley then was as Plettenberg Bay had been twenty years earlier, before crass commercialism scarred the beauty of one of the most striking bays on this earth. Sixteenth-century Portuguese sailors had called it Bahia Formosa (the Bay Beautiful) when they first rounded the Cape, the southern-most tip of Africa.

June Wilson had taken me to Plettenberg Bay during my high school and university years to spend tranquil, enlivening holidays with her and her family. At that time, remote Nature's Valley was a favoured picnic spot I occasionally visited with the Joneses while on our holidays at Plettenberg Bay. I am grateful that I came to know the natural beauty of Plettenberg Bay long before the shopping malls and hundreds of luxury holiday homes had spoiled the indigenous wonder of the flora and fauna.

Memories are with me still of sunset walks on the curving three-mile beach of white sea sand, of clambering on and fishing from the Robbeberg Nature Reserve, of pansy shells, sandpipers, whales birthing in the bay, of my maturing relationship with June and my growing friendship with Diane, and of my introduction to the great mystery of the forests and the call of the Knysna loerie.

Nature's Valley lies in a steep mountain valley at the sea's edge. Climbing up from the valley to the north is the Grootriv-ier Forest Reserve and to the south the De Vaselot Forest Reserve. Thick forest walls and a canopy of branches mark the turnoff to Nature's Valley. The Grootrivier is a swelling stream on the left side of the road and soon becomes a wide lagoon. It is flanked on one side by a few wooden cottages built on stilts and across its width in the distance by a wall of tightly knit forest branches intertwined with creepers. The Perlmans' cottage is on a knoll overlooking the lagoon, just high enough to catch a glimpse of the sea beyond the dunes and below the sandy orange cliff that marks the river mouth.

Because Nature's Valley falls within the De Vaselot Forest Reserve, building rights are restricted, and building is strictly controlled. There is only one general store and no hotels, and the holiday homes are set into the forest. There are no tarred roads or electricity. Energy is obtained from propane gas tanks; paraffin lamps softly light the cottages in the evening.

In Nature's Valley you walk and bathe on the two-mile beach

and fish from the jagged black rocks into the sea and from huge smooth rocks into the deep swells at the wide mouth of the Soutrivier. Colorful sea anemones wave to you from the rock pools, sea birds dive for fish. You can walk by moonlight through the forest scrub, barbecue under the clarity of a startlingly starry southern-hemisphere sky, or laze around under the blazing sun at the edge of the Indian Ocean, sipping coffee on the deck in the early morning while watching the grey-white wraiths of mist on the lagoon, listening to the birdsong, and, perhaps, glimpsing a bushbuck at the forest's edge.

The forest comes right up to the door of the Perlmans' cottage. Once when I had to call London, I remember marvelling at the technological wonders of the Communication Age. For there I was, standing in bathing costume and ragged shorts in the doorway of a cottage in a remote region of remote Africa, with the forested mountains that had existed for millenia beckoning at my doorstep. A gull sifted through the ash of our outdoor cooking place, two wood doves called gently at the edge of the forest, a troop of vervet monkeys played in the creepers a hundred yards away. And in the face of all this, my direct-dial call rang in cold, wet, miserable London.

". . . We are not able to come to the phone right now. . . ." The disembodied voice of the answering machine echoed in my ear, and I was so disconcerted that I put down the receiver. But I had to call again, and this time I had my message prepared. After accomplishing that disorienting task, I collected my family, and in bright sunshine we headed for the forest.

I had not seen a Knysna loerie since that blazing day in Krantzhoek twenty-one years before, although I heard them often over the years. I had introduced their call to Sandy and then to each of our sons as we walked together in the forests since they were a few months old, initially carried in a pack on my husband's back and then walking on sturdy legs that kept growing longer and stronger.

We chose for our afternoon walk that day the trail that winds around the far side of the lagoon and forms the initial miles of the eight-day Tsitsikama Trail and the last few miles of the famed Otter Trail, a four-day coastal trail. We were in a section of the Tsitsikama Forest. (Tsitsikama is the Hottentot name for the honey bird and knysna the Hottentot name for a big stretch of water. The Knysna Lagoon is thus linked, at least semantically, with Lake Nyasa in central Africa.)

The walk took us deep into the forest, through the milkwoods and ironwoods, the Cape beeches and chestnuts. The path wound its way past giant thousand-year-old yellowwoods and the rare stinkwood. Mosses, ferns, and fungi grew on decomposing branches and tree trunks. The air was still and heavy. Brightly coloured butterflies and dragonflies darted across our way. Roger, eleven years old then, led us until he was caught in his second spiderweb of the afternoon, evidence that no one had walked this path that day. Many birds called around us. The light varied from patches of dazzling sunlight, startlingly bright after the gloom of the inner forest, to dappled splotches in the deeper wells, to diffused murky gloom where the tightly packed foliage seemed to be breathing.

A family rule forbade talking at more than a whisper in the forest, and then only if it was information concerning the walk. We had evolved a series of hand signals to convey information about birds, small animals, and plants. Another family custom was to stand still every few minutes to listen, really listen, to the sounds of the forest.

There had been no loeries calling that afternoon. Nine-year-old Tony suddenly tugged at my shirt. Stopping, I glanced at his face, which was red with excitement, his hazel eyes dancing, and then I followed his pointing finger. To our left, in a huge gnarled old yellowwood, which grew from a deep incline a hundred feet below us and still towered over us, a flock of six loeries had settled. How I, walking in front, had missed them I do not know. I must have been gazing in the other direction. Standing as still as our excitement would allow, we watched as another three birds alighted on the branches. I did not know what was more important to me, the joy on the boys' faces, reflecting my own, or the sight of the elusive birds. Sandy, bringing up the rear, froze when he saw us standing so still. He nodded his head when he saw the loeries and winked at me. Slowly we lowered ourselves to the ground and watched this truly unforgettable tableau. The birds hopped among the leaves, quarrelled noisily, made spectacular, swooping red-winged dives, and for fifteen wonderful minutes gave us unadulterated pleasure. I hugged to myself a feeling of joy.

A few days later I was in the forest alone, early in the morning. There was so much sensory stimulation that my inner being was aquiver with awareness. Quite unexpectedly as I mounted a little rise I saw two loeries on a branch ahead of me. They were scarcely four feet away, looking the other way, unaware of my approach. This time we were in such close proximity that as I gazed hungrily at them their bejewelled beauty was revealed to me in all its spectacular glory.

Some weeks after that sighting, shortly before we left the valley, we took a day drive through the back roads, meant for lumber trucks, of the Outeniqua Forest. At Millwood, a tiny ghost village left over from an abortive gold rush in the 1860s, we picnicked alongside a stream, supposedly the source of the short-lived hopes for a substantial alluvial gold deposit a century ago. The forest soared hundreds of feet above us on all sides. A loerie was sunning itself on a rock in the stream. It flew off as we approached, leaving behind, etched in our memories, a flash of brilliant red.

Africa, lost Africa. The fish eagle swooping for bream, the vast sea of floating green papyrus grass, the white-red, bejewelled, fingernail-size tree frogs clinging to the reeds with tiny five-fingered hands outstretched, the thousand-bird-wing rush at dawn, the glowing fireflies at dusk, the musk-scented flagrant-crimson flowers, the sun filtered through the haze of wood smoke, dark grey-green mist wrapping the tall, unmoving Livingstone palms, lilac and pink water lilies, soft in the pools, mirrored and mirroring—watery land, land of water.

The fish eagle cries from the tall lightning-struck tree at the water's edge, stridently emblematic of another place I love, the Okavango Swamps.

In July 1978 I was with Irene Menell in the Okavango Swamps of northern Botswana. The swamps are not swamps at all, but the only inland river delta on earth. The Okavango River has formed myriad channels and islets here, and birds and game abound.

We had left husbands and children in Johannesburg, taken

our malaria pills, and were a party of eight led by a game
ranger and five polers of the Kavango tribe. "Polers" were men
who poled our mokoros (dugout canoes) through this watery
wonderworld for five days.

Makabela was the headman of the village and the head poler.
We did not choose him; he chose us by placing our bags in his
mokoro. This pleased us for it meant that ours was the lead
mokoro, giving us the initial view of all that lay ahead on the
watery pathways that crisscross the Okavango Delta. Makabela was tall and lithe, in his early fifties, we thought, with the
demeanour of the clichéd nobility of the natural man.

Irene sat up front at first, her bare feet on either side of the
prow, with a straw hat and large dark sunglasses, her old
Gucci hold-all a backrest. She seemed, perhaps for the first
time since I'd known her, at peace. Behind me Makabela stood,
balanced on the stern; he handled the pole expertly with his
right hand. He wore faded dark grey shorts, a white T-shirt,
and a soft dark brown sun hat. His body was lean and muscled,
and his strongly featured ebony face looked steadfastly ahead.
He seemed at peace, too. He knew I was watching him and
pointed to my right with an imperious gesture of his hand. In
the papyrus, growing thickly six inches away from me on
either side of the mokoro, I saw many tiny tree frogs. I plucked
one off the grass stalk, grinning delightedly at Makabela. He
nodded his head.

The light at dawn was soft and yielding and bathed the tops
of the papyrus fronds with a yellow glow. At dusk the sky was
more dramatic, purple, red-orange, and then a mauve haze as
the stars pricked out the darkness. One evening Irene joined
me at the water's edge; we watched the fireflies and did not
speak. Indeed we spoke little on that trip. In the distance a lion
roared, then a hyena laughed. We heard a snuffling in the thick
reeds and grasses behind us, between us and the roaring camp
fire. We returned to the others then. In the morning Makabela
showed us the prints of a hippo in the mud near where we had
been sitting. They were at least fourteen inches across.

Once we were behind three other mokoros, and the symmetry of the movement of the polers was caught and refracted in
the symmetry of the curving waterways and the curving banks

of reeds, now bending toward us, now bending away from us.

We saw the rare lechwe and the shy sitatunga, the kudu, the impala, and the timid bushbuck. We saw the rare honey badger, giraffe, zebra, and a glimpse of elephant through the reeds and trees on Chief's Island. We heard lion every night, and twice we saw hyena in the early dawn.

We saw kingfishers, marabou storks, the African jacana or "lilytrotter," pygmy ducks, many other species of waterfowl, the mighty fish eagle, other birds of prey, and at night, alert, the great eagle owls.

There were insects too—spiders, tsetse flies, mosquitoes, butterflies, moths, ants, scorpions. But we were not bothered by them, although we were both bitten by tsetse flies. We slept at night on the ground under mosquito nets strung from branches near the campfire. One of our party did not let down her mosquito net on the first night. She had an allergic reaction to the mosquito bites and came out in ugly red, itchy welts.

We were told there were snakes too, but we did not see any.

On a humid afternoon, when we were resting under a grove of trees at the water's edge, I waded to the mokoros to fetch another beer from the cooler bag. My return to the bank elicited screams of horror and general consternation. My alarm was greater than that of my companions when I saw, clinging to my legs, several large, rapidly swelling leeches. Many hands held cigarettes and matches to my legs and burnt them off me. Somehow I did not react with the atavistic revulsion I thought I would feel. It is the large, hairy spiders found often at Nature's Valley that evoke those fears in me.

Early one morning, after breakfasting under an ancient wild fig tree, we set off on our twenty-mile trip back to Xaxaba. Makabela led the party as usual. We were not on the water for more than twenty minutes when I felt Makabela stiffen behind me. He sniffed the air like an animal himself.

"Buffalo!" I could not smell anything significantly different. But Makabela headed for the nearest bank and leapt from the mokoro while swooping for his old two-barreled rifle at our feet. He motioned urgently for Irene and me to follow him. He made off through the thorn trees, paying scant attention to us or the rest of the party, which was only now coming into view around a bend in the river.

"We'd better catch him," I said to Irene. "We can't stay here alone."

Africa suddenly seemed inimical in the glazed early-morning light. The silence was oppressive. "You go," Irene said. "I can't keep up with Makabela on the trot."

I was torn between being with Makabela and staying with my friend. The other mokoros were making for the bank while Makabela gestured impatiently from a rise through the thorn trees. After one look back, I ran to join him.

We moved quickly through the bush, weaving and ducking our heads to avoid the acacia thorns. Now I too could smell them, the distinctive smell of many sweaty hides. Makabela held up his hand. I stopped. Ahead of us, in a denuded area sparsely dotted with low thorn trees, a herd of about five hundred buffalo stood, immobile. The leader, a magnificent bull, had picked up our scent. He stood across the clearing, sniffing at us.

We could hear the sound of the rest of the party coming nearer, crashing through the grass, calling loudly and excitedly. The old bull snorted. As one the herd seemed to melt into the surrounding thicket. Makabela called in his native tongue to Dave, the game ranger. We waited for the fitter members of the party to join us. Makabela spoke sternly.

"No speak!"

We nodded our heads. At a steady pace we set off after the buffalo. My heart was pounding with excitement. The danger of having been that close to so many huge wild animals seemed enormous.

The buffalo took Makabela by surprise this time. We walked right into the middle of the herd. Makabela froze and gestured for us to stand stock-still. Most of us had stopped breathing anyway. The buffalo stood a few feet away from us on all sides.

Suddenly Makabela shouted something that sounded like "Hi, hi, hi!"

The buffalo began to move off. We were adrift in a river of trotting animals. Across one side of the mass of heavy bodies working their way around us I could see Dave and Irene and the others, looking concerned. Then, as quickly as we had blundered into them, they were gone. For the first and only time, I saw Makabela smile. He leaned the butt of his old rifle into the sand and reclined back onto it. He and Dave shared an excited conversation when the rest of the party joined us.

"His old rifle would have blown him up first if he'd had to use it," Dave told me later.

My most compelling memory of that incident, besides the buffalo themselves, was that for the first time in my life I felt my scalp tingle.

Later Makabela, feeling pleased with himself, sang the lead in a tribal chorus answered by the other polers as he skillfully used the current to carry us downriver. I smiled at Irene sitting behind me; calmer now, she smiled back.

Africa, gilded in the bright morning sunlight, lay still, breathing quietly around us.

Years later, another African sunset became the backdrop for another quintessentially African scene, this one in Londolozi Game Reserve, about 40 miles from Kruger National Park.

Dusk—an almost cloudless sky, a cool breeze in the late autumn air, the plain in front of us. In the middle distance a herd of wildebeest rested near a water hole. Five male sentinels stood guard at the periphery of the herd. The younger animals were ensconced amid the others.

"Shall we have our drinks here?" asked Pete, the young blond game ranger.

It would be magnificent to watch the sunset from here. Already the far rim of hills was a black silhouette. The grasses, waving gently in the breeze, tossed back at us the pink glow of sunset on their feathered plumes.

A primeval African plain at sunset.

Lucas, the black tracker, went to the back of the Jeep to take out the cooler bag with the drinks. In a low, urgent voice he muttered to Pete in his native Shangaan.

Pete turned slowly in his seat and then started the engine. Lucas assumed his station on the hood, his legs resting over the grille on the front fender.

"Cheetah," said Pete, "over there . . . they're stalking."

My heart beat faster. Cheetah were the rarest and the most sought-after game to view. I had seen them before, but only in the distance, in Wankie, in Kruger, but not like this, from an open Jeep in a private game park.

Roger and Tony were rigid with excitement. They were both passionate about cheetah, whose pictures festooned their bedrooms. A favourite fantasy game of theirs, when they were preschoolers, was to spend hours stalking around the house on all fours, communicating with high-pitched squeaks and whistles. "Cheet," Tony would call lovingly to Roger. "Come here, cheet." They had not seen a cheetah in the wild before.

"There he is," breathed Pete, having turned the Jeep in a half-circle.

We followed his pointing finger but saw nothing. Then I caught the movement of a flickering ear above the heads of tall grasses. Pete took the Jeep closer. It was a young male. He was sitting on his haunches, his forelegs stiff on the ground. He watched the wildebeest with a frozen stare.

Lucas muttered to Pete again. I followed the general direction of his pointing arm through the binoculars. Far around to our right was another cheetah, inching its way forward on its belly. The sun, a fiery orb across the plain, shone into its eyes. Behind it the eastern horizon was a pink glow, although the sun had not yet reached the distant western hills.

Lucas pointed again: yet a third cheetah was away to our left. It was trotting closer to the herd, its movement scarcely discernible in the darkening, lengthening shadows.

Our cheetah began to move, too, trotting slowly in a line with its companion to the left. They were upwind from the wildebeest, who, although they could not smell the cheetah, were becoming restless. We could hear the guards snorting, the herd shuffling in the grass.

In the fading light we watched the slithering cheetah through the binoculars away to our right. It was obvious that he was going to charge the herd and try to turn it toward his two companions.

Taut with tension we drove on about thirty feet behind our steadily trotting cheetah. We followed him around thorn trees, over rocks and anthills, down small dongas (eroded gullies), and up the other side.

It was dark enough around us for Lucas, now perched at the back of the Jeep, to have taken out the huge spotlights. But he did not turn them on yet. The cheetah was a moving shadow ahead, the herd of wildebeest a blackening stain in the sea of grass. Stars pricked their way through the darkening sky behind us. A band of gold played on the horizon where the sun had set, the glory of its blood-red leaving still reflected in the few wispy clouds over the western horizon.

Suddenly, wheeling as one, the herd galloped off to the west, the one direction where no cheetah lay in wait. In seconds our cheetah was running at full speed, sixty miles an hour. Lucas fleetingly held the spotlight on his streaking figure, but we would not be able to catch him, for he moved with a fluidity that seemed to deny that he was moving at all. The air was full of the sound of galloping hoofs, and we were thrown around in the Jeep while Pete tried to follow Lucas's directions to bring us after the cheetah. The Jeep hit a rock, and we were thrown forward in an almighty jolt.

"Don't you think . . . ," I began, but Pete was not about to listen to my reservations about our safety. His job was to take us to the cheetah. I did not know whether to be relieved or sorry when the Jeep's gears were crashed into reverse and we were off again. "Hold tight, you two!" my anxious voice admonished the boys. "Oh, Mom!" Derision was the tone of their response. We stopped on a grassy knoll.

In the spotlight I saw the herd standing still, grazing peacefully. Before I could ask a puzzled question of Pete, Lucas's handheld spotlight picked out three pairs of eyes on the ground a short distance from the herd. The cheetah were already feeding on a young wildebeest.

We watched them for a while.

The surrounding hills were a dark rim at the periphery of the earth. The moon was rising, three-quarters full, and was beginning to cast night shadows among the thorn bushes.

"Well, I guess that's it then?" Pete, his job done, was inhaling on a Camel, his feet relaxed on the frame of the Jeep. I nodded.

Almost sedately we regained on the sandy road and, under the inverted bowl of the eternal African night sky, finally had that drink.

I have stood at the edge of the world and seen an ocean of cloud two thousand feet below me. It is difficult to find words to describe the beauty of the Drakensberg Mountains of South

Africa, for be it Injusuti, the Royal Natal National Park, or Giant's Castle, there is a splendour to the earth there, where mountaintop meets the aery light of the African sky.

Like a discoverer full of wonder, I want to recount what I have seen that lives on inside me. The colours of the Drakensberg stretch away in front of me, five layers of mountaintops, dark green-gold in the foreground, grey-purple, then purple-black, a lighter blue-grey, and, towering in the far distance, light blue jagged peaks.

Then there is the red-orange and orange-yellow of ericas and aloes, the pink-red of sugar bush proteas, the various shades of everlasting daisies. Blue agapanthus, salmon-pink watsonias, green alpine grasses carpet the lower slopes dotted with tiny ground-hugging yellow and blue wildflowered grasses.

I have also seen baboons, rock rabbits, small buck, and the magnificent lammergeier riding on the air; Bushmen paintings, too, of eland, rhino, and strange men in ritual headdresses at Giant's Castle.

The wind rising against the escarpment can blow a waterfall back up the mountain and send plumes of cloud streaming through chasms and ravines hundreds of feet into the air.

And at sunrise, at the edge of a precipice, at the edge of the world, layered bands of dark clouds catch the rays of the sun, turning crimson, orange, then gold as the sunlight changes the cloud ocean below into a solid plane of shifting colour.

In the cool of the late afternoon, sitting at an ice-cold rushing stream, you can watch the magnificent white thunderheads build and build behind the mountain ramparts, while at night, if you stand in the cold stillness of the brooding mountain quiet and see the stars, I mean really see the stars, the night sky will dazzle you with its remote alien beauty, for as John Buchan wrote, "the southern constellations blaze in a profound sky."

Come, walk with me along any of the mountain paths, through the mountain forests and grasslands, for this six-hundred-mile mountain range is wild and beautiful, is Africa, is the country to which I belong and which I love.

Sunnyside, a guest farm, is a four-hour drive from Johannesburg. It is nestled in the Maluti Mountains, thirty miles from the Lesotho border, on the "other side" of the Drakensberg, in a remote southeastern corner of the Orange Free State. We often spent long weekends there.

The region is made up of sandstone hills with granite and igneous rock mountain peaks. The walks around Sunnyside are more of a rambling sort than serious climbs, but when you feel the urge to challenge yourself, there are a few splendid paths that wind around the edges of plunging chasms and venture into the upper peaks.

It is the colours of the sandstone cliffs that make this remote corner of South Africa eternally fascinating. The sunlight, through its daily cycle, reveals a wondrous palette of earth colours—from grey-blue through ochre and red, natural colours dye the cliffs.

Sunnyside is the original 150-year-old farmhouse; it is surrounded by cottages built of stone blocks. Indeed, a stonecutter still shapes giant building blocks at the base of a sandstone cliff, where huge rocks frequently tumble to the ground. The cracks of his chisel strokes echo in the valleys.

Fossilised dinosaur bones were found on the farm.

Basotho tribespeople squat there, working in the kitchen and cottages and in the fields, in a century-old exchange of labour for land usage. The Basotho women, dressed in patterned calico wraparounds, their hair strung with brightly coloured beads, serve in the dining room. A weekly roster of meals and duties is never changed so that, even over a period of years, the women always seem to be the same people, standing in the same pose you last saw them in, months, perhaps years, before.

Denis and Ann Boland ran the farm. An elderly artist permanently rented one of the cottages. At twilight he would sit on his terrace, sip a drink, and watch the sunlight on the sandstone cliff across the valley while playing classical music on his portable gramophone. He became aware that one of the local herdboys would inevitably appear at his terrace at this time, seemingly entranced by the music.

The artist taught him to speak a little more English than he already knew, as well as the rudiments of piano playing. The herdboy, Matlose, would entertain invited farm guests. A musician from Durban heard him play and arranged for him to have lessons in the conservatory there. Public recitals followed private appearances in elegant homes. The boy, an adolescent in the late seventies, travelled with the artist to Europe and the United States. He was given a scholarship to attend a famous music school in New York.

We too heard the herdboy play, with the French windows open to the terrace and the last rays of the sun lighting the sandstone cliff in a golden shower.

At moments of my greatest enjoyment of the physical beauty of my motherland, paradoxically, resignedly, I was always aware that at places like Sunnyside (as part of the South African way of life) there were no black guests and that, the musical herdboy aside, the black children living on the farm led a life of deprivation and rural poverty. For if I took my eyes off the sandstone cliffs, I saw rural schoolchildren walking miles from their rudimentary schoolhouse to their family kraals. Three, maybe four years, was the extent of the education they received (if they were lucky), and then they faced the prospect of lifelong unemployment. For there was then and still is, increasingly, little paying work on the farms, and South African labour laws forbade "illegal" influx to the cities.

The ugliness of apartheid pervades even the heart of the physical beauty of South Africa. The Edenic beauty of the land, sadly, is rotten at its core. For these groups of schoolchildren on the country roads around Sunnyside are an ever-growing presence in every rural corner of every part of South Africa. These children grow into a footloose, hungry mass of people who wander aimlessly between rural outposts and alien cities.

Urbanisation in South Africa increasingly means vast squatter camps growing in the whites-only periurban areas of the cities. Sprawling, unplanned shantytowns, like the famous Crossroads Camp in Cape Town, with no infrastructure and no services, are a phenomenon whose existence the white South African regime has not yet admitted, standing King Canute-like, trying unsuccessfully to turn back the inevitable tide of long-suppressed black anger and frustration with forced resettlement of people and forced busing of urban squatters to so-called rural "homelands." The world has seen these actions perpetrated again and again by the state authorities at places such as Crossroads, where shanties are torn down by bulldozers and people are bused to the Transkei and the Ciskei. But, like the ebb and flow of a wave, they always return, in ever-growing scores of thousands.

This is a phenomenon with which South African governments of the future—be they black or white—will have to contend, for the demographic projections for this country make startling reading: today's population of thirty-one million will become forty million by the year 2000 and eighty million by 2020 if every female of childbearing age has only two children.

At the Giant's Castle Game Reserve Rest Camp, the accommodations are upmarket, and because the state subsidises the national parks, the rental of a hut costs a minimal amount and includes the services of a Zulu cook "boy." The accommodations are strictly for whites only. The fear that facilities such as these camps and parks will be swamped by a wave of black masses ensures that they remain racially exclusive to the letter of the law. For the government responds to this fear and narrow self-interest by passing laws to legally ensure the whites-only privilege and keep amenities separate for racial groups.

Separate, I need not remind you, is never equal, and the apartheid regime makes no grand gesture to the contrary.

I would estimate that if every Drakensberg accommodation facility was utilised every day of the year, only about eight thousand white people, out of a total population of thirty-one million, enjoy the mountain splendour.

From the rest camp, set high on the edge of the escarpment beneath the highest peaks (in range of a good day's hike), there is a magnificent, sweeping view across the hilly river valleys. Laudably, great effort has been made within the reserve to conserve the flora and fauna and the mountains themselves, but outside the reserve small villages of Zulu people dot the valleys. This is rural Kwa-Zulu. The land is steadily eroding, the hillsides are being denuded by overgrazing, and the trees, used for fuel, are disappearing.

The contrasts between the overcrowded, overgrazed, hilly "homeland" and the splendidly grassed conservation areas,

Mrs. Marais's Nursery School, class of 1950. (I'm at far end of side fender.)

I'm with my brother Roy; Galway Road, Parkview, Johannesburg, 1950.

I'm five years old here at
Muizenberg Beach, Cape
Town, 1950.
(Note unknown "nanny" in
the background.)

With my parents, Solly
and Eileen Berman, at
the annual family
vacation at Muizenberg,
Cape Town, 1952.

I was captain of the first Tennis Team, Emmarentia Primary School, 1958.

Emmarentia Primary School, Scholar Patrol, 1958. (I'm in back row at right of teacher Mr. Broderick.)

With my friend Natalie Goate (left) in 1963, at the swimming gala of Parktown Girls' High, where I was Head of House.

My mother, Eileen Berman, and I at a family function in Johannesburg, April 1970.

Sandy and I, eight months after our own wedding, at my brother's wedding in Johannesburg, January 1972.

Robert Kennedy's visit to South Africa, 1966.

Helen Suzman and I chatting outside polling booth on Election Day, 1970.

The Knysna loerie.

With my sons Tony (left) and Roger
(right) at Nature's Valley, 1977.

My visit to Okavango Swamps with Irene Menell in July 1978.

A gathering at 38 Ivy Road: Janet (centre) with Houghton workers.

Helen Suzman, the long-serving PFP Member of Parliament for Houghton and my political mentor.

The Star, Johannesburg

Irene Menell, friend and political ally.

The official portrait of the city council of Johannesburg 1983–84.

Alderman Sam Moss, PFP leader in the Johannesburg City Council, my caucus "boss" and friend.

Alderman J. F. Oberholzer, Chairman of the Management Committee of the Johannesburg City Council, one of my most intractable political opponents.

"Lack of municipal services", says Levine

Council moves spell new hope for city hawkers

Residents battle to save park

Norwood refuses to give up fight on bus depot

As a Johannesburg city councillor from 1977 to 1984, the everyday work for my constituency involved a wide variety of local issues.

Three of the Ma-Afrika Taxi Ltd. directors (left to right): myself, Milton Mdakane, Ezekiel (Windy) Mdletye.

Ishmael (Mylie) Richards, chairman of the so-called "Coloured" Management Committee, a political ally.

Mamphele Ramphele,
Lenyene doctor and
committed activist.

Joseph Mavi, leader of the
Black Municipal Workers'
Union, shortly after his release
from prison after the 1980
"strike."

Percy Qoboza, editor of *The Sowetan,* my editor on
Post before it was banned.

Afrapix, Johannesburg

The dumping grounds—a familiar scene in the "homelands" in the late seventies and through the eighties.

The Star, Johannesburg

Len Apfel, "the Jewish missionary," founder of Imqualife, with crafts from the rural areas.

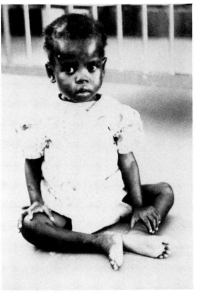

Len Apfel (foreground) and
Mary Hanna (background)
February 1984.

At St. Brendan's Mission,
Lebowa, a four-year-old girl, a
"kwash" victim, showing the
ravages of malnutrition.

An early morning line at the clinic at St. Joseph's Community
Centre, Thohoyandou, Venda.

Helen Suzman and I in Straus Library at Milton Academy in April 1988. She was there to deliver the Alumni War Memorial Lecture.

Mvelase, a black exchange student from South Africa, joined our family in our Milton, Massachusetts, home for the 1986–87 school year.

often on opposites sides of the same roads, are too obvious to ignore.

"See how those blacks ruin the land!" remark the white visitors.

My blood pressure rises at such comments, for it is these Zulu people who for centuries carefully and lovingly tended the land that fed and sustained them. Enter the apartheid regime, whose ideologically excessive "resettlement" policy upset the balanced ratio of people to land area by dumping many more people on the land than it could ever hope to sustain.

The contrast between Giant's Castle Game Reserve and the Kwa-Zulu homeland is but one chapter of a desperate saga found over the length and breadth of South Africa.

Closer to home for me lies another example of this chasm caused by the race-obsessed ideology of the South African government. At the Perlman cottage in Nature's Valley, Dora Hartz came every second day to tend to the household chores. Ina had warned me that Dora was a "fixture" of the cottage and there was no avoiding her. She had been in the service of the previous owners as well.

Dora was an elderly grandmother, a "coloured" woman. (In South Africa's political lexicon, *coloured* legally means a separate "mixed-blood" racial group of about three million people, distinct from the "white" group and the "black" group. Historically there are few "blacks" living in the Eastern Cape.) She was seventy-two when I met her. She had a weather-beaten lined face, and her wispy, light grey hair, escaping from her doek, was tinged with black. She walked with a limp.

"An accident, madam," she explained to me in the local patois of mixed English and Afrikaans words, "killed one of my boys and injured me. Three months I was in the hospitaal there by Port Elizabeth. It was after a church meeting, there by The Crags, you know?" I nodded. "The driver was dronk. We went off the road, there in the pass, near the river." She shrugged her shoulders. "The driver was not hurt, but he was killed later, another accident."

Dora would catch the South African Railways bus at six-thirty in the morning and be at our cottage by eight. There is no rail link between Port Elizabeth and Knysna; too many precipitous gorges and wide river mouths precluded the building of a line. Instead, a daily Railways bus service ferries passengers along the two-hundred-mile road. Dora and the other "coloured" passengers would sit at the back of the bus.

Dora lived at Coldstream, a small cluster of foresters' bungalows in the Lottering Forest Reserve. Her husband had been a forester, and her two married sons and three sons-in-law were foresters. She lived with her two unmarried forester sons in a green-painted bungalow with a tiny garden and a TV antenna on the roof.

Lottering is a series of state-owned timber plantations with miles of conifers planted in neat corduroy rows. Yet pockets of indigenous forest are still to be found dotted around the plunging ravines.

At Coldstream the bungalows for the "coloured" foresters were built at some distance from the white foresters' compound. The whites encampment had within its barbed-wire confines the post office, butcher shop, general store, drank winkel (bottle store), and garage. Here stood the modern wooded facade of the whites-only Dutch Reformed Church.

Among the cluster of bungalows where Dora lived one could make out the cross over the tin roof of the white-painted "coloureds"-only Dutch Reformed Church. (The churches were racially separate by decree of the predominantly white, reactionary, ruling synod of the church.)

On Sundays, the same hymns, sung in the same Afrikaans language, at the same time, would sound forth from both of these buildings. Dora told me that she had once attended a service in "die wit mense se kerk" (the white man's church) and that the white minister occasionally delivered a sermon in her church. It would never enter her head to want to attend an ordinary service there, she said. "Die wit mense bied alleen." (The white man prays alone.) She cackled with laughter in answer to my question. Her understanding of the sad reality of living inside apartheid was underscored by her ironic, laconic comment.

Sandy and I would vie with each other to take Dora home. It was more than enough for me that she insisted on tending the cottage at all, let alone brushing the carpets on her hands and knees. I would not let her limp the two miles to the general store to catch the bus.

We would wind our way from the forest floor at Nature's Valley to the top of the Grootrivier Pass, drive over a wooded plateau for a few miles, and then descend to the Blaawrivier, twisting our way through steeply forested glens.

"Dis die plek, die ongeluk. Hier is my seun doed." (This is the place, the accident. This is where my son died.)

Dora pointed down a steep bank to a deep pool where the river slowly meandered. She shook her head sadly.

On the first day that she showed me the place, I stopped on my way back. It was still and hot in the forest, the sky a narrow blue band between the two sides of the forest wall three hundred feet above me. Birds called in the stillness. A malachite kingfisher sunned itself on the rocks at the river's edge to the sound of a baboon barking close at hand. Dora's life drama was far away.

By the second week of our drive to Dora's home, her two sons and two friends (I limited the numbers) met us at the entrance to the Blaawkrantz Pass for a ride home as well. They were working in the forest thereabouts. Although they answered my pointed questions about their lives in the segregated village, they were noncommittal and I did not elicit any emotional responses from them, particularly the resentment, or anger, I was anticipating.

But Dora, although she bore her lot in life with Christian forbearance, let me glimpse her state of being.

"My madam," she would say referring to Ina Perlman, "smokes too much, even when she's at the valley. It's because she works too hard for the black people in Jo'burg. It's an evil place there; the government is evil there."

"It's the same government as here, Dora."

"But we've lived together too long here—kleurling en wit mense [coloured and white people]. We're too far from Jo'burg. The government in Cape Town is becoming bad too, though. Our young coloured people are fighting with the government in Cape Town. There's trouble coming, big trouble. Maybe even here," she gestured out of the car window at the tapestry of forest, shrugging her shoulders. "Already the coloured children burn the school and throw stones in Knysna."

It seemed a remote notion, I reflected to myself as I drove back from Dora's village, that the unrest that had affected the rest of the country since 1977 could rear its head in the remote forested reaches of the Tsitsikama Forest and Coastal Natural Park.

In captivity the Knysna loerie dies.

CHAPTER 7
38 Ivy Road

It took me four years, 1966 to 1970, to become involved in mainline politics again after the disheartening, at times frightening, political forays of my university years. During that period, however, my liberal idealism never wavered. My conviction that many more whites (including me) had to involve themselves in the political arena, engaging the Nationalists on every platform and in every forum available to us, strengthened inexorably.

The apartheid regime had things its own way in South Africa mainly because it was prepared to use reactionary institutionalized violence. But that did not preclude whites' fighting the Nationalists all the way in their own forums. Some perversity made the powers that be preserve the outer shells of democratic procedures—elections and councils of government run on strict parliamentary procedures. And a valiant, though hamstrung (through limited state censorship), liberal press stood firm in endeavouring to bring the word of liberal resistance to other South Africans and to the international community. There were opportunities for activist liberals, if not to bring down the government in the reactionary climate among white voters, then at least to make it accountable in some way for its actions, through documented answers in Parliament, by being "put on the record" on details of policy in political debates.

These thoughts sifted slowly through my mind over my postuniversity years, but I see now that they set me on an inevitable course. What I really wanted to devote my energy to was fighting the government. I chose to join Helen Suzman and the Progressive Party to do so.

During those four years, I also began my teaching career. Several experiences in my first year stand out as catalytic in reinforcing my sense of certainty—even urgency—about the political path I was choosing. The fact that the government's tentacles reach into every South African's life became a reality for me when they impinged on my own life. My student activism had ensured that the apartheid regime's beady eyes would watch the progress of my life, for I was assigned a teaching position in a National Party stronghold at Witbanksehoerskool (Witbank High School).

"Witbank!" my mother shrieked when she heard the news. "How can they send you there with those raw Afrikaners? You'll never meet anyone. Your politics will get you into real trouble there."

She still shakes her head today at the thought of me in Witbank. And I was as appalled as she was at the thought of going to live there.

Witbank was the heartland of one of the most politically reactionary and conservative areas of the country. How would I react in such an environment? Could I really teach those schoolchildren, who I knew would be the ones forming the guard of honour, Nazi Youth League style, waving flags and saluting various National Party leaders as they attended party rallies in the town hall to rousing choruses of "volksliede"? No, I could not see myself sitting in the faculty room of Witbanksehoerskool making small talk with other faculty members, or being friendly to my students' parents, or being able to find a rapport with my students themselves. But overriding all else was the appalling thought of having to bury myself in the narrow Calvinistic dogma and Puritanical racism of that community and that place. That undid me.

Certain Afrikaans-speaking schools were openly assigned the best teachers from the training colleges. It was to be my fate, in graduating as one of the top five English teachers of my year, to teach English to Afrikaans-speaking children.

In order to teach in a state school, one had to have a diploma from one of the state education colleges. Payment for tuition was in the form of a contract to teach for the Transvaal Education Department for the equivalent number of years of one's training. My contract was for one year. I had to teach at whichever school I was assigned in the Transvaal.

It occurred to me that my assignment to Witbank might be a form of political exile, banishment to a rural Nationalist stronghold where many eyes could be kept on my activities. This impression was reinforced when I tried to have my assignment changed to one at several of the English-speaking high schools in Johannesburg, where I knew the principals had applied for my services.

Finally, I went to Pretoria in person to plead my case, trying to make use of any slim excuse—my father was dying (which he was), my mother did not drive (which she did not), my Afrikaans was not good enough (which it was not).

In a Kafkaesque daze I wandered from one office to another, from one hostile bureaucrat to another, in a hollow building with alarmingly long corridors and seemingly innumerable offices, where women in crimpilene dresses and beehive-style hairdos sat and knitted. Eventually, on entering the office of a scowling, fairly senior bureaucrat, I heard the truth.

He was of medium height, in his mid-thirties, with wavy black hair slicked down over his forehead with hair grease. He wore the ubiquitous safari suit of his breed—khaki shorts, open-necked khaki shirt with short sleeves and a row of pens clipped to the breast pocket. A thin black comb was stuck into the side of his knee-length khaki socks. His sallow face was pitted with large blackened pores. He sported, along with his safari suit, the equally characteristic Hitler moustache. His small dark eyes stared fixedly at me over my file, numbered

11096. Looking at him, I knew why the entrance to the building was dominated by a huge metal sculpture of a grotesquely twisting bull, its overlarge genitals glinting like steel in the bright Pretoria sunshine. It was the emblem of the cast-iron nonvirility of this place.

"Juffrou . . ." (He spoke to me in Afrikaans. I spoke to him in English.) ". . . there is a black mark in your file, for your student activities. There is no question of you teaching where you want to go. You will teach where we send you."

He did not bother to disguise the threat in his words. I walked out of his office, determined about two things: not to be bullied into going to teach in Witbank and to find a way of teaching in a state school in Johannesburg.

Of course I had other options. I could have returned to university to do postgraduate work, applied for a post at an independent school (although these were hard to come by at short notice), gone to live in the more liberal Cape Province, where my teacher's certificate was valid and a black mark in my file hopefully not as condemnatory. I could have gone to London, which I longed to do, but my father was too ill. Anyway, I had a point to prove to the authorities: I wanted to teach in Johannesburg on my terms.

A colleague and artist, Arlene Burstein, had acquired her first teaching job at Krugersdorp High School that year. (Arlene lives in Perth, Australia, now.) The principal was short of three English teachers, and she told him of my plight. After our interview, he mysteriously but inevitably, in view of his faculty needs, managed to change the official attitude toward me, and I began teaching at his school.

The children I taught were from a lower-middle-class white background, the offspring of railway and factory workers. The stories of my experiences there are many. Suffice it to say that I struck up a strong rapport with the students. They had a real love of literature, especially poetry. And that is how I acquired my second black mark in the Transvaal Education Department (TED).

In class I had read a poem by Jonty Driver, the exiled ex-NUSAS student leader, linking his memories of his homeland to his first impressions of his new home, England. He writes of the "stratification of the white cliffs of Dover."

An explanation of the word *stratification* led to a discussion of geology, then fossils, then archaeology, then the theory of evolution. I was aware that I had strayed from the domain of English subject matter as laid down in the syllabus, but I believed, as a maxim of my teaching, that I must answer any question from any child, if I could, no matter where the discussion took us.

On the faculty was one Ampie de Ridder, an Afrikaans teacher, reputedly a member of the Broederbond, a secret society of Afrikaner Nationalists and the most powerful body in Afrikanerdom, its leaders even more powerful than the parliamentary Cabinet. The Broederbond's members infiltrate all levels of political, religious, and academic life. Admittance to the society is by invitation only.

Ampie de Ridder, tall and thin, was treated with an absurd degree of obsequious deference by the other teachers. He had cold light brown eyes and an infuriating manner of sidling right up to you when he spoke, whether you were both seated or standing. He knew a great deal about me and made it his business to draw me out on political matters almost as soon as I arrived at the school.

Rumours of his cruel disciplinary techniques were legion among the students. It was said he would punish boys and girls alike, hitting them across the tops of their fingers with a ruler, driving their fingernails into the flesh of their fingers. One of his rules held that any student who dropped something from the desk had to hit the ground before the object. Legend had it that he once pushed a boy out of a second-story window, and the boy broke an arm. No one told me if de Ridder was even reprimanded.

These facts made it difficult for me to assimilate another side of him, one of which I was earnestly and repeatedly made aware by other faculty members—Ampie de Ridder, the caring, patient helpmate of an invalid wife. Even more disconcerting to me was the way the skin around his eyes crinkled when he smiled, reminding me of Mr. Broderick, my childhood hero and teacher. I wondered at my finding a likeness between this smiling bigot and the enlightened guide of my childhood intellectual endeavours.

On the day Robert Kennedy was assassinated there was scattered applause in the faculty room when the news came over the radio. Losing control of myself, I switched off the radio and stormed and railed against the bigotry, conformity, and reactionary shortsightedness evident among the faculty. In the silence after I had finished speaking, before conversation could begin among the small groups again, de Ridder strode over to me and wagged his finger under my nose.

"Meisiekind, ek soek jou, wees noukeurig." (Girl, I'm looking for you, be careful.)

Sometime in October of that year, the principal, Mr. van der Merwe, called me to his office.

"Janet," he said, "I'm sorry to have to tell you this, because you have the makings of a good teacher, and I like you. But I have to tell you that the department has blacklisted you. You can no longer teach in TED schools."

His words were not entirely unexpected. Ampie de Ridder had been avoiding me for some weeks, and I knew that something was about to happen. My blacklisting was shocking and frightening to me, though, because of the finality of its message. It embodied the paranoid obsessiveness of the apartheid government, its driving need to leave no stone unturned in its bid to twist South Africa into a conformist, racially segregated society.

Fortunately, I had already arranged a teaching post for myself at a Catholic parochial school for the forthcoming academic year beginning in January. It was simply not possible for me to teach in the stifling atmosphere of the state school system.

"I have persuaded them to let you stay here until the end of term," Mr. van der Merwe continued.

"Is it possible for you to tell me why I have been blacklisted?"

"Not really, but I'm against this sort of witch hunting, so I'll bend the rules. I won't tell you, but you can read the report if you want to."

. . . complaints have been filed against the above named for exceeding her subject matter in the classroom . . . teaching evolution, political indoctrination and racial attitudes. . . .

. . . the above named, who already has a record of student activism, is thus suspect. . . .

. . . on investigation by a member of your faculty the above mentioned complaints were found to be of substance. . . .

. . . further evidence was forthcoming of her subversive activities among faculty members. . . .

Mr. van der Merwe looked rueful. My fright gave way to fury. The accusations were absurd but invidiously condemnatory. Ampie de Ridder shrugged his shoulders when I confronted him, and he paid scant attention to me for the remaining two months of the school year. I was of no consequence to him; I posed no further "threat" to education in state schools in the Transvaal.

Most of the other faculty treated me as if I were a leper; only the principal was courteous. Fortunately, I had a small cadre of friends there, three other young teachers who had been at Teachers' Training College with me: Arlene, the art teacher; Rudi, a vocational guidance teacher and a zealously evangelistic Jehovah's Witness (who had enough sense to keep his missionary zeal out of the classroom); and Helen, another English teacher. We had formed a car pool to travel from and to Johannesburg each day.

In 1968 I went to teach at Marist Brothers' College in Linmeyer, Johannesburg. If my first year of teaching had been less than satisfactory on a number of fronts, my four years at Marist Brothers' College were fulfilling. The brothers themselves were cooperative, tolerant colleagues. One of them, redhaired Irish madcap Brother Paul, became a firm friend. Our relationship culminated in our codirecting an exciting production of *The Wizard of Oz*.

By 1970 I had made the decision that led me on my inevitable path: I decided to become politically active by working for the liberal Progressive Party. It was not with unalloyed enthusiasm that I made this decision, for I had qualms about putting myself into the whites-only political arena. That uneasiness waxed and waned over the ensuing years but never left me. Yet liberal party politics did present avenues for directly engaging the government, and it did present a platform for expressing my deeply held liberal values.

By 1970 Helen Suzman was the lone member of her party to win a seat to Parliament in twelve years. This was a sterling achievement in the face of white obduracy and conservatism. Indeed, it is my conviction that it is only because of her efforts during those years, and the unique role history granted her, that the vocabulary of liberalism is still evident in South Africa today, whereas all the other vestiges of it have long been swept away. Without her methodically plugging the holes in the dam walls by challenging the details of every bill destroying human rights that was passed, the flood of white reactionaryism would have swept all before it during the sixties. Helen has her place in South Africa's history.

The idea of working with this great lady in some capacity thrilled me. I remembered vividly the excitement and feeling of triumph that had pervaded Helen's Houghton headquarters at 38 Ivy Road, Norwood, on the night of the 1966 elections. Young Progs leader Johnny Fedler, Steven Suzman, and I went together from the Greenside School polling booth where we had been working. Johnny was the Parktown Young Prog chairman.

38 Ivy Road was a small house that had been converted into an election office some years earlier. During the ensuing years it was to become the headquarters of the "left wing" of the Progressive Party and the political home of not only me but also many of my closest colleagues and friends. On that 1966 election night we gathered in the yard under the early summer highveld night sky. The air was warm and carried the night scents of jasmine, roses, and honeysuckle. Few of us had slept the previous night, for we had been decorating the polling booths. Most of us had risen at five o'clock to be at the polls.

We sat in a circle around a fire, toasting marshmallows, drinking cheap, astringent red wine, and singing with Des Lindberg, a Young Prog (already becoming South Africa's most famous folksinger) who had brought a guitar. Our singing was interrupted only by the beeps on the radio, the precursor to an election results announcement. The worse the results were for Progressive candidates around the country, the more frenzied was our singing and the higher our excitement.

Beep, beep, beep, beep, beep—"Here is the result of the election in the Transvaal Constituency of Houghton." Not many of us were breathing easily. "Mrs. Helen Suz—" The rest of the announcement was drowned in a wave of cheering and expressions of mad euphoria.

A few minutes later Helen and her entourage of election agent Max Borkum, polling agents, and supporters arrived from the Houghton School, where the count had taken place. The cheering from the yard had not abated, and now it reached unimagined dimensions. Smiling, a little bravely, I thought, Helen looked tired and drawn. Although she had doubled her majority, she had still won by only a few hundred votes.

"Four more bloody years" were the opening words of her remarks to us, and we cheered madly. She spoke a little longer, but I could not hear the rest of what she said. My head was swimming from too much cheap wine, too much excitement, and not enough sleep. Irene Menell, a stalwart political force in Houghton, came out of the front room of the house and embraced Helen closely.

"A cousin," said Steven, who was standing next to me, in a somewhat sardonic reference to Irene, "on the other side of the family."

"Any other family members here?" I asked him half-mockingly. "Plenty," he laughed. "The place is full of them—Suzmans, Gavronskys, Bernitzes, others." He dismissed them all with an elegant flick of the wrist. "How the hell else do you think she wins?"

He was joking, I knew, but later, when I came to know the inner workings of the Houghton office, I often thought that Steven's revelation had more than just a grain of truth. The fierce pride Helen's family took in her achievements would not allow them to let her lose Houghton.

So, in 1970 I decided that if I was going to work for the Progressives, it was going to be in Houghton. For in April there was to be a whites-only general election.

Filled with trepidation, because wherever I had worked

before I had known the people and had not simply barged in, some weeks before the election I went to Helen's campaign office.

The key Houghton workers were a formidable group of powerful women. People with a strong sense of political involvement gravitated to Helen. I felt their dominance immediately. The white-painted spaces overflowed with them, not to mention the desks, telephones, election propaganda, maps and election posters, and other office necessities.

"You, can you spell?"

Those were the words first spat at me as I stood apprehensively on the threshold of Ivy Road. Tall and elegant Ellen Hellman, with the ever-present cigarette in her mouth and an equally inevitable perfectly coiffured hairdo, had snarled at me. Her words reduced me to the gangling seventh-grader I had been in my English class at Parktown Girls' High School.

"Well, I teach English, and I write articles, so I guess you could say I can spell." I laughed nervously.

"Good, because at this time of the day, in the 'flow,' there's only the filing of the cards to be done."

I was to learn that the cards, canvass cards, were essential components of an elaborate system. Canvassers recorded vital information about voters on these cards. Clerical workers deciphered, annotated, re-sorted, and filed them in a cycle of meticulously applied attention to detail that went on throughout the campaign. This obsessiveness, this head-by-head counting, was one of the factors that enabled Helen to win, however narrowly in those years, again and again. To be involved in one of her campaigns was adrenaline-producing, heart-thumping action. We simply dared not let her lose if liberalism was to have any credibility in South Africa. For in the South African context then, parliamentary representation made the difference between a bona fide viable political party and Mickey Mouse operations. Voter contact, arguing issues with the public, gave me a real charge, a sense of grass-roots reality that I had never experienced before. I disliked braving the rottweilers and Dobermans in people's gardens, but I enjoyed talking to (most of) their owners.

The office was quieter than I had expected it to be, most of the day clerical workers having left and the evening canvassers not yet arrived.

"Gerda's in the strongroom with her cards, batching."

Following Ellen's upright figure to the back rooms, I wondered who the next ogress would be. Gerda Koeningsfeld, grey-haired, with large glasses over sympathetic eyes, a cigarette also dangling from the side of her mouth, did not look pleased to see me.

"This is . . . what's your name, girl?"

"Janet, Janet Berman." (This was eighteen months before I married Sandy.)

"Janet says she can spell, so she'll be okay for the filing."

Gerda barked, "Batching's behind, we've a huge canvassing drive tonight . . . I can't stop now to show someone filing."

The tension between the two women (sisters-in-law, I later learnt, and good friends) was palpable. I intervened.

"I know a lot about filing. I filed for eight weeks once, a vacation job . . ."

Gerda rounded on me.

"This filing's filing—categories, shoelaces, boxes for recanvassing. It's Helen's election, not a vac job!"

All right, I thought, I can come again when everyone's not so busy. But I would avoid these two bitches.

"I can see you're busy now. I'll come again . . ." My words were nervous and hesitant. It is ridiculous, I thought, to be so defensive.

Then Gerda smiled. Ellen left in a haze of cigarette smoke.

"Okay, you can help me batch."

Cornered in the strongroom with this strange, formidable woman, I wanted to run away. Gerda bent over the trays of white and blue canvass cards, a pose I was to see many times in the ensuing years, and snapped instructions at me. I finished my batching as she had told me to.

"That street's done . . . ah, Mrs. . . . ah, Gerda . . ."

"What? Impossible! Impossible to be done so quickly. Here, let me see what you've done. . . . Seems okay, no numbers out of place . . . okay, here's some more to do."

Gerda pushed a whole tray of cards in front of me. Although it was foolish to feel elated about her approval, I valued her acceptance. I was even more pleased when she praised me to Ellen Hellman. Obviously, it was important to me to succeed in Helen's office, which had a reputation in political circles of being a well-oiled machine, a model election office.

Until Ellen Hellman died some fifteen years later and despite the fact that I came to know her well, my discomfited awkwardness toward her remained with me. She was a highly regarded, knowledgeable member of the liberal opposition and an academic sociologist with an international reputation for her pioneering work in studies of urban black people in South Africa.

Gerda Koeningsfeld, her brusque manner evident only when she was pressured at election time, was a warm, friendly, sympathetic woman, an indefatigable and selflessly reliable worker. Fortunate to have Gerda and a handful of other workers of her calibre and dedication, Helen was aware of their contribution to her career and took great care to ensure their continued loyalty and support.

It was at this time that I began to know Irene Menell well. She was vice chairman of the constituency and one of Helen's top election organisers. Thirteen years older than I, Irene often used to bring the younger of her five children to Ivy Road with her. I envied them a little, growing up with political activism as part of their everyday lives.

Irene and I became friends, and from 1970 until I left in 1984 there was little we thought or did politically in which in some measure we did not each have a part. Latterly our political discussions usually ended (and still do) in fairly heated disagreement, as I grew more impatient with whites-only politics and more radical and Irene remained (and remains) steadfastly loyal to Helen and the moderation of the Progressive Federal Party. But tacitly we have agreed to respect our differences, and our ongoing relationship is something I value.

Helen's opponent in the 1970 election was Brigadier Louis Steyn, a United Party man, a retired police officer. In a newspaper interview at that time Helen said of him, "Well, I don't feel sorry for him. If he wants to take on an old dragon, he must be prepared to be consumed by fire."

And consume him she did, trebling her majority over her

narrow 1966 victory margin. Again, Progressive Party candidates lost around the country, but many made important gains in several constituencies, clearly bringing them within the party's grasp. Especially bitter for Helen was the loss of Colin Eglin in Sea Point, Cape Town. He came within 232 votes of winning the seat.

Helen could not help blaming herself a little for that loss. Two nights before the election, at a hugely successful rally in Cape Town, she had allowed a heckler to bait her into stating that the Progressive Party would allow the Communist Party to operate legally in the country. Indeed, that was Progressive Party policy, but in redphobic South Africa, on election eve, her statement was a gift to Colin's opponents. They smothered the telephone poles of Sea Point with posters of a white hand shaking a black hand and the slogan "Eglin Supports Communism." Whether or not that incident had made a difference in the outcome of Colin's election niggled away at Helen.

A painstakingly prepared scrapbook I kept of the Progressive Party effort in the elections bears the following gracious inscription on the final page. (Helen was being prudent. For if she had bumped into me in the street then, she would not have known who I was.)

To Janet, who helped so much, Helen Suzman.

CHAPTER 8
The Election, 1974

"Which one is Biko?"

Unable to contain my curiosity any longer and willing at last to admit to my ignorance, I turned to Johnny Matisonn.

"He's not in the hall, but I'm meeting him at lunch. And he's speaking this afternoon."

It was a winter day in July 1972, when I was pregnant with Roger. Johnny Matisonn, a young reporter on the *Rand Daily Mail* and a political colleague, had invited me to accompany him to Hamanskraal, a black township north of Pretoria, where he was covering a South African Students' Organisation (SASO) conference.

There had been much newspaper coverage of both SASO, since its inception in 1969, and its first president, Steve Biko. Steve was hailed as a "young Mandela," the next great black leader of South Africa. In the media he came across as a forceful ideologue, an effective and charismatic leader. I was eager to see in action, among his followers, the man who was the moving spirit behind the development of the Black Consciousness (BC) philosophy.

The theme of the conference was "Creativity and Black Development." I had come for the final day's proceedings.

Tables were placed along one side of the hall for the press, a rostrum stood at the front for the speakers, and chairs in neat rows were arranged in the auditorium. Most of the delegates sat on the floor at the front of the room. The walls were draped with banners bearing BC slogans, Azanian flags in the colors of the African National Congress (ANC), and a small, illegal ANC flag.

The students were dressed casually, many of the women wearing the colourful, flowing dresses of their West African counterparts. When we arrived, the audience was concentrating on a report being presented by one of the SASO leaders: ". . . the material at present given to black children inculcates self-hate and psychological oppression. . . ." The speaker called for the composition of black nursery rhymes, black children's stories, and black child art.

He sat down to thunderous applause. The report was opened for discussion. Many students stood at the rostrum awaiting their turn to speak. Most of them spoke in English, others in Zulu, Xhosa, SeSotho. There was no translation, but no one seemed to mind not understanding all of what was being said. Most of the speakers were articulate and confident, some more strident than others. The virulent antiwhite rhetoric made me feel as uncomfortable as I did when I heard Afrikaner Nationalists indulging in antiblack rhetoric.

I had studied the faces of the SASO leaders on the rostrum, trying to decide which one could be Steve Biko. One man in particular had a look of strength and resolution about him. Biko, I thought. But when he stood up to propose the formal adoption of the report, he was introduced as former SASO president Barney Pityana.

Another lean, lithe man walked to the microphone with an air of consequential authority. He summed up the discussion, which had highlighted the gulf between the intellectual elite and the people in ordinary black communities. But he was not Biko either. "Bro' Jerry" he was called, Jerry Modisane, the newly elected SASO president. Modisane asked that a commission be appointed to investigate the possibility of creating "a free black university."

Steve Biko was a little taller than I, with a slightly round face, a wispy beard, and wisely humourous eyes. It was difficult to talk to him at lunchtime, which was a gathering of delegates on the dusty ground in front of the hall, for a continuous stream of people came up to him to pat his shoulder, shake his hand, say a few words. There was no doubting his popularity and the magnetism of his understated personality. He had an aura of confidence and self-purpose.

When he began to speak that afternoon, a summation in English of the conference's proceedings, I was aware of the almost total concentration on him by the people in the overflowing hall.

> . . . the call for Black Consciousness is the most positive call to come from any group in the black world for a long time. It is more than just a reactionary rejection of whites by blacks. The quintessence of it is the realisation by the blacks that, in order to feature well in this game of power politics, we have to use the concept of group power to build a strong foundation for this.

Steve spoke quietly, calmly, in a well-modulated tone that was easy to listen to. He held his audience's rapt attention.

> Being historically, politically, socially, and economically a disinherited and dispossessed group, we have the strongest foundation from which to operate. The philosophy of Black Consciousness, therefore, expresses group pride and the determination by the blacks.to rise and attain an envisaged self. At the heart of this kind of thinking is the realisation by the blacks that the most potent weapon in the hands of the oppressor is the minds of the oppressed. . . .

In further well-reasoned arguments, his intelligent face mirroring his own concentration on his ideas, he went on to underline the importance of the conference in terms of addressing the psychological bondage of black people to white political power. He said that "mental emancipation is the precondition to political emancipation" and added that the relationship between white control and black fear must be broken. Blacks had to overcome the alienation created by that fear—for themselves, by themselves. Black Consciousness must be used for that purpose.

One could easily sense an iron will forged in the soul of Steve Biko. Nothing was going to deter him from spreading his word on Black Consciousness. He embodied its meaning. Steve Biko was the medium of his message.

On our way back to Johannesburg, Johnny and I discussed the reasons why the government did not seem to be taking SASO and BC seriously. Why was Biko, with his easily understood and powerful message, unbanned and walking the face of South Africa? Did the government feel so secure wielding absolute power that it did not want to bother itself with this populist black student activist movement?

In 1973 the government finally took action against the movement. Biko was banned and confined to the rural area of King William's Town. Nine SASO and BC leaders were arrested for treason.

By then, however, Biko's advocacy of black pride had become ingrained in the minds of a whole generation of young South Africans. Grass-roots Black Consciousness committees were operating all over the country. The Soweto Students' Representative Council (SSRC), the student body that was to control the student revolt in Soweto in July 1976, was composed of Biko disciples. The leader of the emerging black trade union movement were Black Consciousness adherents. The virulently anti-white student bodies of the late seventies and eighties—the Council of South African Students (COSAS) and the Azanian People's Organisation (AZAPO)—took their philosophy from Biko's pronouncements, too.

SASO, Biko's brainchild, was formed when black students broke from NUSAS because they felt NUSAS was white-oriented: "Whites may talk about the erosion of freedom, but for blacks there is no freedom."

SASO members were aware that the creation of separate student bodies fell within the design of apartheid. The preamble to SASO's constitution states that black students believe that countries should have only one student body, but that was not currently possible in South Africa.

SASO rejected working with white liberals because "White liberals work toward repealing the oppressive legislation and allowing blacks into a 'white society.' What must be created now is a common society."

According to Biko, "It is impossible for white liberals to identify with our oppression, for this system forces one group to enjoy privilege and to live on the sweat of another group." On another occasion he said, ". . . even those whites who see a lot wrong with the system make it their business to control the response of blacks to the provocation," and "liberalism dangles before freedom-hungry blacks promises of a great future for which no one seems to be particularly working."

Other SASO leaders made similar pronouncements. Said Barney Pityana, "We blacks must stand on our own feet; we must reject all value systems that make us foreigners in the land of our birth and reduce us from common humanity. We must develop toward a realisation of our potential and worth as self-respecting people." And fiery Jerry Modisane, SASO president in 1972, concurred: "We do not need the cooperation of the white man anymore—and we do not want him. We can find liberation from perpetual servitude on our own."

Not all BC formations were so fiercely nationalistic. Saths Cooper, an Indian office bearer of the Black People's Convention (a BC offshoot) and a dedicated opponent of the apartheid regime who had been in and out of solitary confinement for most of his adult life, said in 1972, ". . . the big mistake SASO has made is their belief that they can go it on their own, without the whites. The irresponsible talk by young black leaders vying for power will only prove detrimental to their cause."

Steve Biko's brief years as a public figure were in all senses of the word revolutionary. Perhaps the most important manifestation of his message among black people was that after Biko the term *black* was no longer a racial categorization as much as a state of mind. Biko's movement had begun to free black South Africans from the limitations of their mental oppression. The seeds he planted then flower now in South Africa in the revolutionary climate he helped to foster.

After having seen Biko in action, I could understand the power of his appeal to black students and intellectuals. Self-assured, competent, articulate, with the ability to present his argument in powerful, rational terms—the traits of leadership were his. It was his belief in the validity of his philosophy that made him outstanding.

Mulling over his words, I found myself returning again and again to his assertion that it was impossible for white liberals to identify with black oppression, that whites were forced to enjoy privilege and to live on the sweat of others. It was obvious to me that from any perspective he was correct. I was white; therefore, I was privileged. White society, as I knew it, existed because of the sweat of other racial groups. Yet I wanted—as much as any black South African activist—to rid my country of the apartheid scourge. I abhorred its presence in our lives. Overt political acts of "terrorism," leading to martyrdom and prison, were options I had rejected since my days of student activism. What were my other options? My quandary was the disturbing search for identity of the white liberal. And although I continued to develop and embrace the identity of a white liberal activist, it was always with gnawing doubts eating away at the edges of my persona. Like many other liberals I knew, I had become a convincing rationaliser.

For example, while deeply questioning my burgeoning party political involvement, I rationalised my inclination to grow even more involved. Political activism was challenging and fulfilling on a personal level. Politics was in my blood. And despite having to acknowledge that I could not be part of the black struggle, as much as I might want to be, I saw that there was much I could do in the liberal pursuit of human rights for all South Africans. The Nationalists had to be battled on every front: liberal ideals had to be held up before South Africa as an alternative to white or black nationalism. If I could not be part of the black struggle, I could still engage the Nationalists in the quasi-democratic forums of public office.

I decided that I would stand for public office at the first opportunity available to me. The camaraderie and sense of intense involvement generated by election campaigns were my life source. The parry and thrust of political debate were nectar to me. And I knew myself for what I was: a mainline political junkie.

In Houghton I found sustenance for my political craving, for Helen Suzman imbued her constituency office with a real sense of idealism and purpose. If she suffered the angst of identity of other liberals, I was not aware of it. She always seemed self-assured—even dogmatic—about the place of the liberal in South Africa's political dynamic. And her surety swept us along with her. As long as she was in Parliament, white liberalism had a toehold in the public life of South Africa. But we all knew that it was imperative for the Progressive Party to win more seats. In 1972, Selma Browde, a lifelong liberal, a passionate Zionist, and an academic physician, was responsible for that breakthrough. She won a seat on the Johannesburg City Council for the Progressive Party.

Selma's was a different political personality from Helen's. She had not involved herself in the party political arena, preferring to work in the field in grass-roots medical activism. She stood for the Progressives only to do her friends on the constituency committee a favour, on the assurance that she could not win.

Selma was tall, attractive, and warmly concerned about people and local issues. Her opponent, Aleck Jaffe, was an ex-mayor, a popular United Party hack, who had served on the city council for almost twenty years. He was regarded as a shoo-in.

During her election campaign, from the tally I patiently collated each morning I could gauge that Selma was gaining ground. I began to predict, quietly, that she was going to win. My gut feeling became even stronger when I listened to her genuine personal interest in the voters she canvassed on the phone.

An archetypal voter, a Mrs. Blumberg, a widow and a United Party diehard, would assuredly vote for "the good doctor" and tell her friends to do so, because "the good doctor" had spent five minutes listening to Mrs. Blumberg's woes and accounts of her ailments without once trying to sell her the Progressive Party.

Aleck Jaffe, thinking he was a shoo-in, did not spend much time and effort speaking to the Mrs. Blumbergs of his ward. When the election fracas was over, Selma, a political novice, began her battle in the city council to much acclaim and fanfare—a lone liberal voice in one of the most important public forums in South Africa.

But the Progressive Party's finest hour was in the general election of April 1974.

Analysis of the election results of 1970 had shown that in the urban English-speaking areas of the country the Progressive Party had its best chance yet of winning several seats. There was a feeling of buoyancy and anticipation in campaign offices around the country.

In Orange Grove, a constituency bordering on Houghton, the Progressive Party candidate, Rupert Lorimer, aided by the major South African Sunday newspaper, *The Sunday Times*, was running neck and neck with a United Party veteran, Etienne Malan. For the first time Malan's anti-Semitic sentiments were being publicly hung around his neck.

In another adjoining constituency, Johannesburg North, Gordon Waddell, son-in-law of the mining magnate Harry Oppenheimer (and therefore in the public's eyes a member of South Africa's royal family), was giving the United Party incumbent a real battle.

In Parktown, a retired editor of *The Star*, a large Johannesburg daily newspaper, was pitted against another long-term United Party man, Sonny Emdon. Other candidates around the country were carrying the Progressive Party flag in United Party and Nationalist strongholds.

In Houghton the United Party had to struggle to persuade someone to stand against Helen. Finally they came up with Jake Senekal, a minor party official. Helen said that she felt "sorry" for him but "was sure that even if they put up a donkey it would still get a couple of thousand votes."

Nineteen seventy-four was the first year in which elections for the provincial councils were being run in conjunction with the parliamentary elections. Selma Browde, "the good doctor," was Helen's running mate.

As I was then in the last stages of my second pregnancy, I did not play too active a role in the April 1974 campaign. In the past years I had held various offices in the constituency and had come to know many of Houghton's voluntary army of workers. Houghton had over three hundred workers in the field on Election Day, spread over four polling booths—one worker for every fifty voters.

Helen came into the control room at one of the polling booths where I was working. She was accompanied by Irene Menell, the constituency chairman that year. Irene came over to where

I was sitting, and we spoke excitedly of the prospects of some of our other candidates.

"Have you heard from anyone else? Colin?" Colin Eglin was our party leader, a friend of Helen's. He was fighting for his seat in a Cape Town constituency.

"Hold thumbs for Colin; he's feeling confident. His figures look wonderful. And Gordon too—apparently Anglo [Anglo American Corporation, the Oppenheimer head office] has just about all its staff working for Gordon—a fleet of hundreds of cars cruising around, picking up voters."

Then, together with Helen, she was gone, taking an aura of purpose and excitement with her, to meet Selma at another polling booth.

My fetal baby was restless. I did not feel a part of the proceedings. I went home to Roger, my seventeen-month-old son.

It had been decided that Ivy Road was too small to hold the traditional postelection workers' party. Many more people from all over the city were working for the Progressive Party that year. A huge marquee where Helen's operations had been conducted during the day had been taken over that night to accommodate the hundreds of workers who gathered to listen to the election results.

I almost did not go to the postelection gathering. Heavy with my baby, I was dragging myself around. Sandy persuaded me to spend a few hours there.

It was after ten when we arrived. The tent was a seething mass of bodies. More and more people kept arriving with radios, beer, wine bottles. Most were exhausted from the day's rigours, but most were smiling. The atmosphere was one of excited anticipation. After a while I too began to feel excited. These were my comrades, my political allies. For so many years we had carried the small flame of liberalism in the country—maybe tonight we would be rewarded. I would not, however, think of the grand possibility of another seat in Parliament, because we had been disappointed so often. Another seat in Parliament was a vision of grandeur to me, for then Helen would not be so alone, and we would have proof that our liberal voice in the arid air of white nationalism was finally being heeded.

An hour later there was a commotion at one end of the tent. Someone, wildly excited, was standing on a table surrounded by frenziedly cheering people. Everyone was screaming the good news.

"Waddell, Nixon, they've both won, won!"

Sitting down abruptly, I felt tears prick my eyes. At last, at last. Gordon Waddell, the crown prince of South African business, was now a member of Parliament. Peter Nixon, his provincial running mate, a contemporary of mine at university and a staunch Progressive worker, was the first Progressive elected to the provincial councils.

Then came Parktown's result: Progressive Rene de Villiers had won. There was pandemonium in the marquee.

A short while later Rupert Lorimer, the giantkiller of Orange Grove, was carried in shoulder high. The cheering went on for many minutes. If Rupert could win, then we had a chance in many other seats.

Helen and her entourage arrived from their Houghton count. Both she and Selma had won. Helen was so overcome by the knowledge that she now had colleagues in Parliament that she could not speak to anyone; that in itself said volumes about how she felt. Watching Rene de Villiers embrace her in a bear hug, tears streaming down their cheeks, was a poignant moment.

The celebrating went on in earnest. No more seats had been won in the Transvaal, but the party had registered gains in many areas and had come whiskers close to winning in several others. The drought was over. Voters, in their many thousands, had voted for the Progressive Party.

Later the results in the Cape Province were announced. In a Cape Town constituency, a presentable young Afrikaner academic, Frederick van Zyl Slabbert, had won his seat in a surprise victory for the party.

"Who's he?" was the question asked around the tent.

(In 1980, in a "Young Lions" coup, van Zyl ousted Colin Eglin to become the leader of the Progressive Federal Party. And in February 1986, in dramatic fashion, he resigned from Parliament and the leadership of the party, stating that Parliament was irrelevant in the current racial conflict that was tearing the country apart. Colin Eglin then resumed the leadership of the party. In July 1987 van Zyl courageously led a group of Afrikaner community leaders to Dakar to meet with members of the outlawed and exiled ANC.)

One result kept everyone waiting in the marquee that delirious night—Colin Eglin, the party leader, in Sea Point. Several people called his office, only to be told that there was a recount, then another recount. It was three in the morning. Sleeping bodies were stretched out on the ground.

If I had been reluctant to come to what became the most memorable celebration of my life, I was now reluctant to leave. But my own good sense, Sandy's persistence, and the advice of several "good doctors" present sent me away. Much later that morning I learnt that at six o'clock Colin had been declared the winner. There had been three recounts, one of them caused by a government official suffering an epileptic fit and inadvertently knocking over the ballots.

A month later came the cherry on the top. Alex Boraine, in a by-election, won a seventh seat in Parliament for the Progressive Party. The victory margin was thirty-six votes.

Johannesburg belonged to the Progressive Party on postelection day. Suddenly everyone was a Progressive. Newspapers carried the stories of the election battles in banner headlines. The blue and white of the Progressive Party was seen on lapel buttons, bumper stickers, ties, handkerchiefs. Ordinary black people smiled at ordinary white people in the streets.

While floating on a self-satisfied euphoria of vindication, I knew the election results to be only a tottering step, when giant strides were needed if South Africa was going to turn back from the road of white totalitarianism to a nonracial accommodation of the aspirations of all its peoples.

For black leaders in South Africa, the general election of 1974, like all other elections, was a nonevent. To black politicians, elections were a game the white man played. To paraphrase Biko, whites enjoyed the privilege of playing election games, while blacks sweated on.

But in the ferment of white politics the Progressive Party's successes sent shivers down the spines of the government's right-wingers. Despite all their efforts, the liberal will was alive and functioning in society.

Toward the end of that year the Progressive Party held a triumphant congress in Bloemfontein, the capital of the Orange Free State, the judicial capital of South Africa, and a citadel of Afrikaner conservatism.

Although my new baby, Tony, born in July 1974, was only five months old, I found the pull of the congress irresistible. It began in dramatic fashion. The party had invited a number of black guests as observers. After the opening session in a public hall in Bloemfontein on Friday night, the Bloemfontein City Council, in an emergency decree, prohibited the party from using public facilities if "members of races, other than the white race, will be present."

At a function at the English-speaking Bloemfontein Country Club later that night, the party leadership went into a huddle after receiving this decree. It was decided that, despite the drawbacks of overcrowding, the Congress would remove itself to an Anglican church hall, where the black observers would be welcome.

The local authorities had done the party a favour. The atmosphere at the congress was positive and defiant. The cramped, stifling venue made the proceedings intense and intimate.

It was in this favourable atmosphere that I gave my first public speech, a short one in support of a resolution on press freedom. The government had made its annual threatening noises about the English-language press, stating that "its house needs putting in order." The National Press Union, fearing further legislative restrictions, agreed with the government and drew up a controversial press code to control its own activities. By this appeasement it hoped to preempt government action against itself.

The congress, to resounding applause, unanimously supported the resolution. I was pleased, but definitely surprised, by the reaction my speech evoked. Several party leaders, men whom I had admired from a distance, made an effort to speak to me.

"Did you write that yourself?" asked one, his praise inherent in his question.

"A strong statement," said another, "in the Houghton tradition of strong statements."

"Are you interested in joining a party discussion group I run every second Sunday evening?" asked another, a wealthy ex-parliamentarian interested in building his own power base in the party.

"Join our table tonight?" asked a party powermonger.

A heady response, but my best moment came when a hard-bitten journalist came over to me and said, "Good speech. May I have a copy?"

As if I had been told, instinctively I knew that the press was as important a platform to me as any the party offered.

The very success of the Progressive Party in the 1974 general election heralded its demise.

United Party public representatives in seats now vulnerable to the Progressive Party, in an act of self-preservation, formed themselves into a Young Turks movement within their party. In a neatly orchestrated clash with the Old Guard they broke away from the United Party and formed the Reform Party, which began a courting dance with the Progressive Party. Rumours of an imminent amalgamation began to circulate.

Together with a number of other Progressives, I was bitterly opposed to this move. The Reform Party members were the main party hacks and Tammany Hall types, political survivors. For years they had harassed Helen in Parliament and Selma on the city council. The Progressive Party had fought many unnecessary and vituperative election campaigns against these very men who were now to be our allies. It was preposterous that we were to be political bedfellows.

Deeply suspicious of their commitment to human rights, I could see the party, with an infusion of Reformists, becoming a bland version of the National Party, concerned only with garnering white votes. Gone would be the challenge to the government, the role of protest politics, the bridge to black liberals.

Houghton became the rallying point for national grass-roots party opposition to the amalgamation, a stand the ex-United Party Reformists never forgot. They in turn were deeply suspicious of us and scornfully castigated us as the extreme left wing of the party.

At a special national congress convened to debate this issue, I publicly accused the national executive of already having decided in favour of the move and of using the congress as a sop to grass-roots members. I went on to say, "Who of us would dare speak against the move, knowing that our opposition will be remembered at the formation of the new party and at the election of positions within the new party?"

My remarks touched a raw nerve among the fifteen hundred delegates. The congress, which had been tame until then, suffocatingly stuffed with reasoned arguments as to why this amalgamation was a good move, erupted in applause. It had taken a large measure of courage for me to make that speech, but I was more shaken by the applause and support from the floor than by my act of defiance. The floodgates were opened. Delegate after delegate expressed feelings of regret and apprehension. The resolution to amalgamate had to be defended by the party leadership. Along with many others, I felt that the leadership was being led by the nose by the vision of the party's current seven parliamentary seats becoming eleven, a number that would put them within reach of the status of the official opposition in Parliament. The resolution was carried by only a narrow margin.

Years later I would meet people who had been delegates to that congress. They would ask me if I remembered my "Who of us would dare?" speech. Ruefully, I would remember the occasion with mixed feelings.

Many liberals left the party then. Most of them began to work in other change-oriented bodies such as the Black Sash and church groups. Still deeply suspicious of the motives of the Reformists, I wanted to resign as well. At any time in the past fifteen years they could have simply joined the Progressive Party if their convictions about race relations and the ineffectiveness of the United Party were as strong as they professed. They need not have waited until Progressive Party inroads in their constituencies made possible the loss of their seats in upcoming elections.

Helen's attitude persuaded me to remain. If she was prepared to work with them, she would need support. I also had my eye on a Johannesburg City Council seat in the upcoming elections of 1977. I could hardly wait to be a Houghton public representative.

Houghton, more than ever before, became the symbolic (and

real) home of white liberalism in the South African party
political process. Being called the left wing was an easy label to
bear. For if our actions were prejudged by the party, we could
act with impunity as left-wingers should.

At times I was desperately unhappy with having to be associated with the Progressive Reform Party, but at all times I
was proud to belong to Houghton.

At the First Transvaal Provincial Congress of the South
Africa Progressive Reform Party in October 1976 I was asked
to propose the Houghton resolution calling on the party to
"immediately establish multiracial bodies with the leadership
of the black, coloured, and Indian communities in the various
Transvaal regions."

In my speech I called the cities "the crucible of South African
politics" and said that as a party of moderation we should be
establishing formal links with black liberals and creating
aligned political groupings that would be islands of constancy
in a sea of racial violence. Because the Improper Interference
Act prohibited political contact across racial lines, this was a
direct left-wing challenge to the party. Establishing such
informal linkages might have constituted civil disobedience,
and no one had tried to do so before. But I felt that we had to
begin some dialogue, even if only in this circuitous way.

The applause after my speech was muted, and though the
resolution passed without any dissenting votes, the attitude of
some of the delegates told me it was a hollow victory. Some
congratulated me, but others pointedly asked whether I was
playing with fire. "We can't afford to isolate our white voters to
gain black sympathies," they said.

It was as I had feared. These Tammany Hall placaters would
hold back the party from crossing the racial divide at a crucial
moment. They had no conviction, no political faith, no insight
into the fact that the Progressive Party had begun to make
headway among the white electorate only because of its unswerving commitment to human rights and the rule of law.
Their attitudes of political expediency would hasten the demise
of the white liberal in South Africa. And no further action was
ever taken to implement the resolution passed on that day.

When I look back at the exigencies that framed the amalgamation of the Progressive Party and the Reform Party and that dictated the acute arguments over the identity and direction of the party, I see it as simplistic to label all the Reformists as backsliding party hacks. There is a certain merit to the argument Reformist pragmatists used that an enlarged Progressive presence in Parliament would put a brake on government excesses and provide a platform from which to try to ameliorate white racist government attitudes. (In light of events in South Africa especially since 1984, that argument has been proven wrong.) Understandably, a bias toward policies and pronouncements in tune with white electorate attitudes was of cardinal importance to them. The fact that to me and other "left-wingers" this was too high a price to pay for alienating black liberals is not really a satisfactory resolution of the dilemma. The two factions within the Progressive Reform Party struck up an uneasy peace.

Inwardly anyhow, I had acknowledged to myself that my call to the congress was already too late. For in June 1976 Soweto had exploded.

It was not surprising that my "new" party colleagues were taken aback at the stridency of my speech. None of them had firsthand knowledge of what had already become known as "Soweto '76," whereas, together with Irene Menell, I had been into the still smouldering township five days after the worst clashes between the police and the students had taken place. It was what I had seen and heard there and my political activities in Soweto over the past months that had put the stridency and urgency into my words.

CHAPTER 9
The Scars of Soweto

The vast majority of white South Africans have never been inside a black township. Soweto lies nine miles from the centre of Johannesburg, and with the exception of government officials and those few whites (on government sufferance) who work with blacks on social welfare and education programs in Soweto no white Johannesburgers venture there. In the beginning my visits to Soweto held great mystery for me, but I soon became used to its dull appearance. What I never became used to were the raised eyebrows and comments of my extended family and some friends when they learnt that I was "going in" (to Soweto) on a regular basis. It made me feel out on a limb, radical, when all I was doing was trying to teach Shakespeare to matriculants who happened to be black and living there.

The year before Soweto exploded in June 1976, at the request of a nonracial education institution I had been running workshops on Shakespearean plays, required readings in the matriculation syllabus. Soweto was becoming familiar to me, its drab grey and brown monotones part of my landscape of living. At first I saw the uniformly tiny houses, the rare bedraggled eucalyptus tree, the rutted and potholed sand roads as an unrelenting affront to my growing sense of impotent morality and justice. But after a while the poverty and depression of it all, the barren sterility, simply stopped registering as anything other than what it was—Soweto.

By contrast, the students I taught were bright and articulate, interested, academically ambitious, and far more politicised than their parents. Biko's Black Consciousness movement had taken sway of their imaginations. Throughout Soweto, student leaders were organising students into the Soweto Students' Representative Council. The tensions of rhetoric and political discussion were always thick as I walked into a classroom; something big was building.

In that year as well, I was elected to executive office in my party, and Irene Menell was voted our regional vice chairman. Often at regional council executive meetings I would report on the political movement I saw growing in the schools. One of our MPs, Rene de Villiers, acting on my and other reports, warned the government in Parliament of what was coming in Soweto.

Fortunately, I was not in Soweto on June 16th, when the first clashes occurred between the police and the students. I say fortunately because in the confusion of that day, whites who were in Soweto were lucky to escape with their lives—several did not. Women from the Black Sash who had been visiting at crèches and schools told of how young blacks had jumped into their cars and directed them away from the trouble spots and out of Soweto on back paths they never knew existed. Yet other whites had felt the fury of the mob and had been dragged from their cars and burnt. Like rats in a maze suddenly let loose, the fury of many young Sowetons, unable to hit back at the heavily armed police who had killed their fellows by the score, had found unfortunate targets.

The police had killed over a hundred placard-wielding students taking part in a peaceful march, while suffering no deaths themselves.

In the days after the first clashes, roadblocks and police cordons prevented anyone from entering the township, and only a few residents were allowed to leave. Soweto was besieged. As news began to filter through from the battleground by word of mouth, I was appalled by the fate of the students.

Some of those I taught were among the student leadership. I felt a great need to see for myself what had happened and what was going on. As all telephone contact had been cut, I could not verify the reports I was hearing, and the media coverage was strictly controlled. Readily Irene agreed to accompany me in "going in" as soon as we were allowed. As a senior party office bearer she believed the party should have an eyewitness report as soon as possible. The government had no right to refuse access to a "trouble spot" to a representative of a party with parliamentary representation, and I believed strongly that I should be able to go anywhere I wanted to in my own country. After all, we were not at war with anyone, and Soweto, where I conducted at least part of my daily business, was not a war zone. Perhaps going into Soweto was acting with questionable bravado, but I was determined not to be scared off by the government bully boys.

To almost all whites in South Africa my foray into Soweto was seen as white Americans would have viewed a white teacher or journalist going into Harlem or Watts immediately after Martin Luther King, Jr., was assassinated.

Somberly Sandy nodded when I told him I was going to Soweto with Irene. "I'm not that crazy about the idea, but if you feel you must, then you must go and see for yourself. But be careful."

Smiling with reassurance I did not really feel, I left for Irene's house. We all knew that taking care was only relative in this tense situation, with the police so trigger-happy. It was on the fourth day that we were allowed in.

As we drew nearer to Soweto we became extremely conscious of our whiteness (the first time for me). We spoke about it to one another, but it was only cold comfort. A burly, heavily armed black policeman checked our papers and waved us through the roadblock on the edge of the township.

"You sure you know what you're doing, ma'am?" he asked Irene, who was driving. "It's not a picnic in there, you know!"

Irene nodded politely and drove on. Her face was set, and I knew she was as tense and angry as I, but she always believed in being polite.

"No sense in confronting him," she remarked cursorily. I had

wanted to exchange words with the policeman. She drove
slowly so that we could take visual note of the street scene.

Buses and large trucks were stranded at the sides of the road,
looking eyeless with their windows and headlights smashed.
The streets were dotted with other burnt-out and overturned
vehicles. But the houses showed no outward evidence of the
clashes. Aside from police and army vehicles roaring by on
either side of us with guns bristling from behind wire-mesh-
covered windows, there was little vehicular traffic.

"Bastards!" I muttered under my breath. "Fascists!" They
were behaving like an occupying army on foreign soil. We felt
conspicuous in Irene's silver-grey car. Many pedestrians wandered through the streets. Days earlier, after several buses had
been damaged, the bus company had refused to allow its buses
into Soweto. Commuters had to walk to the outskirts of the
township to board the buses. School children too, of all ages,
roamed about. The schools had been closed indefinitely. They
seemed cheerful enough, stopping their impromptu games to
wave, grinning at us, some even raising their fists in a black
power salute, shouting "Amandla, amandla awethu!" (Freedom, freedom now!) after first looking to see if any policemen
were about. We waved back.

It was only deep into Soweto that we saw burnt-out buildings—offices and beer halls of the government's West Rand
Administration Board. Some school buildings were also damaged—by the police or the students? We commented in surprise
to one another for the state media had led us to believe, through
dramatic pictures filled with flame and fury, that there had
been indiscriminate arson and looting. It was obvious to us that
the targets of the uprising had been the symbols of government
oppression and had been carefully selected. Preselected, we
decided. For churches, houses, and shops alongside gutted
government buildings remained intact and undamaged.

Through a phone call the day before we had arranged to
meet Julia Mavimbela at the Salvation Army Headquarters in
Mofolo opposite the Eyethu Cinema, the only movie theatre in
Soweto. Julia, a spritely grandmother, was a social worker.
Looking nervous and tense, she was waiting for us in her office.
Our presence was a worry to her, drawing the attention of the

young radicals as well as the police. But she repeatedly told us
how much she valued our coming into Soweto to see for ourselves what was happening there. An unmarked police car
carrying heavily armed, uniformed men cruised up and down
the sand road outside of Julia's office all the time Irene's car
was parked there.

"It's been terrible, terrible—bullets, tear gas, so many children shot, killed." Julia spoke with tears in her voice as well as
her eyes. "It's war. They've made war on our children. You
should see the injured at Baragwaneth; the hospital is full. The
police shoot them like animals from their cars—even when the
children are only crossing the road."

Irene and I looked at each other. We had heard rumours of
this indiscriminate shooting, of long lines of injured children at
Baragwaneth Hospital—some with horrible wounds from
dumdum bullets, bullets that exploded once inside the body.

"Come, I'll take you to the clinics, some schools. We'll go in
the Salvation Army van."

Julia drove us through the back streets of Soweto, over
twisting, rutted sand tracks between ramshackle, cheek-by-
jowl houses. The garbage had not been collected for days and
lay in huge rotting piles at the corners of main roads. Even the
straggly trees looked desolate, their bare branches covered in
dust.

We saw injured, bewildered children and sullen adolescents
in the clinics. I was haunted by the blank dullness of their eyes,
almost as if they had drawn a blind down over themselves.
Irene commented on the contrast between these children—
overt victims—and those we had seen looking so "wonderfully
cheerful" on the streets. Then we went to some nearby schools
and spoke to teachers and a few students who were in the school
buildings, off the streets, in order to avoid the police.

Neither of us had been prepared for the magnitude of what
we were beginning to piece together. It was sobering to see how
the people had hardened in the aftermath of the clashes.
Subdued as we drove home, when we spoke at all it was of what
we could try to do for the schoolchildren.

My firsthand look at what had happened in Soweto during
those tense days—however devastating they first appeared to

me—proved to be perfunctory. The depth of the agony of Soweto '76 was revealed to me at a meeting I attended a few nights later.

Molly Kopel, a women's rights activist, an ex-Reformist, and now a Progressive Reform Party colleague, had invited Irene and me and other concerned people to her house to meet with representatives of women's groups in Soweto. She hoped that together we could structure some initiative to assist the injured schoolchildren in Soweto. I had expected to meet with a handful of Soweto mothers. But when I arrived, Molly's small house was teeming with Soweto parents and children. As I moved from group to group, listening to their stories, a picture of brutal police abuse emerged. We began to assist a few law students in taking these personal accounts of police victimisation.

As the government gave lip service to the independence of the courts, affidavits were of utmost importance in bringing criminal charges against, in this instance, the police. In South African law, affidavits are vital to prosecution. The law students were there on behalf of various legal aid bureaux that were prepared to act for the victims of police brutality. For at that time, if the police could be proved to have acted in any way beyond their duty, the minister of police would have to compensate the victims or their families. And, of course, court hearings that were covered by the media brought international attention to the police excesses.

One group of agitated adolescents (who recognized my name from some articles I had written for a black magazine) pleaded with me to contact the African National Congress on their behalf to learn the "safe" illegal route across the South African border to Botswana. I felt helpless and inadequate. I had no contact with the ANC, and that type of "cloak and dagger" activism had never come my way. Perhaps that in itself is a comment on the impotence of liberalism.

For these desperate children, any lead was a potential lifeline to which they tried to cling. The young men said that they could not get that information for themselves for they feared the "informers." They also told me that hundreds of their colleagues had fled the country and were already safe in Botswana and Zambia. They were staying in refugee camps until they could be trained as freedom fighters to return to South Africa to help with the struggle.

"This Bantu education is not for our generation," they told me, referring to the racially separate educational system the apartheid regime rammed down their throats. A sweeping rejection of this system was at the root of the current "unrest" in Soweto.

A middle-aged man had been waiting patiently and politely to speak to me. Introducing himself as Alfred Mkize, he said softly "I am here for my son, Reginald, who has fifteen years. He was shot three days ago, here." He indicated his right arm and his back. "His mother sent him to buy bread. The police shot him as he was crossing the street. It wasn't a police car, and he ran to get out of its path. The men who shot him were not in uniform."

Alfred paused and sighed. "There was not much bleeding on the back. At the clinic they took out many small bullets." (Birdshot, I noted.) "But his arm, his hand, he can't move it. It is frozen, like this." He made a claw with his own hand. "The doctor said a bullet cut the nerve. Reginald won't come out of his room. He is a good boy, kind, respectful, and he plays the piano well, very well. It's his life. But he won't play again, the doctor said. That's why he is staying in his room."

Noting where I could reach Mr. Mkize at work, I moved on to the next group. I spoke to an angry, embittered woman. The woman's nephew, eight years old, had been killed by the police, shot in the back. His family wanted to know if they could sue the police. I told her I would hand her affidavit to a lawyer and she would be contacted.

Another account, this time from a group of fifteen-year-olds, told me how they had carried their dying friend from a school playground where he had been shot from a roving police car. Another group of policemen had ordered them to leave him in the street or be shot too. They had waited behind a nearby house and seen their friend die in the sun and the dust. They wanted to know how they could recover his body from the police morgue for burial. He had no parents and had lived with the family of one of the boys. They had been to the morgue that day and had been told that only the family of the victim could claim the body. "Otherwise we have to pay fifty rand for the body," they told me. The eyes of the children were flints in their steely faces. I gave the boys the name of the lawyer to whom I would give their affidavit.

Another group of schoolchildren told me of how the police, with fierce dogs, had raided their classrooms while they were still having lessons on the first day of the clashes. The police barred the doors and set the dogs loose in the classrooms, forcing the terrified students to jump out of second-floor windows.

A young science teacher, unable to keep the bitter tears out of his voice, gave me an affidavit detailing how the police had smashed into his school laboratory, one of the few at any school in Soweto, and destroyed the equipment in the darkroom with their rifle butts. "The only school darkroom in Soweto," he said. It had been built after five years of fund-raising. "I am thinking of leaving now, going into political exile, working with the ANC. I'll teach again after the struggle is won."

On my way home I felt numbed, emotionally exhausted. But I was certain of one thing: the scars of Soweto 1976 would never heal. The wounds ran too deep. A fuse of anger burned in my soul. There was nothing I could do about the dead children, but I could do something for Reginald Mkize. He would play the piano again. Something had to be salvaged from the ashes of so many lives.

After gaining Alfred and Eileen Mkize's permission, Reginald's agreement, and Irene's cooperation in attempting Reginald's recovery, we contacted David Saffer, a neurologist at Baragwaneth Hospital, and he conducted extensive tests on Reginald. I often drove Reginald from his Mofolo home to and from the hospital. Irene contacted Vivienne Cohen, a Houghton Party member and a physiotherapist, who agreed to treat Reginald on a daily basis. She disagreed with Saffer, who did not think that Reginald would move his hand again. Irene's driver daily drove Reginald to and from Soweto to Johannesburg for physiotherapy. This proved to be too onerous for

Reginald, who had been mentally shattered by his encounter with the police. He had trouble speaking, stuttered, and was tense and uneasy.

Robin Harvey, another friend of mine, on behalf of her elderly mother, a well-known mentor to musicians in Johannesburg, offered Reginald residence in her home until he had recovered. When he felt he was ready to start to learn again, I would visit the Harveys' home and direct Reginald's interrupted eighth-grade studies. After many weeks of patience, treatment, and his own assiduous devotion to his physiotherapy exercises, Reginald plucked up enough courage to try the Harveys' grand piano. Hesitantly his clawed fingers sought the notes he knew so well. Slowly, over the months, he regained almost complete movement of his fingers.

Helping Reginald was important to me, yet I knew there were hundreds of Reginalds who needed but would not get individual attention. The best I could do for them was to respond to invitations to work with groups in the white liberal Johannesburg community whose activism had been spurred in the aftermath of the "unrest" in Soweto. I had little time, but I began to work with Isongo, a community-based self-help group whose founder, Jean Graham, was to become a close friend, and with an emergency six-week Winter School Programme at the University of the Witwatersrand for five hundred Soweto matriculants.

I also assisted Julia Mavimbela of the Soweto Salvation Army in a successful attempt to turn an acre of fallow land belonging to that organisation into plots of family-cultivated vegetable gardens. And through the Mayoress's Programme. which raised funds for new school equipment in Soweto, I was introduced to two young artists, Dumisane Mabaso and Ben Nshua, who taught art at the Mofolo Art Centre in Soweto. Drawn to their talent and the dedication and perseverance they had shown in keeping the art centre alive, I took on the special project of supplying the centre with art materials.

Within a couple of months American and British journalists and politicians began approaching me as an "expert" on Soweto. As I drove them through the township we would invariably stop at the Mofolo Art Centre. As a result, scores of offices and homes in the U.S. and Britain now boast a picture by Mabaso or a small wooden sculpture by Nshua. One visitor, a trustee of the Reckitt Trust in England, was so impressed by Ben's work that he helped raise funds for Ben to attend the Slade School of Art in London in 1981.

Soon thereafter I was forced to curtail my activities in Soweto as I had been nominated as a candidate in the forthcoming city council elections in Johannesburg and had to spend my time and energy in the ward where I was standing. Having committed myself to liberal activism, I saw public office as a natural next step and a perfect platform from which to continue my work.

Although I was standing in a ward in Helen Suzman's constituency, the Progressive Party had never won that particular part of her constituency. The election was in early March 1977, and I knew if I was going to win the ward (and I could not imagine running if I was not going to win) I would have to see as many people as I could to convince them to vote for me.

Peter Janisch, a friend of many years, a political ally, and now my election agent, joined me in pounding the pavements of Norwood and the surrounding suburbs. Between October 1977 and the end of February 1978, I met members of two thousand households—an enjoyable, if tiring, experience that allowed me to take the political pulse of my constituents. I began to map out an agenda that would take care of their concerns, which revolved mainly around sidewalks, street gutters, streetlights, traffic lights, the condition of the parks, noise pollution, air pollution, and the like.

On the eve of the election our office tally put me marginally ahead of my United Party opponent but with a significant percentage of the canvassed voters still "doubtful." Helen would turn over the canvass cards and look quizzically at me. "Lots of 'againsts' have become 'doubtfuls,' " she would say, "and so many 'doubtfuls' are now 'fors.' You've been busy, seen so many people?" She raised an eyebrow. "How do you feel about it?"

"Okay," I replied, exhausted and tense. "It felt solid, speaking to people."

"It will be a good win," Helen smiled, "after nineteen years of losses."

During the campaign I had two platforms, one of issues of

local community interest and the other of race relations in Johannesburg. Helen aptly expressed my stand in a letter to the voters:

> ... Janet is as concerned as you are about matters which affect the community life of your part of Johannesburg. She has a particular concern for the future of our country. Her presence in the City Council will serve two important purposes. Firstly— active, dedicated service to the people living in her Ward. Also the clear expression of a political policy which is an alternative to the shortsighted and dangerous policies of the present government that are leading our country into increasing instability...."

In a standard interview the *Rand Daily Mail* conducted with all municipal candidates, I said that Johannesburg could become a showcase multiracial urban complex, an example to the rest of South Africa.

Most of the other candidates from my party were ex-Reformists, bland and cautious in their pronouncements on race relations. Their political background would not allow them to make statements or take stands that could jeopardise them in the eyes of their white voters. Our party had drawn up a blueprint for our local government policy, including such initiatives as desegregating the buses, city recreational facilities, and swimming pools. None of the local government bigwigs had, however, articulated that policy publicly, although they had committed themselves to doing so.

I was conscious of a credibility gap every time I spoke to voters. I wanted them to know that if my party was running Johannesburg we would embark on a rigorous programme of desegregation and normalisation of race relations in the city, within the jurisdiction allowed to us by the central apartheid government. At least we could try and, if thwarted, then lay the blame for not succeeding on onerous central government legislation, which would always override any we passed. What made me angry and impatient was concealing our objectives from the voters.

After discussing this with Irene in her capacity as a senior party official—and she felt as I did—I decided to go ahead with what I knew would be a controversial speech. On one auspicious night in February 1977 I addressed a house meeting in my ward. The meeting went well, and I do not think the voters present found anything startling in what I said. The next morning the *Rand Daily Mail* ran my speech as a front-page lead—"PRP Favours Shared Public Amenities" was the headline.

The article made the point that my statement had filled a significant gap in PRP policy in the election. I had made my speech because I believed we needed a mandate to institute changes that would be seen by white South Africa as sweeping and radical—racial intermingling in the parks, blacks in the public swimming pools, and so on.

Of course the "Reformists" were furious. They could not conceive of what they called "excessive" honesty in campaigning and accused me of sabotaging the whole election plan. Several of them, who were shortly to become my council colleagues, never forgave me. I had to fight a bitter vendetta with them all my years in the council.

In contrast, the old "left wing" of the party congratulated me: "It's about time someone said it publicly." At least in Johannesburg, however, we "left-wingers" were outnumbered. When the election results came in, most of the PRP candidates had lost, with only eighteen of us elected out of a council body of forty-six.

Many of the ex-Reformists took an "I told you so" stance, using the election results as proof that my speech had sounded the death knell for the party's chances in the election. Accusing fingers were pointed at me and the Houghton "mafia," as we were known in the party. Neither Irene nor I was reelected to the regional offices we had held in the party's organisation. Even Helen, whose reputation apparently was beyond damage, was voted only as an alternate to an important party body. It would be five years before Houghton members stopped being "punished" and were allowed to play a full part in the regional affairs of the party.

This acrimony unsettled me. All I had done was to tell the truth from which the others were scuttling away. And after I had suffered a crushing, skillfully engineered defeat by the "Reformists" in an inner party election, I shied away from the party organisation. My uneasy rationalisation to stay in the party to support Helen—at least in this area—had proven to be a mistake. A bitter feud, which exists to this day, was always evident between the right and left wings of the party.

Our approaches were so different. Helen, Irene, others, and I were unswerving idealists, always adhering to the liberal values we embraced. Political pragmatism dictated the impossibility of achieving our vision in the exigencies of the present reactionary climate, but our vision was our motivation and rationale for political involvement. Pomp, political perks, and the outer trappings of political office were quite secondary. We knew we were engaged in an unrelenting struggle. The right-wingers, on the other hand, strove to ensure their seats next time around so that they could gain more positions on white public bodies, have more segregated fancy-dress balls and dinners, enjoy more perks, and capture the public eye as often as possible. Talk of fiddling while Rome was burning!

Our caucus meetings were always filled with the tensions of this two-way tugging. In the vacuum left by their reluctance to speak on controversial issues, like-minded colleagues (the small minority) and I gained greater media coverage. This made the right-wingers even more bitter and jealous and notched the spiral of inner party tension higher and higher.

I often found myself mired in disbelief, looking around at and listening to the people who were supposed to be on my side. Fighting the Nationalists in the city council was an easy task compared to fighting them.

The repercussions of my speech made my city council election victory less than unalloyed joy. In her letter of congratulation to me, Helen presciently wrote:

> . . . Congratulations on a well-deserved success and on a campaign that many more seasoned politicians would do well to emulate. . . . Don't be too depressed at the human fallibilities you will most certainly encounter in the tough arena you have entered. . . . You've launched yourself on a new and exciting career. Enjoy!

I did enjoy being a public representative, making the best

use I could of my platform to further the ideals of the nonracial society I still believed possible, if not for South Africa, then initially for a sophisticated urban area like Johannesburg.

Two memories of my election victory stand out in my mind. The first is the efficiency and warm support of the skilled team that ran my Election Day operation. After all these years the Houghton team had Election Day routines down to a fine art. It was a good feeling knowing they were behind me.

The second is a mental picture I have of my sons—four-year-old Roger and two-year-old Tony—standing with my mother at the front door of our house, waving good-bye after I had dashed home to change my clothes when the weather turned colder during Election Day.

My decision to stand for public office while they were still so young had been fraught with misgiving. Yet in some strange way I felt that the time I was sacrificing in being away from them would be to their benefit later if I could become one of the movers and shakers, wrestling South Africa out of its racist present. Another rationalisation, another compromise, I reflected. All my early years of motherhood seem to have been a compromise between my guilt at not spending enough time with my children and my guilt at not doing even more than I already was to try to build the bridges, keep the lines of communication open between white and black South Africans.

And I knew then that no matter how much I may have wanted to, I could not have taken public office if it had not been for the encouragement and support of the boys' grandmothers, Eileen and Lydia, and the efficiency, patience, and involved concern of our housekeeper, Annah Kelefetswe.

But in my years of public life it was Sandy who buttressed me, helping me overcome my exhaustion, depression, tension, and disappointment, and who shared my triumphs.

I imagine that political life without intimate personal succour can be devastatingly lonely.

CHAPTER 10

Black Monday and
Mr. Madingwane

My advent onto the public stage of South Africa in September 1977 started on a high note. An early opportunity to test my city council wings arose when my caucus reluctantly agreed to let me put a motion to the council asking that the central business district of Johannesburg be opened to all races. Governed by a coalition headed by the apartheid National Party, the council, while not accepting the motion, did surprise me by agreeing to investigate steps to "open" certain facilities. (It was only in late 1985, eight years later, that some of those amenities were desegregated.)

My speech generated much publicity. The *Rand Daily Mail* called me "a new, avant-garde brand of city councillor" and ran my whole speech on the editorial page on September 12th under the banner headline "Time to Go Open." The next day the paper's lead editorial read:

> As Johannesburg city councillor Janet Levine pointed out yesterday: "The city has many fine restaurants, cinemas and theatres. It provides an everchanging programme of entertainment for its citizens—if they are white."

Toilet facilities are seriously deficient in numbers, restaurants available to blacks are either a handful of the eating-house variety or five-star ("international") hotel restaurants, and there are no recreational amenities apart from a few open spaces.

As Ms. Levine noted, there is a need for the City Council to be enterprising in seeking the lifting of the Group Areas restrictions within the city centre so that individuals can be treated on socio-economic grounds instead of skin colour. The Council needs to enact by-laws to decrease apartheid and ensure the removal of offensive racial signs.

The Star ran this report on the motion:

... Mrs. Levine said there were 900,000 people in Johannesburg who could not use the facilities whites took for granted. . . .

. . . Amid loud interjections including Councillor François Oberholzer telling her repeatedly not to be "a naughty girl," Mrs. Levine said: "We will make laughing stocks of ourselves if we do not accept the motion."

More than twenty years had passed since my political consciousness was born when, as an elementary school girl, I first went to see for myself the trudging bus boycotters of Alexandra. Yet from the outside the attention my speech drew made me look like an "instant" political success. Not only was my new role just another cycle in an ongoing involvement, rather than a stupendous beginning, but the acclaim with which my debut was greeted did not sweep me away. I had long since realised the powerful potential of a positive symbiotic union with the media. And as the state-run radio and television services were not available to "opposition" spokesmen, the English-language press became a vital means of mass communication for me. Helen had often said, "If you want to be quoted, don't comment on the news; make the news yourself."

In doing so through my "open Johannesburg" speech, I drew the notice of the foreign embassies in Johannesburg. Over the years I valued the contact I had with United States, British, Australian, Canadian, and some European diplomats. Interactions with these practised political observers broadened my political perceptions. I learnt much and valued our discussions and conversation. It was part of their jobs as diplomats to contact the widest range of opinion in the community. I suppose they were as grateful for me, a new voice, as I was for them, an international audience to take me out of the often stultifying arena of white politics.

In the embassies and the homes of these diplomats I met a spectrum of other South Africans whom I doubt I would have met in the normal course of events. And it was a real pleasure for me to reciprocate this attention and hospitality by showing the diplomats aspects of South African life that might not have come their way. Often I would invite one or several to accompany me when I attended meetings of, for instance, "removals" resistance committees in the periurban or "closer" communities, when I monitored legal proceedings in Soweto or elsewhere, and when I visited people I knew in various townships.

Coincidentally, as if to highlight the disparate parameters of the political arenas in South African politics, on September 11, 1977, while I was giving my speech, Steve Biko lay dying in a prison cell. Only a handful of Security Police and district surgeons in Port Elizabeth knew of his condition. A day later, he died in the Pretoria prison to which he had been transferred overnight, unconscious, naked, and shackled in the back of a police van. As news of his death emerged in radio and press reports, most of the nation—not including government ministers and their supporters—was stunned. Official pronouncements at first denied and then tried to play down the news of Biko's death. "He died while on a hunger strike" was the smug, official version of the event.

Around the country Steve Biko was mourned and remembered and honoured at services, protest meetings, and mass demonstrations. On the Sunday following his death (the date of his funeral had not yet been set), Helen, Irene, and I, together with hundreds of others, attended a mass multiracial memorial service for Biko. It was a blustery spring day with racing, wind-driven clouds blotting out the sunshine. A shower of pigeons swooped low over our heads as we moved slowly in a solemn line—black and white together—into the Central Methodist Church on Pritchard Street in downtown Johannesburg. Like a black cloud, the pigeons settled in the plaza in front of the Supreme Court opposite the church.

Peter Storey, white, and Simeon Nkoane, black, both Methodist ministers, conducted the service while overseas television crews disconcertingly roamed along the aisles and pews. Several stopped to film Helen, her face sad and grim.

While I listened to Reverend Peter Storey's eloquent eulogy to Steve Biko, I remembered seeing Steve alive and speaking of his political philosophy and vision at the Hamanskraal SASO conference I attended in July 1972. Steve's words that night had reverberated in the consciousness of the black people of his country. His was truly a moving spirit, a guiding light.

Tears pricked my eyes as I thought of his brutally beaten, unprotected body being bumped around in a police van on a thousand-mile journey through the dark night. His death was a personal shock to me and imbued with strong personal meaning. Perhaps I associated myself with him because we were the same age, because I respected his intellect and rational leadership style, because from different directions we were working for what we both believed possible—a free, democratic South Africa. His death shoved in my face the vulnerability of all of us who take a stand against apartheid. How capricious were our lives subject to the regime's ideological whims and strong-arm malpractises. Hindsight lets me see that unlike Steve I was protected by my white skin, allowed by the regime to champion our cause because they knew I was no real threat to them, while he, a crusader in the same cause, because he was black, because he was bright, because he was a leader, because he was perceived as a threat to their white racial superiority, was dead.

Steve Biko's life may have been beaten out of him by the Security Police, but they would never snuff out the spirit of the movement to which his philosophy had given birth across South Africa, particularly among the youth in the townships. There was no doubt in my mind that Biko's Black Consciousness awareness was becoming instrumental in liberating his people from the racist oppression of his white murderers.

"Let no one say he did not know," Storey ended his impassioned chronicle.

Let no one say he did not know of the events surrounding Bantu Steven Biko's death.

Biko had been detained in terms of the Terrorism Act on

August 18, 1977, together with Peter Jones, a Black People's Convention organiser. Until September 5th, Biko had been held in the Walmer Street Police cells in Port Elizabeth. While at Walmer Street he had been kept naked as the police feared "he would hang himself." Contrary to prison regulations but on instructions from the Security Police, he was not allowed any exercise for the eighteen days he was at Walmer Street. He was visited once by a magistrate to whom he complained about being kept naked and being given only bread to eat.

On September 6th he was transferred to the Security Police offices for interrogation. There he was chained in leg irons and handcuffs. Major Snyman led the five-man interrogation team that began questioning Biko on September 6th. Biko was with a Lieutenant Wilkens and two other guards throughout the night. Later, in testimony, Lieutenant Wilkens said that he had noticed a mark on Biko's head when he came on duty.

According to Major Snyman, Steve Biko became violent on September 7th, after allegations had been made regarding his role in compiling certain black power literature. "He had to be subdued by all five members of the interrogating team," said Major Snyman.

After this alleged "scuffle," Colonel Goosen, the head of the Port Elizabeth Security Police, was called to see Biko. (Twenty-eight affidavits made by doctors and policemen involved in the case did not mention "the scuffle." Only Major Snyman did—perhaps inadvertently—under oath at the inquest into Biko's death.)

Dr. Lang, the district surgeon, was called at Colonel Goosen's request. He signed a certificate stating that he "found no evidence of abnormal pathology" in Biko. (Under cross-examination he admitted that the certificate was incorrect, because Biko had refused water and food; was weak in all four limbs; had a laceration on his lip, a bruise near his second rib, swollen feet, ankles, and hands; could not walk properly and slurred his speech.)

On September 8th, Dr. Tucker, the chief district surgeon, together with Dr. Lang, examined Biko. He was still in leg irons, lying on a mat in the Security Police offices. Both the mat and the blanket were wet with urine.

The doctors recommended that he be moved to the prison hospital at Sydenham Prison so that a specialist could examine him, as he showed "possible symptoms of a malfunctioning of the nervous system which could have been caused by brain damage."

Dr. Hersch, the physician, found that Biko was suffering from echolalia (a symptom whereby a patient repeats everything he hears). A lumbar puncture was conducted and a neurosurgeon consulted. Mr. Keely, the neurosurgeon, said that Biko should be sent to hospital for observation as the spinal fluid from the lumbar puncture contained red blood cells, indicating abnormality. Dr. Hersch had signed a letter saying that the lumbar puncture was normal. (Under oath he admitted that the test had shown abnormalities.)

Colonel Goosen refused to allow Biko to be sent to the Livingstone Provincial Hospital, and he was taken back to his prison cell on September 11th.

Colonel Goosen called Dr. Tucker back that day to see Biko. Biko had collapsed, and his condition was "apathetic." He was frothing at the mouth and hyperventilating. Dr. Tucker told Colonel Goosen that Biko should be admitted to a hospital in Port Elizabeth, but Colonel Goosen insisted that he be transferred to a prison hospital in Pretoria. (Under oath Dr. Tucker admitted that the interests of his patient had been subordinated to the interests of "state security.")

The Biko family was not informed of Steve's condition or that he was being taken to Pretoria.

Biko was dragged in a semicoma to a police Land Rover for the thousand-mile journey to Johannesburg. He was shackled naked on his wet cell mats, with a blanket over him. He was given a bottle of water.

In Pretoria he was put into a cell.

Dr. van Zyl, a prison doctor, examined him at 3:00 P.M. on September 12th. He had not received a medical history of the case or been told that it was "urgent." He found Biko on his urine-soaked cell mats "very sick and comatose." He put him onto an intravenous drip.

Bantu Steven Biko died a few hours later.

Giving evidence, South Africa's top neurological pathologist,

Professor Proctor, said "considering the number, extent, and nature of the lesions in the brain, Steve Biko was rendered unconscious at the time of receiving the injuries" (the time of the "scuffle").

Mr. Sydney Kentridge, the senior counsel for the Biko family at the inquest, said in his final address: "The relationship of the district surgeons to Colonel Goosen is one of subservience bordering on collusion. Their obvious neglect of their patient's interests and their deference to the requirements of the Security Police is a breach of their professional duty which may have contributed to the final result."

Kentridge submitted that the inquest had exposed grave irregularities and misconduct in the treatment of a detainee. It had "revealed the dangers to life and liberty involved in the system of holding detainees incommunicado. Any verdict which can be seen as an exoneration of the Port Elizabeth police will unfortunately be widely interpreted as a licence to abuse helpless people with impunity."

The magistrate delivered a three-minute verdict. He found that no one was criminally responsible for Biko's death.

Three searing images of Steve's death drama have imprinted themselves forever on my mind, beyond the general horror of his last days. One is of his battered face as his lifeless body was carried in its open coffin at his funeral outside of King William's Town, attended by fifteen thousand people. Another is of the thin, pinched features behind dark sunglasses of Colonel Goosen and Major Snyman as I saw them when I attended the Biko inquest in Pretoria. The third is of the statement of Jimmy Kruger, the minister of police and minister of justice, when he was told of Biko's death while attending a National Party congress on September 12th. "It leaves me cold," he said to the wild cheering of hundreds of enthusiastic National Party delegates.

Steve Biko's death sparked smouldering resistance in black communities. As in 1976, the police's breaking up mass meetings with tear gas, dogs, batons, and shots became an everyday occurrence. A particularly embittering and provocative action of the authorities was the mass arrest of thousands of mourners at Biko's funeral. Police raids on children in the townships, mass detentions, mass trials of children, and the anguish of black parents marked the times. Thousands of children were held in preventative detention for months, and hundreds at a time were kept in detention at Protea Police Station on the outskirts of Soweto, which was also the headquarters of the police force in the township complex. The Black Sash had a roster of members who would monitor the children's "trials." On several occasions I attended the court proceedings on behalf of the group. Grimly I would sit and take notes.

It was easier at this time of crisis simply to keep on doing what was asked of me than to step back and look closely at what I could see before me. Hindsight clearly shows at least two things: that a civil war had begun in the country and that for white liberals to bear witness as it unfolded was to be one of the most important political actions of all.

The hundreds of children who were on "trial" were kept in a barbed-wire compound within the police station grounds. Aged about eight to eighteen, they sat listlessly on the baked earth in the sun all day and were brought back to the treeless, dusty arena on subsequent days until they were "tried." Every day many women, many of them with small babies strapped to their backs, and a few men searched longingly with desperate eyes through the barbed wire.

When the magistrate was ready, a few children together were marched into the courtroom. Black policemen armed with subautomatic weapons herded away the pushing, pleading crowd of mothers trying to catch a glimpse of the young prisoners from the courtroom doors.

Each trial took less than a minute. Many of the children, tried in groups, pleaded guilty to the "unrest" charges. The older ones were taken away to spend months as prison farm labourers, and the younger ones were returned to the custody of the Prisons Department. Many of these were set free, but no attempt was made to contact their families. Some had been in prison awaiting "trial" for more than three months.

While these and similar trials were going on around the country, other students, those able to be in school and to organise, were ensuring that by the end of September 1977 a full-scale boycott of schools—teachers and students—was in force.

By October, in Soweto, Alexandra, Atteridgeville, and other areas of the Transvaal, in the Cape Province and Natal, it was reported that 196,000 black pupils throughout South Africa were not in school. To counteract this defiance, the government extended its ban on outdoor meetings and stepped up reinforcement of other "unrest" contingencies. But support was spreading for mass action against government institutions, symbolised by the boycott of the black school system. Boycotts, marches, and shootings by the riot police escalated around the country.

South Africa was becoming ungovernable, and inevitably the government responded forcibly, the only way it knows to deal with situations of "unrest": it brought the full weight of its repressive legislative armoury—backed by armed force—to bear on the burgeoning mass black protest.

On Black Monday, October 19, 1977, eighteen organisations were declared unlawful. One was the Christian Institute, headed by an excommunicated Afrikaner cleric, Beyers Naude. The other seventeen were Black Consciousness organisations, including Biko's South African Student Organisation and the Black People's Organisation.

It was a crushing blow to black resistance. It had taken fifteen years, since the events around Sharpeville, the passive resistance campaign, and the outlawing of the African National Congress, for resistance to reach this intensity. The battle lines of the civil war were becoming clearer. And it was the apartheid regime that was drawing them. The message was sharply etched: any black person who tried to oppose the government through legitimate peaceful channels ran the risk of incurring brutal, unrelenting state violence.

The World and *Weekend World*, the country's two largest black-circulation newspapers, were banned.

Forty-seven people, all leaders of the black community— teachers, journalists, church leaders—were detained at Modderbee Prison near Johannesburg under the preventative detention provisions of the Internal Security Act.

Police and justice minister Jimmy Kruger said, "The government is determined to ensure that South Africa is not disturbed by a small group of anarchists using the young to create a revolutionary climate."

Despite these measures, the disruption of black schooling continued.

In December, a meeting of appeasement took place in Soweto among hundreds of black school principals and senior officials of the Department of Bantu Education. It was resolved that the system of Bantu Education would be scrapped and that a delegation would meet with the minister to begin discussing proposals for another system. (Those discussions proved abortive. Black schooling in South Africa has been in disarray since 1976.) I suppose in some measure the children had succeeded in their bid to smash the Bantu Education system. For them, the generation of June 1976, and those who came after, despite the crackdown on black organisations, the deaths, the detentions, the harassment, the loss of years of schooling, South Africa would never again be the same.

The mass black resistance of 1977 was a different story from that of 1962. Back then the government had succeeded in smashing the resistance that threatened its power to govern. Then the African National Congress had been forced underground, and the will of the people to resist was broken. It had taken almost fourteen years and a leader of the stature of Steve Biko to rekindle mass protest in South Africa. In the decade since 1976 that mass protest has been suppressed only by the full weight of all the apartheid government's repressive machinery. If the government unclenches its iron grip for a moment, massive black political protest bursts forth again. And although in 1977 the Black Consciousness movement was destroyed, black protest was already becoming spearheaded by the growing black trade union movement and myriad other smaller community, church-based, and self-help groups. By 1983 the United Democratic Front would grow out of these local groupings. The battle lines were being drawn for the massive upheavals that would shake South Africa in the mid-eighties.

Since the news of Biko's death was revealed in September 1977, I had been in a state of political frenzy, pushing myself relentlessly to meet a schedule of meetings and speaking engagements protesting the government's treatment of political detainees. A month later the deathblow to the Black Consciousness movement came like a physical blow to me. Months of pressure and emotional involvement had reduced me to a state of exhaustion and nervous tension. In the aftermath of the ministerial pronouncement of the bannings, I collapsed, giving way to despair and frustration.

I did attend protest meetings, but only to slump despondently in my seat and to listen to the brave words and outraged reactions of many other liberals I knew well. I felt listless and in deep despair—there was nothing we liberals could do anymore. The government, with its blindly repressive actions, had destroyed any slight chance of a black-white accommodation in South Africa. The stuttering mass black protest of past decades was becoming a low-grade, but escalating, state of civil war.

Almost inevitably the National Party won a landslide victory in the whites-only general election in November 1977. White South Africans were grateful to the government for its strong-arm responses to the upheavals of the past eighteen months. This strong embrace of the government by white South Africans underlined for me the hopelessness of our liberal cause.

In the election, despite ongoing commitments in Soweto and my own political malaise, out of a sense of obligation, I suppose, and because I hate sitting on the sidelines, I managed the campaign of Hymie Miller, an elderly veteran ex–United party member of Parliament. (He was part of another small breakaway group that had joined the party, causing yet another name change. We were now known as the Progressive Federal Party—the PFP.) It was a dismal campaign. Jeppe, the name of the constituency where I was working, was a lower-middle-class, mainly Afrikaans-speaking community. The National Party, busing students from the Rand Afrikaans Universiteit and the Goudstadse Onderwysers Kollege (City of Gold Teachers' College), blanketed the area. The National Party won by a landslide.

On a personal level, I was very pleased that Irene won an election to the provincial council.

It was a measure of my deep frustration, my need to engender some political action and excitement in Hymie Miller's deathlike campaign, that I engaged myself in a bitter clash with Councillor François Oberholzer.

My first clash with Oberholzer—Obie, the legendary, reactionary, long-serving chairman of the Management Committee of Johannesburg—had come in September 1977, when I made my first city council speech. He and his deputy chairman, the council's National Party leader, Carel Venter, became my "pet" targets, and I sought to expose their racism whenever I could. We had some bitter clashes in the ensuing years. It was only my strong belief in my political ideals that gave me the moral courage to challenge these men and exchange the vituperative verbal blows we did.

Taking exception to Oberholzer's having sent a personal letter to the voters of Jeppe on Management Committee letterhead, somewhat impetuously I attacked him in the press, accusing him of "abusing his power" and of "high-handed arrogance."

He did not take kindly to a novice city councillor challenging him so aggressively, and before I knew what had happened he sued me for a twenty-thousand-rand ($20,000; in 1977, R1=$1) libel suit. My guilt at the possibility of landing my family with a debt of that magnitude undid me. I cursed myself for the unthinking way I rushed into things. But my lawyer, a leading Johannesburg attorney, party stalwart, and close personal friend, Barry Jammy, assured me that Oberholzer's damages claim would come to naught. On that basis I agreed to defend the libel suit. Barry was correct; a few months later, Oberholzer dropped his suit.

This happened during the buildup to the November general election. It provided an interesting sideshow for the public, surfeited by the political rhetoric of white election games. It was with this tension between Councillor Oberholzer and me that we met in December for the final council meeting of 1977.

Councillor Oberholzer glowered at me from his seat behind the raised Management Committee bench. He was so pompous, so self-righteous and smug. My nervousness over his libel suit faded as my old urge to puncture his pomposity and self-possession overcame me. Unknown to him, with a bit of luck (being allowed to speak in council), I would again be able to do so that day.

In the days before the council meeting took place, together with the Black Sash, I had been monitoring the actions of the West Rand Administration Board (WRAB), the government agency that administered the black townships around Johannesburg. To my dismay, Oberholzer and the Management Committee—mere elected office bearers, *not* representatives of a government agency—had been colluding with WRAB in evicting people—in the thousands—from their homes in Alexandra Township.

The bulldozers were flattening brick homes as well as makeshift shacks. The purpose of this action was twofold, the authorities said: "to clear Alexandra of illegals" and "to raze the area to the ground" for the proposed construction of a huge complex of high-rise, single-sex "hostels" to house sixty thousand male workers living in Alex.

Apartheid theory had it that only the men, the labourers, were "legal" in the townships. The women and children were not working and therefore could not live there. The "resettled" men were to be housed temporarily at City Deep Hostels, an archaic complex of buildings on an old mine that even the conservative city council health officials had condemned as unsuitable for living accommodation.

We had not quite collated all these facts as I prepared for the council meeting, but when I arrived at the council building I had a message to call the Sash offices. A Sash field-worker, who had been in Alex that morning, brought me up to date. Despite West Rand Administration Board officials' claims that only single people were living in Alex, she assured me that families were being broken up and the homes of married couples were being bulldozed to the ground. "I saw the bulldozers at work, and I've spoken to members of families who are being separated."

Seething with impatience, I waited for an opportunity to speak. I desperately wanted to rub Oberholzer's and his cronies' noses in their lies. I also wanted this opportunity to express in some way my frustration at the whole web of arbi-

trary repression I could feel the government drawing tighter
around us all. In my own small way I wanted to make them
accountable for these (among the thousand others) attacks on
human rights and human dignity.

Under an item dealing with the council's own single-sex
hostels (many with as iniquitous living conditions as those in
City Deep), I seized my opportunity to speak. And before the
mayor could rule me out of order for not dealing directly with
the item, I had delivered a few telling thrusts. Councillors
Oberholzer and Venter, who was also chairman of the Housing
Committee and the deputy chairman of the West Rand Administration Board, were furious.

Venter roared at me, in a finger-shaking rage, to find him a
man "who will be moved who has got a marriage certificate
predating his removal order."

When I sat down after speaking, the council messenger
brought me a note from the *Rand Daily Mail* municipal reporter Chris Smith. In it he asked me to take up Venter's
challenge and go to Alexandra to find such men. He and a
photographer would accompany me.

On arrival in Alex the next day we drove straight to the
church hall of Reverend Sam Buti, where those whose homes
had been demolished were being housed. The large room was
packed with people, some sitting patiently, waiting for law
students to take their affidavits, and many others sleeping on
mattresses laid out in neat rows against the walls. Others sat
staring numbly, desperation and hopelessness covering them
like a pall. Children of all ages crept underfoot, many of them
crying monotonously, a more despairing note against the quiet
murmur of the adults. We walked among the hundreds of
people wanting to tell their stories in personal statements.

One earnest man, Mr. Derobela Irish Madingwane, held both
his framed marriage certificate, which until yesterday had
hung on the wall of his Alex home, and his orders from WRAB
to move to the City Deep Hostels. The photographer took a
picture of Mr. Madingwane holding both documents, and it
appeared on the front page of the *Rand Daily Mail* the following day. In the article under the picture I am quoted as repeat-
ing my challenge to Councillor Venter to come to Alex to see for

himself. I asserted that, despite the board's pledges to the contrary, thousands of women and children were being rendered homeless.

Other English-speaking Johannesburg newspapers, along with the *Post* in Soweto, had similar coverage. In the Afrikaans press, these events simply were ignored. Despite the media attention, the demolishing of houses and the removal of married men to City Deep continued. Councillor Venter never bothered to reply to me.

Among many others, we also met Mr. Wille Majola in the hall. I asked him if he would take us to the site of his demolished home. He took us to 132 2nd Avenue, Alexandra. The street was devastated, as if it had been bombed. Up and down on either side of the road piles of rubble attested to the zealous work of the bulldozers. While the photographer and I looked on grimly, Mr. Majola, standing on top of the pile of rubble and surrounded by nine of his children who had been sitting listlessly on top of the bricks when we arrived, spoke. "Yesterday," he gestured in bewilderment around him, "yesterday, this was my home—two rooms. We all lived here—me, my wife, twelve children. Today it is dust."

He bent down and picked up a handful of rubble, which he let run slowly through his fingers. No one said anything. A kite called in alarm overhead. What if Carel Venter had been there with us? I know I was ready to do or say something drastic.

On the way back to the church hall, Mr. Majola told us that his first wife had died and his second wife looked after all twelve children as her own. He also said that he was fifty-two years old, a labourer, and that he had been trying to obtain a family permit to live in Alex since the early sixties, but had always been refused.

The men I spoke to in the church hall were angry and humiliated, defiant about going to live in a hostel while their families were forced to return to their tribal "homelands." Most of the men and women had never been to their "homeland," having been born in urban townships. The women were no less angry than the men but spoke with a resigned helplessness.

It was December, nearly Christmas. Cardboard cut-out models of the nativity scene and pictures of Mary and the Babe decorated the building—"Peace on Earth and Goodwill to All Men" ran the message on the banner draped across the front of the hall. Beneath the banner bewildered mothers nursed tiny babies, their worldly possessions in cardboard boxes stacked around them. Legal clerks still went from group to group taking affidavits, noting details of marriage certificates and the birth documents of the children.

Together with Chris Smith I drove along some of the back streets of Alexandra. Dust and broken slabs of brickwork lay where the bulldozers had just finished demolishing houses. We passed a house where two children stood crying loudly in the dusty street as their family goods were thrown out of the smashed windows and broken-in doorway by WRAB officials and all the while the lumbering yellow bulldozer waited, its running engine sounding alarmingly powerful and destructive in the summer heat.

A few days later a black reporter and a black photographer from the *Rand Daily Mail* were smuggled into the City Deep Hostels. Their report on the living conditions provoked renewed furor. A senior WRAB official denied that the "re-settled" men would be made to sleep on the narrow concrete cubicles shown in the photographs: ". . . our first reaction was that this mortuary-like sleeping accommodation was not to be used. . . ." Later he said that "about 300 of these beds would have to be used because of lack of space" and added that "6,000 men will be accommodated at City Deep." Referring to the photographs of huge areas of communal toilets, he said ". . . they are adequate in view of the fact that only males are there and that they use the veld [open ground] in Alexandra." He added, "The mine boys have never complained about that type of toilet. We use them in the older hostels in Soweto."

CHAPTER 11
"Money Is Power"

Almost a million township dwellers around the metropolis of "white" Johannesburg commute daily to work in the city. About eight hundred thousand of these come from Soweto. There is only one train line (which is government-owned and-operated) snaking past the outer perimeter of the sprawling "dormitory" complex. Train commuters rise between four and five in the morning to brave the hazardous, overcrowded, crime-ridden journey to arrive at work on time. Many other commuters travel on PUTCO (Public Utilities Transport Company) buses. Putco is a privately owned company with well-known businessmen, National Party stalwarts, on its board and enjoys a government-granted monopoly of bus transport in Soweto and the other townships around Johannesburg. The bus lines are not linked across Soweto; the buses travel from widely dispersed stations directly to the city.

Over the years the Soweto taxi service evolved, filling the vacuum created by the gross inadequacies of the public transport system. Although it was illegal for blacks to own and operate transport businesses, the authorities nevertheless turned a blind eye to the taxis because they fulfilled a useful purpose. Black taxis were not allowed to have meters or carry white passengers. Yet, aside from being subjected to police searches (a daily feature of township life anyway), they were left alone. The fare structure and other regulations that governed the white taxi business did not apply to black taxi operators. The Soweto taxi fraternity—transport entrepreneurs—developed its own structure of taxi associations, usually based on territorial imperatives; its own fare structure created on market demand; and its own methods of retribution for interlopers, or "pirate taxis." Disagreements often escalated into "taxi wars." There were never enough taxis—which were safer than the train, cleaner than the buses, and more convenient than any other mode of township transport—and the informal black taxi sector flourished. The township taximan loomed large in the Soweto consciousness: an almost mythical swashbuckling figure of entrepreneurial independence, a black man who worked for himself and who, together with his "brothers" in the taxi associations, was a law unto himself.

In 1978 some of the onerous business restrictions on blacks were lifted and it became legal for black businessmen to have a majority share holding in a company. The idea of Ma-Afrika Taxi Ltd., a black company, a black taxi cooperative, the first in South Africa, was born in the minds of several black businessmen. A series of coincidental events led to my somewhat bemused involvement in the company, but my association with Ma-Afrika proved a unique and enlivening experience.

By mid-1979, a year into the project, I knew I was in far over my head. Ma-Afrika demanded all of my time, and I could give only bits of myself because I had many other commitments—my family, the city council, my voters, journalistic commitments, other involvements in other antiapartheid bodies. I suppose I could have given up most of these if I had felt that Ma-Afrika really fit me, and I did cut back in many areas. But I stayed involved in these other commitments, which shows perhaps that I was always a little uneasy about Ma-Afrika and my role in it.

Probably I should not have been involved at all. I had no training or experience in business, but when the proposal was first put to me I found it intriguing and exciting. It took me out of the essentially white racial political arena and into an area of black South Africa, where I would be the first and only white interacting with rank-and-file black South Africans in a way difficult for most other whites to imagine—in the subculture of the Soweto taxi world.

By now we had created something from nothing, and it was growing so quickly that it threatened to swallow us all. The idea of uncontrolled growth frightened me. Not that the others seemed perturbed. They would have quite happily gone on acquiring garages and members in a pell-mell rush over all of South Africa's black townships. The cautionary words of our bank manager Henry Lukojolo and our auditors and lawyers seemed to strike fear into my heart alone. I have often wondered why that was so. Was it that as a white I had grown up schooled in the knowledge that bankruptcy in business could mean losing your home and everything else you owned, whereas my black codirectors, never able by law to own land, knew no such fear? It is an ironic thought. For once the law could not touch them because, obviously, business laws had been written for white businessmen, the idea of a black business sector not as yet having entered the lawmakers' heads.

We had been through all the uphill slog these problems caused: No black director had been able to sign a lease for office space downtown, because blacks were not allowed to rent space downtown. We had been unable to raise a loan, because, in a catch-22, loans could not be given without the security of land ownership, and blacks were not allowed to own land. We had been unable to register our company, because we did not have a loan. Despite my presence, we were a black company. Our board had seven directors, and six of them were black. And we were credited with a number of firsts in the black business world, most of them, ten years later as I write, still not emulated.

Ma-Afrika not only was the first black-owned cooperative business venture in South Africa with the first majority black directorship. (Prior to 1978, blacks were not allowed to have a majority share in a public company, and a shop owner was not allowed to deal in more than one business.) We also dealt with the first black bank manager in South Africa, whose bank handled the first-ever share offering to blacks in a black company. We had designed for our members the first life benefits package for blacks—general insurance, health insurance, pension funds, education funds. And we had the support of the white business sector, at least the American part of it: Mobil, Arthur Young, and D'Arcy, MacManus and Masius (currently known as D'Arcy Masius Benton & Bowles). (American companies were beginning to respond to demands put on them by their parent companies in the States. Supporting black businesses looked good to shareholders back home.)

Ma-Afrika had given me a real charge that first year. Being in Soweto on a basis no other white had been—no politician, no Black Sasher, no government official—meant I was breaking new ground, experiencing the grass roots. The taximen called me Thandiwe ("beloved by all"), and who could resist that sobriquet? And I really was happy working with Bongani, Windy, Mr. Zwane, Mannie, Goodman, Milton. For the first time I truly felt that Soweto was a part of me and I of Soweto. It was at our garage and offices there in Mofolo, a stone's throw from the Regina Mundi Cathedral, where I had stood fourteen years before and cheered Robert Kennedy.

At the garage I was the only white among many blacks, buying, waiting, talking. My parents' fears about my throwing in my lot with "the blacks" had taken an unexpected shape. Yet at Ma-Afrika, in Soweto, surrounded by blacks, I was in no political danger from the state. What would my father (ten years dead) have made of his daughter's role in Ma-Afrika?

In retrospect I see those were the good times, despite the time pressures, the responsibilities, always having more to do than I possibly could.

It all began in a crowded hall in Dube, Soweto, in May 1978. I had been invited to the Ma-Afrika launch by a good friend, Bongani Ngcobo, a Soweton entrepreneur. By then I was writing a weekly column for the *Post* called "From the Laager Reaching Out," and I thought that the launch would make a suitable article for the column.

On my arrival I was pleased to see that my editor and friend, Percy Qoboza, was the main speaker. The gist of Percy's speech dealt with the relationship of money and power:

　. . . We must realise that money is power. The kind of power

, black people can use as a lever in industry for the employment of
more blacks in responsible positions. . . . It is essential to build a
strong black business community. . . .

My name was called after Percy had sat down to thunderous
applause. Taken aback, I walked to the microphone; no one had
told me that I would be asked to say anything.

"Money is indeed power," I began, picking up on Percy's
theme. Welcoming the initiative of the organisers, I wished
them well and spoke briefly on the imperative need for black
people to be part of the economy in a capacity other than that of
labour units. Percy's speech and my few words appeared the
next day in most of Johannesburg's newspapers.

Later Bongani called to thank me for my support and asked
if he could bring a few friends around to discuss the next step
of their campaign. "Your experience in political campaigns will
be of great benefit to us," Bongani said charmingly.

Out of a large Soweto taxi they emerged, the men from Ma-
Afrika, into my white suburban Norwood home: There was
Bongani, spruce and eager in his business suit, always impeccably pressed and set off by well-chosen silk accessories. Mannie Sahabodien, a tall, portly, imposing man with carefully
slicked back dark hair and a pencil-thin mustache, was a
sallow-complexioned Clark Gable look-alike, but Clark Gable
gone to seed. Mr. Ellison Zwane, a cadaverously thin, short,
older man, was the "chairman" of several large taxi associations in Soweto, a father figure treated with gentle respect by
the others. Ezekiel Mdletye (Windy), about Bongani's age and
build but not as well dressed and without Bongani's assurance
and aplomb, was shy and diffident but with a sincere, winning
smile. Finally came Milton Mdakane and Goodman Sikakane,
both tall, comely men and taxi owners, Milton owning a fleet of
five taxis. Neither of them would speak to me at our first
meeting because they were embarrassed by their scant knowledge of English.

It was soon obvious that Mannie Sahabodien was the driving
force behind the enterprise. A devout Muslim, a "coloured"
man, he had been in the car business for years in Mayfair, a
"grey" suburb of Johannesburg. ("Grey" Mayfair was a semiin-
dustrial area of small factories, warehouses, auto body shops,

and so on. It was designated "grey" because people other than "white," for instance "coloured" and Indian businessmen, could operate there without official harassment, but they could not own property or live there, and their leases had to be in the name of someone classified as racially "white.")

One person was missing of those I had been introduced to as being part of Ma-Afrika at the launch.

"What about Mr. Mncube?" I enquired about the spokesman for the group in Dube the previous week.

"Oh, he's out. It was said that he kept some Ma-Afrika funds for himself," Mr. Zwane asserted with a reticent shrug. I gathered that Mr. Mncube was out of favour, condemned, on the strength of a rumour. I was to learn only too well the part rumours played in the life of a Soweto taximan.

Mr. Mncube was forgotten as Mannie began speaking. The upshot of our discussion was that Mannie could see "millions" in forging a taxi cooperative of Soweto taxi drivers. Nothing of its kind had ever been attempted, though many regional and subregional "associations" of taximen were already in place. These were nonprofit associations that the members, with similar interests, joined for social reasons. Ideally, Ma-Afrika Taxi Ltd., as a registered company in terms of South African company law, would provide the taximen with political power and financial clout. Mannie, Bongani, and the others were admirably innovative for having promulgated the idea of the company virtually as soon as the law had changed to allow blacks to run a company in South Africa.

According to the scheme, each taxi driver would buy at least one twenty-five-rand share in the company. These shares would become increasingly valuable over time, and the idea of the shares could be sold to the taxi drivers as an investment. A shareholder would be issued a company membership card. Ma-Afrika Taxi Ltd. would negotiate for its members insurance packages, spare parts discounts, medical aid schemes, and so on. But, Mannie assured me, with Bongani's enthusiastic agreement, the "real" money was in advertising and contracts with record companies. "Already," Mannie said, leaning forward confidentially, "the directors have been approached by advertising agencies and record companies."

He sat back in his chair, beaming. It was Bongani's turn to speak.

"Now, Jennet," he said with warmth and sincerity, "we have discussed this among ourselves, and we are in agreement—we want to invite you to become a director of Ma-Afrika."

It was not what I had expected. The offer was flattering and intriguing, but I knew nothing about business. I believed that with my city council responsibilities, my journalistic commitments, my parenting concerns, my commitment to a range of "change" groups and organisations, I could not possibly embark on another venture.

Thanking them for their offer and reassuring them that I would willingly try to be helpful with suggestions on specific problems, I declined. But, with Mannie and Bongani leading the way and Windy adding a heartfelt appeal, I agreed not to close the door and to reconsider the offer.

And the more I thought about it, the more appealing the offer became. I believed in a nonracial country, didn't I? A so-called "coloured" person, a white woman, and five black men—we would be a fairly representative group of South Africans. And it would be a black company.

I enjoyed being at the centre of the stage, and this venture would be making history in South Africa.

Days went by, and the six directors urged me persistently to join them.

Ten days after the launch of Ma-Afrika I received the following letter. The letterhead proclaimed "NATIONAL FRONT ASSOCIATION (SOUTH AFRICA)." It was addressed to me in my capacity as a Johannesburg city councillor.

Dear Madame,
   The Rand Daily Mail, on April 28th, published an article on Percy Qoboza in which he claims, rightly enough, that money is power. You are quoted as saying that "money is indeed power." You should certainly know because it is money that not only gives the World Bankers their evil power to subvert the Western World but money that gives the Progressive Federal Party its power to interfere politically in South Africa far in excess of its worth but an interference designed to subvert the White man's future.
   However we are pleased to know that through the actions of

our movement and other kindred groups the eyes of an increasing number of White South Africans are being opened. Your nefarious campaign is far from being won.

J. N. Noble

The National Front was an English-speaking right wing group that supported the right wing of the National Party. Its members were regarded as fringe reactionaries, allegedly responsible for a number of "intimidatory" actions taken against white liberal activists—shooting at house windows, slashing tyres, killing pets, and so on. Real acts of bravery on their part.

The letter incensed me; moreover, it made up my mind for me. I would become a director of Ma-Afrika. Mr. Noble and his National Front would soon know that my "nefarious campaign," far from not being won, had not yet even begun.

(I suspect that it was this Mr. Noble, or one of his cronies, who called me every year on the anniversary of Steve Biko's death. He would issue death threats to me while asking, amid much heavy breathing, if I had said Kaddish [Jewish prayer of remembrance] for Biko.)

Our first directors' meeting was held in Mannie Sahabodien's cramped, dusty, and grease-stained office at the side of his panel-beating operation in Mayfair. Mr. Zwane, the chairman, opened the meeting—as he would do for the many to follow—with an impromptu prayer in a mixture of Zulu and English.

Then it was down to business—and a complicated and frustrating business it was. Anyone who has ever started a business knows it's no easy task, but in face of the obstacles the apartheid government had installed, our task was formidable. The immediate objective was to have the company registered. Registration would require an initial amount of funding.

It was decided that our first port of call for that funding would be the Urban Foundation, a recently formed organisation to "improve the quality of life of urban blacks." The organisation had been founded and heavily funded by a range of the largest private-sector organisations in South Africa. I agreed to set up a meeting with Mike Rantho, a black field-worker and director for projects in the southern Transvaal region.

Another priority was to find office premises in Johannesburg. Bongani knew of offices in Abbey House, Commissioner
Street, a few blocks west of the heart of downtown Johannesburg. The offices recently had been vacated by a small black
selling enterprise that had failed.

"The landlord doesn't mind black tenants. There are lawyers,
other black organisations, and a Soweto soccer club in the
building." Bongani turned diffidently to me. "But you'll have to
sign the lease, Jennet?"

"Okay, that's fine." I nodded. Bongani had no way of knowing
that I was already the "front" for a black lawyer, two small
black educational institutions, and an experimental black pub-
lishing venture. (By law, black people were not allowed to sign
a lease or "own" premises in the "white" business districts,
although some restrictions were lifted in certain cities and
towns in 1986.)

Mannie then addressed us on the approaches that had been
made by a local record company that wanted to sign a lucrative
contract with us, binding our members to playing only music
tapes recorded by its label's artists. Mannie started building
castles: ". . . we could get an advertising agency to sell space on
the tapes . . . a cut for us and for the taxi driver. . . ."

"Hold on, hold on," I interjected. "If Ma-Afrika is going to
work, we're going to have to organise our systems for all these
things before we go signing any contracts."

If there was one thing I knew about, it was organising systems. Bongani had said that part of the reason he and the
others had invited me to join Ma-Afrika was because of my
experience in election campaigns. I knew that there would be
no surer way to become entangled in an unholy mess than not
to have our shareholders and membership lists systematized.
Maybe I was so insistent because it was a job I knew I could do
well. Perhaps I was still justifying to myself being there at all.

So, as I would do so often, I poured cold water over the group.
I could see that they were conceding to me more out of respect
than agreement with my sentiments. It was the early days, and
we were feeling our way with one another. Mannie agreed to
set up a meeting with the record company. "Can we use your
house, Jennet, until we have our office?"

The next item was that Mobil Oil had also been insistent on meeting with the directors, Mannie said. At the mention of Mobil, Mr. Zwane spoke longingly about Ma-Afrika owning a garage in Soweto, "so our members can have a place to meet" and "to show the other taximen that we are really for them and can do things."

"There will be many other American businesses interested in helping us," I said, "because of the Sullivan Principles. We don't have to put our eggs in one basket."

"The Sullivan Principles?" Windy asked gently.

I explained as well as I could about the Reverend Leon Sullivan in Philadelphia and his Code of Employment Practice for U.S. companies doing business in South Africa. I had a slight sinking feeling. This was going to be a huge undertaking—time-consuming troubleshooting and problem solving. Both activities I enjoyed, but my own time constraints would be a hindrance. And while I could cope with the task of proceeding in an orderly manner to build a cooperative, I was having difficulty in coping with the preemptive input of white businessmen climbing onto the Ma-Afrika bandwagon even before it had begun rolling. My fellow directors were ready to run away with themselves. Could they and should they be made aware of the priorities I had learnt in the building of an organisation? Perhaps I was wrong to want method and order? Perhaps there were other ways of doing things?

Over the following months we moved into our offices in Abbey House. Bongani, Milton, and Goodman found good secondhand office furniture. Bongani managed to charm a salesperson at IBM into loaning us an expensive typewriter. He then installed himself behind a large desk in a private office and was pronounced company secretary. Mr. Zwane interviewed and chose a receptionist/typist for the office.

The Urban Foundation shunted us from one officer to another to discuss our request for a loan of two thousand rand with which to register the company and pay the lawyers. Eventually Dave Millstein, a business officer, told us that without security and a business plan the foundation would have to approve, it would not furnish a loan. In any event, he continued, such a loan would take months to process as it would have to be approved by a series of boards, which met only monthly. So much for the promises of the "enthusiastic involvement" of big business in grass-roots black business ventures. Eventually the attorney in Krugersdorp who had drawn up the Articles of Association provided a small loan that was used for the registration of the company.

It seemed that once we were a registered company we were far more acceptable in the white business community. We were lunched and dined. We were made welcome in directors' private dining rooms. We represented the possibility of a four-thousand-member (by conservative estimate) cooperative in the industrial heartland of the country, the bridgehead into a vast, almost untapped market.

Before our company registration I had often felt humiliated and helpless in the plush panelled offices of the financial houses. It pained me to hear the tone of patronising patience with which smooth young men explained to us why we could not be considered for a loan. They would speak simple, almost pidgin English to my colleagues while addressing me as an equal. I was also disturbed by the mask of obsequious diffidence that even the confident Mannie and the urbane Bongani drew over their faces in the presence of these white "managers."

At this time the office rent, telephone bill, and typist's salary were being paid by a small monthly amount each of the directors "loaned" to the company. The directors had become "A" category shareholders, purchasing many thousands of shares for a small amount. As soon as we could, we bought a book of blank share certificates and in Bongani's copperplate handwriting (his father was a school principal in Kwa-Zulu and had seen to his son's handwriting) began to issue "B" category shares to taxi owners who had bought them at twenty-five rand a share. There had been an initial demand for about four hundred shares, and we were jubilant.

Mobil agreed to finance a luncheon at a downtown hotel for the official company launch, at which we could inform the taximen as to what we were about. We invited twenty local taxi association chairmen and office bearers, representatives of businesses associated with the motor industry and the press.

As I had been prevailed upon to be the main speaker, I sat at the centre of the horseshoe of tables. Looking at the nearly two hundred black men present, at the crowded press table, and at the smiling, trying-to-please white businessmen dotted among the taximen, I could feel the plush conference room vibrating with excitement. Being part of that gathering made tangible for me for the first time that Ma-Afrika was creating something unique and historic in South Africa.

Seated between Mr. Zwane, my chairman and also the chairman of the Naledi African Taxi Association, and Mr. Tabane of the Meadowlands Dube African Taxi Association, I was introduced to numerous other taximen as they came to pay their respects to Mr. Zwane. He told me that the taximen present were representative of about 70 percent of the black taxi population of the greater Johannesburg area.

"Only Jimmy Sejeni's missing," said Mr. Zwane, "and he's the biggest in Soweto. About eight hundred cars and kombis (mini-vans) in his association—Johannesburg Non-European Taxi Association. I hear he's jealous. He wants us to make him a director. Can we do that? There're two hundred people here who want to be directors. Can all members of Ma-Afrika become directors?" He lowered his voice. "Sejeni has a man here, over there, the lighter-coloured one, Patrick Qwabe. Qwabe is bad, makes trouble. He pretends he doesn't know Sejeni, but we know he's a spy. He's spreading stories about Sahabodien, says he has all the members' money in his bank account, says he's making deals behind our backs.

"Qwabe is Sejeni's dog, does what his master wants—pays the bribes to the magistrates and traffic officers when Sejeni's members are in trouble. If Ma-Afrika grows, Sejeni will want to take us over or make war."

Mr. Zwane must have seen the look of consternation on my face. He smiled reassuringly, a grin splitting the leathered skin of his thin, wizened face. "Don't worry, Jennet, all these members here support Ma-Afrika, not Sejeni."

"Maybe we should invite Sejeni around," I said, "talk to him. We can offer him a deal if he has so many members."

Mr. Zwane looked at me with blankness descending over his eyes. Obviously there was far more bubbling away beneath the surface unity of the gathering than I was aware of, or of which

I was being allowed to be aware. I knew that we needed the full support of the extant taxi associations if Ma-Afrika was to succeed, but I was not privy to the internal politics by which they had long operated. But there was more I was unaware of: the suspicion and resentment aimed at Sahabodien. I think it was racial in origin because he was a so-called "coloured," although everyone I spoke to about this denied my accusation.

"Jennet"—Bongani's eyes were dancing—"they want Sahabodien to leave. They say he doesn't belong, he's not black, he's not a taximan, he's a crook, he wants to bleed Ma-Afrika, to bleed them."

Before I could seek out the dismayed Mannie, Mr. Zwane was bringing the meeting to order by asking Qwabe to lead us in prayer. Bringing Qwabe into the mainstream of the meeting was a wily move on Mr. Zwane's behalf. He was now no longer just "Sejeni's dog" but a respected member of the taxi community. Together we prayed for the growth of the seed of Ma-Afrika that was now a tiny plant to become a towering tree. We prayed for the well-being of the directors, the members, our sponsors.

In Zulu and SeSotho, Mr. Zwane called on each of the twenty chairmen of the taxi associations to rise to be acknowledged by the rest of the meeting. Then in Zulu (interpreted by Qwabe into English and by another young man into SeSotho) he outlined our progress to date. He mentioned Mobil's name whenever he could. (Mr. Zwane wanted that garage in Soweto.) Then he introduced me.

Describing some of the trials of the journey and some of the anticipated challenges ahead, I paid tribute in my speech to the vision and perseverance of my fellow directors. I pointed to the major stumbling block black entrepreneurs faced: that because blacks could not own land they could not provide the necessary security for the loans they needed and that, as a result, many a worthy scheme died an abortive death. I also made a plea for other black small businessmen to enter the "free"-enterprise system, to persevere until their successes created great pressure for the legislation to be changed.

The underlying point—indeed, the vision that had led me to get involved in Ma-Afrika—was that the government had to be brought to realise that the people of South Africa, black and white, were one economic unit, that our future should increasingly reflect our interdependence, that the economic truth of the statement that we were a multiracial country had to be shouted aloud, freed of all the artificial restraints that tarnish that truth.

After my speech the meeting went into closed session. In the absence of Mannie, who had had to leave for "urgent business reasons," Bongani summarised the package of benefits we were in the process of negotiating for members.

Mr. Zwane proceeded to field questions from the floor. Bongani, sitting next to me, gave me the gist of the questions and answers. It seemed that if we were willing to drop Mannie Sahabodien from our board, we would have a great deal of support from the taxi associations. The deep suspicion of Sahabodien was clearly evident. Speaker after speaker reiterated that Ma-Afrika was to be a Soweto (meaning black) enterprise and a taximan (meaning Sahabodien was not really one of them) venture. Sagaciously, Mr. Zwane said we would discuss the question of Sahabodien's eligibility at our next board meeting and report back to the chairmen. It was obvious that Sahabodien was a target, for I (white, female, and not a taxiperson) was acceptable, as were Bongani and Windy, also not taxi owners or drivers. Mr. Zwane ended the meeting with a prayer. The meeting broke up on a positive, high-spirited note. I think I shook hands with all two hundred people in the room.

The launch received extensive press coverage with bold headlines and many photos and marked a turning point in our fortunes. The Abbey House offices were now always full of taximen joining up or meeting to shoot the breeze. Numerous white businesses approached us with offers of schemes for the mutual benefit of their profits and our members. Our weekly directors' meeting became twice weekly, one to discuss our day-by-day planning and organising and the other to meet with the proponents of various business schemes. Ma-Afrika was taking over a large part of my life, but it was an exciting ride.

Mannie Sahabodien resigned rather than be voted off the board. He was bitter and acrimonious. After all, the impetus for Ma-Afrika had come from him. I was sorry to see him leave.

We had come to know one another well during his negotiations (with which I assisted him) with city council officials over the lease of land in Riverlea Township to build a mosque and religious school. (He was chairman of the local Muslim community.) He died from a coronary a few months after he left Ma-Afrika.

Once Mannie left the board our membership grew rapidly. I was insistent that we obtain the best professional services.

Arthur Young became our auditors and offered Bongani on-the-job training in the duties of a company secretary.

Standard Bank Insurance Brokers became our official insurance brokers and were most accommodating and innovative in designing packages to meet the insurance needs of the black taximen, none having existed previously.

A major group of attorneys agreed to act for us and almost immediately took successful legal action against several local white-run authorities for overcharging our members on traffic fines and accepting only cash payment, as well as for refusing to issue road-worthy certificates to black taxi owners who had complied with all the stated requirements.

We were negotiating with one company on a two-way radio scheme and with another company for decal side-panel advertising space on "our" taxis. And D'Arcy, MacManus and Masius had approached us with a number of interesting advertising possibilities. These too were firsts for the private black transport sector.

It seemed to me that we had more than enough on our plate when Mobil reentered the picture; this time it offered a garage in Soweto if we could find the initial backing of twenty-five thousand rand as security for Mobil to provide the first petrol deliveries and for rent.

Mr. Zwane and the others were jubilant. Full of trepidation at the enormity of this responsibility in what for all of us was uncharted water, but persuaded by the others, I agreed to our taking on the running of the garage. But I told the board that I thought we were growing too rapidly and that as none of us had the expertise to run a cash business we were looking for trouble. There was no gainsaying Mr. Zwane, Milton, Goodman, Windy, and the taxi association chairmen, who had become our field liaison officers. Obviously garage ownership to a taximan was full of an emotive symbolism of which I had little knowledge.

I had never envisaged that I would be a part owner of a garage concern in Soweto. My colleagues' ebullience was infectious. I committed myself to assisting with the raising of the initial loan and with setting up our credibility at a bank in Soweto. But I emphasised that my interest in the company lay, as it always had, in building up the membership and in obtaining life membership benefits (life insurance, health insurance, medical aid schemes, so on). It was agreed that Bongani and I would work out of the town office and travel to Soweto for meetings, so that Mr. Zwane, Milton, Goodman, and Windy could be at the garage.

News of the garage deal swelled our membership ranks. We were now approaching the two thousand mark.

On the recommendation of Standard Bank Insurance Brokers, Standard Merchant Bank immediately agreed to a loan of twenty-five thousand rand and said the loan could grow with the growth of the business. Scarred by our initial experiences in seeking a loan, I had been uneasy about finding this one and amazed at the ease of the transaction. Bongani and Mr. Zwane looked so much more the part now. In the glassed-in eyrie of the Merchant Bank boardroom high above Johannesburg, they drew on Cuban cigars and signed the papers.

It was even easier to choose our bank. Although many of the other Soweto businesses banked in the white suburbs nine miles from Soweto, following our own inclination and the nudging of our auditors we went to the newly opened Standard Bank in Jabulani in Soweto. This was also a first—the first black-managed bank in South Africa—and Henry Lukojolo was the bank manager. (Land at Jabulani had been set aside as the site for the first massive shopping complex in Soweto, but as this book goes to press in 1988 it has still not been built. Modern bank and building society buildings had mushroomed there in 1977-78 as part of the authorities' intention "to do something positive about Soweto.")

Lukojolo was excited about the Ma-Afrika/Mobil venture. He hoped that our banking with him would encourage our members to bank there, too: "Too many of our people believe that they have money only if they have cash under their bed," he said.

Knowing that one of Mobil's senior financial staff members had been lent to the garage for four months made me feel more secure about our venture. For among many other things, none of the directors of Ma-Afrika had any experience in dealing with the daily large cash amounts of three to five thousand rand generated from the petrol sales. It was gratifying that the taximen were supporting Ma-Afrika Service Station to the extent they were, but we needed help in dealing with this new world: security guards to collect the cash, twenty-four-hour burglar alarm systems to protect the cash, high insurance rates against the risk of criminal action against us because of the cash.

Windy Mdletye, the quiet man of the outfit, came into his own at this point. He was being trained as the garage manager and displayed a knack for paperwork—figures and systems—that delighted his Mobil mentor, Geoff Armstrong. After we linked up with a wholesale spares company to create Ma-Afrika Discount Spares, it became apparent that Windy, in order to be free to deal with management problems, was going to need a bookkeeper to assist with the daily accounting. Milton and Goodman, besides running their own taxis, had taken on the running of the spares division. Ma-Afrika members received additional discounts on the spares. We did a roaring trade.

Mobil wanted us to employ an Indian trainee clerk in its program, but we wanted a Soweton. After we had interviewed many applicants, the gap between white and black education became manifest. The Grade 12 level of bookkeeping (our minimum requirement), while adequate for white applicants, was inadequate for our purposes in black applicants. And black university graduates with the requisite training did not want to work as bookkeepers. So we employed an older woman, Gertrude, who, despite the law reserving such work for whites, had been trained in bookkeeping in a garment factory in Germiston.

A few weeks after we opened in Soweto, Bongani organised a tree-planting ceremony in the lot adjoining the garage. This was a successful public relations exercise and gave the company a further boost in the public eye.

Mobil was so pleased with its experiment with Ma-Afrika that it offered us another garage in a township east of Johannesburg. I put my foot down: there was simply no way we could stretch our resources to run another garage.

"If we take this one on, count me out. I didn't join Ma-Afrika to go into the garage business. I joined Ma-Afrika to help to build the first major black business cooperative. We have been lucky so far, but we must continue to build our foundation, or else the structure on top will collapse."

Our auditors backed me on this issue. Reluctantly Mr. Zwane and the others agreed not to take direct control of the other garage. Instead we offered the ownership to the chairmen of three of our affiliated associations working in those areas—Mr. Nkosi of the Germiston-based Natalspruit African Taxi Association, Mr. Mlokothi of the Daveton African Taxi Association, and Mr. Sibiya of the Daveton Taxi Association. Soon associated members to the west of Johannesburg began pressing us for their own garage.

Once again, after the garage had opened, I began almost daily trips to Soweto. On occasion I would escort foreign journalists or businessmen. The story of Ma-Afrika fascinated them. Stopping at the bank in Jabulani to have tea and a chat with Mr. Lukojolo, visiting the garage with its long lines of taxis waiting for petrol and other lines of taxis queuing in front of the workshop presented a picture of something they had wanted to see in South Africa: a burgeoning, successful black business enterprise growing with the cooperation of white business expertise.

Now, a year after Ma-Afrika had begun, ostensibly everything looked rosy. But there were many undertones in the inner dynamics of the company that bothered me. There was the ugliness of the internecine taxi warfare: rival taxi associations would hold shootouts, individual taxi drivers would be waylaid and beaten, members of associations would attack "pirate" taxi drivers, those who encroached into territory designated to one association by some unwritten agreement. Men I knew would be killed; others would disappear for months until the "heat" was off. A type of reckless, uncaring violence was never far below the surface. I dismissed the thought that I might be in any physical danger, but whenever I learnt of another taxi war incident, which was frequent, the thought niggled away at me again.

Among the directorship there were constant confrontations over petty jealousies and accusations of thieving or embezzlement. And we did have one major incident of embezzlement. At root, maybe it was the fact that we all lacked business management training and experience. Henry Lukojolo often said sadly to me, when I told him of the problems we were having in directors' meetings, that blacks could never succeed at running a venture like Ma-Afrika because they could not trust one another. He made me angry, and he made me despondent, because I did not want to believe his judgment to be true. Deep down I knew that in the case of Ma-Afrika he was probably correct—the lack of trust among my codirectors was a decidedly negative factor. Too many hours and too much energy had to go into sorting out insults, accusations, slights, and suspicions, cast either in anger or in pained dignity. It was time and energy we needed if we were to build Ma-Afrika. Yet to the outside world we were a success story.

At twice-yearly general meetings of Ma-Afrika the hundreds of taximen present were reasonable and polite, respectful to the chair, and "almost adoring of this unique young white woman who rolled up her sleeves and worked with them in the dust of Soweto," as one magazine article described me. But I knew of the violence that boiled away below the surface calm.

Despite the fact that our meetings always began with a prayer for peace and goodwill, every item on the agenda would produce heated words, threats, almost blows, shouted arguments conducted in Zulu, whose course I could follow only through the body language of the participants. In the African tradition our meetings would go on for hours until a consensus among all parties was reached. Other commitments would often force me to leave the meeting, only to return much later to find the other five still going over the same ground of the argument I had left hours before.

One day I was called to an urgent meeting at the Mobil headquarters in Johannesburg. I arrived to find a serious Mr.

Zwane and our auditors already there. I was dumbfounded as the story unfolded. Apparently Windy and the driver of the Mobil delivery tanker to Ma-Afrika Service Station had succeeded in devising a way of subverting the petrol delivery system. "Illicit" petrol was being sold without any record being registered at the pumps or at Mobil's storage depot. Windy and the driver were sharing the proceeds of these sales.

"I have to give them points for cracking the system. It has been foolproof for years in every country around the world where Mobil operates," Geoff Armstrong said with a grin. He had arrived early one morning at the garage and walked in on Windy and the driver dividing up their spoils.

The board immediately relieved Windy of his responsibilities and his directorship, and afterward he came to my home. It was a sad meeting. He knew of my feeling for him and said over and over that he had let me down.

"Not me, yourself," I told him. Windy had blown his own credibility.

When I asked him why he did it, he simply said it was for the money.

He went to see his family in Kwa-Zulu. A few months later I began to see him forlornly hanging about Bongani's office.

Then he seemed to simply fade out of all our lives.

After the Mdletye incident I was more aware than ever of how we lived on rumours at Ma-Afrika. Bongani was a master rumourmonger. Rumour had it that our membership numbers were stalled because Sejeni, the head of the rival taxi organisation in Soweto, had been telling taximen that the directors were pocketing the share money and not using it for the benefits the taximen had been promised. Rumour had it that Sejeni and Patrick Qwabe were telling people that the garage profits were being used to buy more taxis for the directors. And so on.

Something had to be done to counter Sejeni. Mr. Zwane, a wily survivor in these matters, moved to split the Sejeni-Qwabe team. He started his own rumours about deals that Qwabe had set up for Sejeni, which Sejeni had profited from without giving Qwabe his share. It was not long before Qwabe, with the backing of more than half of Sejeni's members, was approaching us to be taken onto the board.

While Mr. Zwane and the others were playing power politics

among the taxi fraternity in Soweto, I was proceeding in my
way to try to counter the rumours of the directors' private
gains from the company share issue. Henry Lukojolo agreed to
handle all the finances involved in any share transactions for
the company. He was only too happy to oblige me, for this was a
first for him—the first share offer of a black company at the
first black-managed bank. He hoped that the share transactions would be the bait with which to catch the taximan and
educate him in the benefits of personal banking practises.

Henry, Bongani, and I embarked on a series of educative
seminars in most of the townships around Johannesburg—from
Carltonville in the far west to Springs in the east. We explained
about shares, investment, banking, and the life benefit schemes
available to Ma-Afrika members. The seminars were successful, and I enjoyed them. It was for this sort of beneficial educative process that I had joined Ma-Afrika. Once again, our
membership figures began to show a steady increase. Lukojolo
reported a commensurate increase in new personal accounts
being opened at his bank.

Patrick Qwabe became a director of Ma-Afrika. At the time
it seemed a reasonable idea because Qwabe brought with him a
large constituency. There was now no question that Ma-Afrika
had by far a larger black membership than any of its predeces-
sor associations, besides being the only black cooperative in
South Africa.

Patrick Qwabe was an interesting man. He was a fluent
linguist, speaking English, Afrikaans, Zulu, SeSotho, and
Xhosa. He was a good public speaker and a good organiser.
Initially he played a valuable role in the directorship, backing
Bongani in consultations and negotiations with white
businessmen.

Unfortunately, he and I had a personality clash. He was
deeply troubled by my presence, and I found him a threat to my
influence on the other directors and the company. From the
beginning I was suspicious of him. During the initial weeks he
was among us, I watched him sowing dissent between the office
in Johannesburg and the office in Soweto. He cast doubt, suspicion, and mistrust among the directors. First I would have to
smooth Bongani's ruffled feathers because of the things Pat-

rick had said about him to Angela, our receptionist. Then
Milton would call with tales of Goodman's wrongdoings that
Patrick had pointed out to him. Eventually I confronted Patrick in a directors' meeting. In the heated argument that
followed I became so angry with him that I found myself rising
from my chair, storming across the room, and, shaking with
fury, pulling him by his suit jacket collar to his feet. I was
appalled at what I was doing. After apologising to Patrick and
the others, I left the meeting.

Perhaps it was time for me to leave Ma-Afrika. I had finite
amounts of time and energy for the company. If I was to be
spending them in clashes with Patrick Qwabe and not on
positive Ma-Afrika work, then I could no longer justify staying
in the company.

Neither Patrick nor I would back down. Directors' meetings
became coldly civil affairs. I missed the open emotion and
volatility of our previous meetings, and I knew lobbying for
decisions and even decisions themselves were being made out
of meetings.

When I talked over the situation with Dudley King, our
auditor, he advised me to leave.

"You've done what you set out to do. The company is on its
way."

It took me a while to put my decision to resign into action.
While I was procrastinating, Mr. Zwane, Bongani, and I invited Mr. Sejeni to lunch. His cooperation would be another
building block in place. At a subsequent joint meeting it was
agreed that, while our two groups would not merge, we would
also not compete, but respect each others' autonomy.

Mr. Sejeni said that he would encourage his members to join
Ma-Afrika in order to take advantage of the benefits we had
forged for the taximen. Qwabe and Sejeni were reconciled.
Inevitably Mr. Sejeni's name started coming up at directors'
meetings to fill the seventh directorship on the board—a seat
long vacated by the deceased Mannie Sahabodien.

There was also a move to rationalise the whole Ma-Afrika
operation into the garage. Mobil seemed willing to stand the
cost of building additional office accommodations on the same
land for us. The move made sense to everyone but me. The

directors and members lived and worked in Soweto. While the garage was only twelve miles from my house, because of the appalling roads and traffic congestion going into and leaving Soweto, those twelve miles could take me an hour either way. I simply did not have that time to spend on traveling to meetings, to the bank, to fulfilling my other Ma-Afrika duties. I decided I would resign when the office move became a reality.

One evening, while I exhaustedly dozed by the television set, I was called to the telephone.

"Next time you walk into Abbey House, look behind the stairs. There's someone waiting there for you—with a gun."

The guttural words chilled me. From the accent and voice I knew my caller to be a black male with little fluency in English. I tried to engage him in conversation, but he repeated his threat and rang off.

There had been a taxi war in Soweto over the past days, and several people had been killed, including one of Milton's young drivers. Previous politically motivated death threats had not frightened me, but this one did. I knew of too many people with whom my fellow directors had been associated who had been killed in a taxi war not to take this threat seriously. It sounded real to me, the final straw. It was after that call that I decided to quit, effective almost immediately.

Bongani reacted most strongly to my resignation. Of the directors he was the one who saw beyond garages and taxis to what a strong, well-organised Ma-Afrika could symbolise for the advancement of black people in South Africa.

Windy Mdletye then appeared out of the limbo to which he had exiled himself and came to see me. He had found a job as a packing clerk in a warehouse. "It is sad for Ma-Afrika, sad for black people that you are leaving us, Thandiwe." He spoke, as he usually did, in tones of gentle warmth.

I had a picture in my mind of Windy, the confident manager, ordering me to bring him a case of whiskey "to bribe those Boers. Ndlovo will get his work permit by tomorrow." Hercules Ndlovo, one of the few fully trained black mechanics in South Africa, had been refused permission to work for Ma-Afrika in Soweto. The Pass Office official had simply said, "You're a homeland Bantu." A few days after I had produced the case of whiskey, Ndlovo was at work with the precious stamp of permission in his pass book. Windy, the stores clerk, would never display to his white overseer the confidence and authority he had shown to me when he was Ma-Afrika's garage manager.

Henry Lukojolo was much more direct. "Without you Ma-Afrika is dead. You'll see—they'll be fighting among themselves. Black people never trust each other. Black people can never build a business."

"As long as Mr. Zwane is there to talk to all the different factions," I replied, "Ma-Afrika is there."

The white businesspeople we dealt with—Mobil, insurance companies, advertising companies, our spares dealers, others— were openly sceptical of Ma-Afrika's future. Their attitude made me angry. To each I asked the same question:

"If you have only been supporting Ma-Afrika because I was there, what is your attitude to your long-term business future in this country? Either you believe in multiracial enterprise and invest in ventures like Ma-Afrika, or else you see your future tied into the maintenance of white exclusivity with the growing reliance on reactionary white militancy that entails. If you can't have faith in Ma-Afrika without me, you can't have faith in your own future."

In due course the offices at Abbey House were relinquished and Ma-Afrika moved to Soweto. Mr. Zwane became ill, weak, and virtually bedridden. In the ensuing scramble for the chairmanship of the company, Patrick Qwabe and Bongani were forced out of the company. Milton and Goodman fell out with each other over accusations of pilfering of cash. As Bongani had feared, the rivalry between the various taxi association "bosses"—without Mr. Zwane to hold them together—resurfaced. The organisational membership flow systems—of which Bongani and I were so proud—fell into disuse. Ma-Afrika could not meet its debts. Lukojolo refused to extend the overdraft. Mobil stepped into the garage, installing its own management with Mr. Sejeni nominally in charge. Most of the taximen of Soweto—at different times—boycotted the petrol pumps of Ma-Afrika Service Station.

Within six months after I left the company, by mid-1981, three years after it had begun, the high-flying dream of Ma-

Afrika crashed to the ground. At the time I felt saddened, otherwise emotionally numbed. For two-and-a-half years Ma-Afrika had been a daily factor in my life.

Looking back now, I see some of the business reasons why it collapsed. None of us really knew what business we were in, none of us had business management experience, Ma-Afrika grew too quickly, and so on. Even obvious factors like the lengthy travel time to meetings because of the sorry road conditions in Soweto mitigated against our growing successfully.

Ma-Afrika's demise distressed me personally because I had invested so much time and energy and many dreams into its growth. I knew that the business reasons for its demise would be ignored by detractors of the capabilities of black people. Its collapse was seen by white South Africans as an example of the black man's inability to function in the modern western world.

Bongani—entrepreneur extraordinaire—put to his own use the contacts and personal skills he had acquired during his Ma-Afrika years. One of his more successful schemes was to hire a train from South African Railways and rent out compartments in it to Sowetons for long weekends in Durban, the premier South African holiday resort, but off-limits to black people because by law it exclusively offered whites-only hotel accommodation.

In the ensuing years, Bongani and I saw each other often and reminisced of the glory days of Ma-Afrika.

Henry Lukojolo remained a friend. He lived in Alexandra Township and would call on me for assistance whenever he had a "township" problem—drainage, sewerage, unexplained actions by West Rand Administration Board officials. He also asked me to assist him in placing his three adolescent daughters in white convent schools in Johannesburg. (The apartheid government was turning a blind eye to white independent schools admitting black students.) He often visited me and would shake his expressive, sad face into his beer mug while commenting on the difficulty of educating "black people to trust banking."

"How are we going to progress, Jennet, if we can't even trust a bank?"

The road not taken.

I often wonder if I should have divested myself of other commitments and thrown myself wholeheartedly into Ma-Afrika. I almost did at one point—we had people joining Ma-Afrika from Natal, Lesotho, and Botswana, as well as from all around the Johannesburg industrial heartland of South Africa. Our membership was well over two thousand and growing. We had sold many thousands of shares, and the profits from the garage were being used to set up an educational fund for members' children and for many other benefits. Ma-Afrika was on a roll.

Perhaps I held back because of my subconscious knowledge that if I used all my energy to build Ma-Afrika into what I saw it could be, I would be no better than any other white paternalist.

Percy had said that money was power, and on one level he was demonstrably correct. The potential money-making ability of Ma-Afrika garnered great power and influence for the black taximan. It opened doors, it gave us platforms, it brought others with ideas and know-how to our side. But money is also the root of all evil. (My father used to quote this truism from an old song he knew.) And on another level, that was also demonstrably correct. Hatred, jealousy, bitter rivalry, and embezzlement thrust themselves upon us, helping to sow the seeds of our own destruction.

To my knowledge, and the knowledge of Bongani Ngcobo and Henry Lukojolo, there has been no other attempt to build a black business cooperative in South Africa.

Since its demise, Ma-Afrika has been only a name on a garage in Soweto.

Perhaps Ma-Afrika was an idea whose time has still to come.

Perhaps Ma-Afrika was an idea that came too late.

CHAPTER 12
The Floodgates Opened and Ten Thousand Council Workers Poured Out

Money is power, Percy Qoboza said. If he had been talking about the burgeoning black trade unions instead of the beginnings of Ma-Afrika Taxi Ltd., he might have added the corollary that organised labour is power, too—power eventually, perhaps, to bring the apartheid regime to its knees. By allowing black workers to join trade unions for the first time in 1978, the government acknowledged the growing political pressure in the workplace. Through a series of unprecedented wildcat strikes in the seventies black workers had demonstrated their discontent. The government sought to channel and contain that restlessness by legitimizing black trade union activity. It tried to produce a lamb but instead has unleashed an angry lion whose tail lashing and fang baring thus far are, I believe, but a prelude to the worker/state struggles that lie ahead in South Africa.

Many observers in the 1980s see the growing power of the black trade union movement in South Africa as the greatest threat that the apartheid regime has yet encountered. The eighties have seen phenomenal growth in all aspects of the black trade union movement, though thousands of activist

202

unionists have already been jailed. Many union leaders operate from underground, and the movement continues to grow. In Johannesburg much of the impetus for the rising tide of union activism was set in motion in July 1980, when an unprecedented ten thousand black municipal workers went on strike.

The buildup to the strike and the way it was handled by the Management Committee of the Johannesburg City Council were of great significance to the development of the burgeoning black trade union movement. The strong-arm action taken by the police—abetted by management—to break the strike and the fact that the strike could not be settled within the framework of the state's own industrial relations system highlighted the contradictions in the state's industrial relations policies and its intentions toward the black labour force. Of special significance were the findings at the trial held in the aftermath of the strike, in which the state had determinedly, but unsuccessfully, sought the conviction of the municipal workers' "leaders."

What proved true then holds true today: industrial disputes cannot be settled in an atmosphere of state intimidation. As of 1988 over two thousand black trade unionists have been arrested without trial under provisions of the Draconian states of emergency. Many of them are still in prison. Among those arrested were officials of the national Black Municipal Workers' Union (BMWU), which had its beginnings in the Johannesburg City Council and which in Johannesburg, in July 1980, underwent a baptism of fire that thrust it prematurely into the national spotlight.

My involvement in the cause of the strikers held great significance for me. On a personal level it forced me to persevere with the bureaucracy and to take a high public profile in a way I had not been called upon to do before, to achieve my objectives on behalf of the strikers. I felt my cause and the actions I took began to embody aspects of the great liberal precept of freedom of the press, and that precept became real and alive to me in a way it never had before. There is no doubt that our cause would have been lost without the press. In a very real way I gained an intimate knowledge of the great potential for justice of even a relatively free press inside apartheid. Without this essential freedom there can be no truth, no justice, no peace.

That July was to have been a period of rest for me. We had moved into another house in June; though there was much to be done, I enjoyed painting and papering. I imagined it would be a kind of therapy.

Although the council was in recess until August, I still tended to my ward residents' problems. But aside from the upcoming month-end meeting, there were no council or committee meetings to attend. Two years since our founding in 1978, Ma-Afrika Taxi Ltd. was ticking over efficiently. I had taken leave for a couple of weeks, although Bongani called me constantly. There were other matters to attend to, of course— my weekly column, other committee meetings—but I stayed home as much as I could and for the first time in months felt relatively unpressured.

We began redecorating. Painting rooms gave me a sense of achievement. It was Friday, July 25, 1980, a dry, cold winter day with a bright blue sky. At about five-thirty in the afternoon, as I was relaxing with a drink and chatting to the boys, the phone rang. It was an agitated young engineer who worked at the city council's Orlando Power Station on the outskirts of Soweto.

"Councillor, this is Jeff Rabie speaking. I know this call will probably lose me my job, but I have to tell someone who'll do something. Hundreds of our black electricity workers have gone on strike. Already they've been locked out of the compounds. They seem angry. My shift boss boy told me that the strike will spread. They're saying that by Monday no black workers will report to work in the Electricity Department at all."

Another crisis. My heart sank. Jeff Rabie's voice faltered at my noncommittal answer:

"Thank you for telling me. I'll make a few phone calls, find out if there's anything I can do, anyone I can speak to. I'll be careful not to implicate you. Phone me again if you think events warrant it."

It was difficult to rouse myself to make those calls that night, for passively I had decided to let things take their own course.

It was recess—a time to disengage. My mind was not in gear

to cope with this crisis. But by then I knew that at least part of the challenge and excitement of politics lay in the unexpected nature of events, in exactly this type of sudden crisis, this adrenaline rush of new demands. Hindsight shows me that I was also reluctant to engage myself because I was so tired, physically and emotionally. Ma-Afrika was hard work, and there had been other recent crises, including a government clampdown in which, among many others, two of my friends, Mylie Richards and Mohammed Dangor, had been detained. In an emotional confrontation with Councillors Oberholzer and Venter in the council chamber, I had pleaded with the council to intercede with the state for their release. (Around 1976, the powers that be had responded to pressure from the Indian and "coloured" communities in Johannesburg by allowing those communities for the first time to elect their own representatives, who would serve on the so-called Coloured and Indian Management Committees. However, those committees were mere puppets, with as much standing as an ad-hoc committee, an advisory body, to the City Council. Both Mylie and Mohammed were members of the "coloured" committee. Later in 1980, I fought this iniquitous and unfair system and demanded that members of both committees be allowed to take their rightful seats in the City Council. Led by Chairman Oberholzer, the council quashed the proposal.) That July, I felt drained, my energies at a low ebb.

Not being on the Utilities Subcommittee, I had no dealings with the Electricity Department officials. Additionally, although I had spoken in the council chamber on labour relations and the council's 14,500 black employees (out of a total of 20,000), I was not, nor was there, an official party spokesperson on such matters. It was true that the year before I had intervened on behalf of forty-four black artisans who had been fired, and they had been reinstated in the council's service. Rabie had probably called me, rather than anyone else, because of my growing reputation for political fearlessness.

It was clear that I needed time off and therefore, unilaterally, I decided that Rabie's report was probably only of a minor disruption of a local nature that would be sorted out by the officials at the power station. Almost desperately, because I did not want to become part of another drama, I concluded that it was unnecessary to reengage myself.

On Saturday I received a phone call from Winston Hertzenberg, a fellow councillor about my age who did serve on the Utilities Committe. His normally cautious, noncommittal tone was agitated and excited. "I've just heard of the strike at Orlando," he said. "Barnard [the city electrical engineer] has called in the council's security people, and there's been fighting. They've refused to allow the strikers into the compounds to fetch their belongings. They're militant, the strikers, threatening to go to all the compounds and hostels to bring the whole work force out on strike."

"We must do something," he continued. "You speak to Sam. He's well liked and respected. Perhaps the strike leaders will listen to him. You speak to him; he'll listen to you."

Sam Moss was our caucus leader. He was a tall, well-groomed, heavily built man with prematurely white hair. A frustrated actor, he used his leadership role on the stage of local government politics to great effect. Sam and I shared a warm friendship. He respected me, he told me often, for my political courage, my intellect. I respected him for his decency and integrity in the leadership of what was often the gutter of politics. Not many of our colleagues could understand our friendship. In the uneasy conglomeration of the Progressive Federal Party, few others had been forged between a protagonist of the "far left" and a conservative, hardheaded pragmatist of the comfortable "middle."

Shortly after the municipal election of 1977, when I had succumbed to mental and physical exhaustion and was in bed for three weeks, it was Sam—the only one of my "new" colleagues—who came to visit me. On the first occasion he brought me a bunch of freshly cut flowers from his wife's splendid garden. The gesture and the flowers filled me with warmth and joy. Because Sam was my friend, and because I disliked seeming to take advantage of our friendship, I reluctantly agreed to speak to him.

No, he said, he hadn't heard of the strike. And no, he didn't think he should offer to speak to the strikers. "Why should we bail the Management Committee out of a crisis? Let things develop a bit, and we'll discuss it at our caucus meeting on Monday."

"No, Sam, act now," I urged him. "You'll gain credit for the party, perhaps prevent a much larger strike."

"No, I can't act without the caucus."

"Can Winston and I go and find out . . ."

"No, I don't want any of our caucus interfering—and no press statements either." Urbane, avuncular Sam, of whom I was so fond, sounded stern and formidable.

"Okay, suits me. I don't want to get involved . . . but I still think it's the wrong tactic. Someone from our side should have liaison with the strikers."

Unease, which I had been brushing aside, filled me. I knew we should be taking some sort of action. On Monday, with a sense of dread, I finished painting my dining room. In the late afternoon I had an unexpected phone call from Jeremy Keenan, of the University of the Witwatersrand's social anthropology unit. A dark-haired, good-looking Englishman of about my age, Jeremy had married and settled in South Africa. He was an expert on the urban black work force. I was surprised to hear from him, but the purpose of his call was immediately clear. Had I been able to monitor the strike? he asked, because he had information from BMWU field organisers that suggested it was growing at an alarming pace.

"On Friday the six hundred workers on strike at Orlando were joined by eight hundred from van Beeck depot, three hundred transport workers, about five hundred others from the Gogh Street workshop.

"This morning about three thousand workers met at Selby Compound; they've been there all day. My latest information is that about five thousand men are on strike—from electricity, transport, gas, traffic, and sewage."

It was with mounting apprehension that quickly became horrified shock that I heard that figure. This strike drama was looming larger and larger, and I really did not want to be involved. Explaining to Jeremy, whom I knew only slightly through the work he had done during a colleague's election campaign, that I was bound by Sam not to initiate any action, I asked him to come round with the information he had if he felt it to be worthwhile. He came after our caucus meeting that Monday.

It was a revealing meeting for me. I had been unaware of the extent of the ferment among the council's black labour force. The BMWU had been only a vague presence in my mind, an image garnered, among much else, from my quick reading of the mountain of paper I received from the council each Friday. I knew that in recent months, in line with the government's new attitude toward black trade unionism in the wake of the 1979 Wiehahn Commission's recommendations, attempts were being made, both by shopfloor activists and Management Committee stooges, to unionise the Council's black labour force, but I had no idea of the extent of those efforts.

(The council's white workers had been unionised for years. Until 1978 when the first black trade unions were formed, it was illegal for black people to belong to a trade union. The new trade union dispensation for blacks, while a breakthrough for workers' rights, was bound by numerous restrictive conditions. For instance, only those black unions that registered with the government's Labour Bureau and were therefore taken up into the mainstream of the Industrial Court's lengthy, cumbersome settlement procedures were regarded as "legal.")

In the Johannesburg City Council, the Management Committee, while placing obstacles in the way of those trying to organise the BMWU, was trying to woo black workers into the Union of Johannesburg Municipal Workers (UJMW), a "sweetheart" union of its own. A few hundred "stooges" in the Health Department bought the Management Committee's union, but many thousands of labourers, despite the duress, signed up with the BMWU.

Jeremy had been advising a number of black council workers on the organisation of the BMWU, and he filled me in on the history of the union, the key organisers, and the events surrounding the current strike situation. The initial spark had been provided by a wage dispute at the Orlando Power Station.

The council granted increases every July, after the annual budget debate in the council in June. In June 1980 Councillor Oberholzer had said that the council would be paying "equal pay for equal work irrespective of race," effective immediately.

In the case of the Orlando workers, at the top level, although black and white electricians had been put on the same wage scale, the former had been slotted in on the lowest "white" pay scale. The effect was that, although the black electricians had received a wage increase, despite the "equalisation principle," their maximum pay was 590 rand a month, 50 rand less than the minimum pay of their white counterparts' 640 rand a month. The differential was explained by the council as a "proficiency barrier," yet no whites were below that barrier, even those with one month of council experience, while no blacks were above it, even those with ten years of council experience.

On July 1, 1980, the weekly paid workers at Orlando (and elsewhere) found that their 30-rand weekly wage had been increased to only 33 rand. At a meeting called by the Orlando employees, they agreed to strike for a minimum wage of 58 rand a week and that the newly constituted BMWU (the inaugural annual general meeting had been held on June 23, 1980, barely weeks before) should negotiate on their behalf.

At a weekly BMWU executive meeting the Orlando dispute was discussed, and the executives resolved to try to persuade the sixty electricians and six hundred Orlando labourers against striking, while the BMWU approached the council on their behalf. The workers agreed to call a moratorium on the strike until July 24th and gave Joseph Mavi, the president of the BMWU, the mandate to act on their behalf.

The city council refused to meet with Mavi, stating that it would not deal with "an unregistered union." This information was conveyed to the Orlando workers on July 16th. They opted to see what they were to be paid on July 24th. If it was unsatisfactory, they said, they would strike.

The demands of the Orlando workers were not met. Nor had the question of the "equalisation principle" been resolved. About 640 workers downed tools on July 24th.

Jeremy said that what had happened then at Orlando was not yet clear. It was known that the workers were addressed by the Orlando compound manager, Mr. Kleynhans, and by the head of the Electricity Department, Mr. Barnard. Barnard threatened that if all the workers were not back at their jobs in thirty minutes he would "repatriate all the migrant workers and dismiss the rest." Meanwhile the West Rand Administration Board police had been called to Orlando. A police spokesman acted as the liaison and took twenty-two elected "on the spot" members of a "worker's action committee" to Barnard. They demanded equal pay for equal work, a minimum, unskilled pay rise of 25 rand per week (to 58 rand), and an immediate meeting with the Management Committee. Barnard, after calling other council officials, said that the demands could not be met. The talks ended in a deadlock.

The workers refused to return to work without more pay. They were locked out of the compound where all their belongings were stored. Most of them went no further than the veld around the compound to spend the night. In the morning they returned to the compound, which had been secured and was guarded by heavily armed police. Kleynhans told them that if they entered the compound to fetch their belongings "they would be forced to work by the police." The workers told Kleynhans that they wanted to work, but only for more money. They also demanded that the council negotiate with the BMWU.

On that morning, Friday 25th, eight hundred electricity workers at van Beeck compound went on strike "in sympathy" with the Orlando workers, also insisting on a wage hike to 58 rand. By lunchtime Mr. Roberts, the compound manager, told them, "You are all fired."

News came that three hundred workers at the Transport Department "had gone on strike."

Unknown to me (and I found this covert secrecy highly disturbing) and all the other councillors, a secret meeting of the Management Committee had been called on Friday afternoon, at which the town clerk's decision to reject the workers' demands was endorsed.

Over the weekend, as news of the Management Committee's hard-line attitude spread, so did worker anger. On Saturday another four hundred transport workers went on strike. On Sunday eighteen hundred black workers at four of the city's five cleansing depots downed tools.

"In the meantime," Jeremy said, "the council has been busy.

There have been paymasters at all the compounds and buses to take the migrants back to the 'homelands.' They have concentrated on van Beeck compound, trying to break the strike. They have sealed off the compound with police and are blaming the strike on a few agitators, saying that all the other workers at the other compounds have gone back to work. They've threatened workers with a loss of wages, gratuities, jobs. They've said replacement workers are already on the way from Venda and other 'homelands.' "

Jeremy shook his head. "I think they were surprised today that, despite all their efforts, the strike has grown."

I was incredulous at the fact that what I had been hearing from him had been developing under our noses for weeks—and no councillors aside from the Management Committee had any knowledge of the furore. "What now?" I asked him. The situation was taking on alarmingly huge proportions.

If the strike grew in numbers and went on for any length of time, Johannesburg would be paralyzed. Maintenance of essential services—water, electricity, garbage clearance, and the like—would cease. Inadvertently, white Johannesburg would know how black Soweto and Alexandra lived and what Mrs. Nthuli, all those years ago in her crèche in Alexandra, had had to contend with. What really alarmed me, though, was my certainty that the state (abetted by the Management Committee) would intervene and that the police and even the army would be brought in to deal with the strikers. Wholesale killings in council compounds, street battles involving hundreds of innocent bystanders, black and white—I could see it all in my mind's eye. Jeremy was appealing to me. I needed to do something, or prevail on someone else to do something, to prevent the carnage I could see was coming. But I felt so inept and inexperienced. What reaction did Jeremy and others expect of me? What did I expect of myself?

Jeremy continued, "The BMWU is in an extraordinarily difficult position. They've been constituted for only a month. They didn't call a strike. Management Committee won't meet with them. Already Mavi and the other office bearers are being cast as agitators and ringleaders. And the strikers are insisting that only the BMWU can talk for them. Gatsby Mazwi, an executive member, my main contact, tells me that they were able to slip into most of the compounds over the weekend and that the mood of the work force is 'militant and defiant.'

"If the strike grows through tomorrow, the Management Committee, for sure, will call in the South African Police Force. Then . . ." he shrugged his shoulders ". . . there could be bloodshed, misery . . . I'm desperately worried about Mavi and the others." He appealed to me. "Can't you, the PFP, do anything to intervene, to get the BMWU, Mavi, speaking, if only informally, to the Management Committee?"

I hoped Jeremy could not read on my face the consternation that I felt inside me. I had feared something like this request. Now we, the PFP, would be caught out in our impotence. I tried to act coolly and suavely, as though we had gone over this and other possibilities. "My caucus is playing this one cautiously. Sam is going to bring an urgent motion tomorrow at the council meeting asking management to convene a meeting of all concerned and to reinstate all the sacked workers. I'm down to speak, but I won't get a chance. The motion will be overruled." I dropped my voice conspiratorily. "An absurd caucus decision has it that none of us are allowed to talk to the press, only Sam. Obviously I'll tell him what you've told me. Perhaps he'll use it. Otherwise I will in my speech, if I can." I smiled at Jeremy with much more conviction than I was feeling. "Just keep me informed of everything you know. The more information I have that the Management Committee doesn't know I have, nor where I'm getting it from, the more effective I'll be. Okay?"

Jeremy smiled back, his good-looking face relaxing for a moment. He trusted me. "Okay."

Later, reluctantly, I called Sam. I did not want to put him on the spot, but with Jeremy's urgent words ringing in my ears I had to do something. As I anticipated, Sam was not responsive. We had had a rumbustious caucus meeting. He had had to defend me in the face of the baying opposition of some of my blander colleagues, who in true fashion, never wanting to take a stand on anything, were against our becoming involved in the strike at all. They accused me of "using it [the strike] for her own self-glorification."

Sam, a "dove" by inclination, had found himself in the difficult position of having to defend a "hawk" because of his personal loyalty to me.

Cautiously, feeling my way with him, I told him only a little of what Jeremy had told me. I did not want him to be able to put a ban on my using all I knew. Again, I urged him to intervene, to make a public statement. He seemed oddly hesitant and indecisive.

"We've decided in caucus what we're going to do."

"I know, but this is vital new information. You must use it. Won't you please meet with Mavi? The PFP must become actors in this, not idle spectators and commentators."

"No! I won't do anything else without caucus approval. I certainly won't meet with Mavi. What if he is an agitator, being used by some organisation?"

"But you're our leader, Sam; sometimes you must act on your own." There was a moment's silence. Before he spoke I knew I had gone too far.

"Okay, as your leader then, I forbid you to meet with these BMWU people or take any action on your own until the caucus meets again."

"Okay, Sam," I answered, and muttered almost to myself as I put down the phone, "but if things get much worse . . ."

Tuesday I seethed and fretted until the council meeting in the afternoon. Jeremy kept me abreast of developments as he received them. During the morning, striking workers converged on Selby compound, the administrative nerve centre of the council's black work force. By noon the crowd at Selby numbered three thousand men.

That afternoon Keenan received reports from the various departments. Adding up all the figures, it appeared that a frightening 10,000 workers out of a black work force of 14,500 were now on strike. It was worse than I had feared. If the strikers became belligerent when the Management Committee called in the police, as inevitably it would, then we could have a bloodbath in Johannesburg.

Jeremy had been informed that in the morning the Management Committee had travelled secretly to Pretoria to meet the minister of manpower utilisation, Fanie Botha, to brief him on "the strike." Obviously the government was watching the

events closely. In meeting clandestinely with a cabinet minister, the Management Committee had bypassed the government's own industrial conciliation machinery with its courts
and procedures, ironically the very act the responsible minister, Fanie Botha, was later to accuse "the strikers" of.

By the time I spoke to Jeremy from council and received that
information, frustratingly I could not use it, for our motion had
already been overruled. Only Sam had had an opportunity to
speak—briefly.

During this entire period of crisis, true to form, my caucus
was governed in its decision making by one major motivation, a
fear of doing something that could "backfire politically" (in
other words, upset white voters). I found this attitude so alarmingly shallow and inappropriate that I threw caution to the
winds. Supported by one or two other voices during interminable caucus meetings called in the exigencies of this time, I tried
shaming my colleagues into action by berating them, attacking
them, and pushing them into doing something other than feeble
fence-sitting. Inevitably I antagonized many of them and made
the obdurate, fearful ones even more obdurate and fearful.

According to the party political system in South Africa, you
have to abide by a majority decision of your caucus and vote for
that decision no matter how opposed you are to it. Caucus rules
forbid you to vote against your party. To do so means you have
broken with the party and will subsequently resign and wander in the wilderness of political independence. If my one vote
on this issue in council would have made the difference in the
actions the council took, I think I would have broken with my
caucus then. But my vote would have meant nothing in practical terms. Far better to give the case for the strikers a hearing
in the media. From the first moment when Sam Moss would
not speak to the strike leaders, through the cowardly caucus
decision to let only Sam speak for us and the equally cowardly
and shortsighted decision not to take any direct action to
intervene between the strikers and the Management Committee, I was in resolute disagreement with my caucus.

"See you keep your muzzle on," Aleck Jaffe, one of my colleagues, hissed at me, when he could see my seething disap-

pointment at not being able to speak at the council meeting. "Remember, only Sam can make statements on the strike." Later I overheard him telling a chortling third colleague of how he would "get that leftist bitch."

As always, it hurt me to the quick when Jaffe and his ilk deliberately chose to misunderstand my motives and reactions. But I refused to be drawn into their vituperative world. I hoped none of them were ever aware of my hurt—my anger, but not my hurt.

Again, privately, I pleaded with Sam to use the information I had from Jeremy. He was firm. "If necessary, we'll call another caucus meeting on the weekend to discuss further action."

As July council meetings usually are, this one was a short one. It was late afternoon when I returned home and found that Keenan had phoned again.

"It's quiet but tense all over. Jaap de Villiers, chairman of the staff board, has said that all the BMWU executives have been dismissed from the council. They can't set foot on council property. How'd your speech go?" He was devastated when I told him that I had not been allowed to give it and was not allowed to speak to the press.

"Can't you issue a statement?" I asked him as we tried to find a way to publicize the strikers' side of the story.

"No, I can't blow my profile, my fact-gathering ability. Besides, I won't carry any weight. You'll have to, you must. You're the only one with the guts in your caucus to do it."

He was probably right about that. And my earlier reluctance to be involved was giving way to frustration and impatience at the one-sided view the public was receiving of the unfolding drama. The evening's TV and radio news and the newspapers were full of the strike again. The Management Committee and council officials were succeeding in building a convincing case, blaming the situation on "agitators." Joseph Mavi and his executive committee members were being tried and condemned without a word being said in their defence. The inequities of the council's wage structure and the appalling living conditions in the council's hostels, two fundamental causes of worker dissatisfaction, were being ignored.

It was with a heavy heart—for I hated courting the opprobrium of my colleagues, and I hated defying Sam—that I
prepared a press statement.

The telephone rang. It was a senior political reporter from
the *Rand Daily Mail.*

"I hear you have some facts for us on the strike," his imper-
sonal voice asked me. I could have kissed Jeremy. He had found
a way for both of us and the strikers. No one had specifically
told me not to *respond* to the press.

The front-page headline the next morning, Wednesday,
screamed "Many Workers Still on Basic Rates." In the article I
made "startling" allegations about the paltry council black
wage structure and warned of the violence that lay ahead if the
strike was not settled quickly and negotiations entered into
with Mavi and the BMWU. I told the reporter that 12,500 of the
black workers were "daily paid staff," which meant that even if
they had been working for the council for over twenty years
they never received an increment on their basic wage and were
still earning 33 rand a week.

Irene, friend and Houghton colleague, called as I was reading with great glee the newspaper report a little after seven in
the morning. It was the usual time for our almost daily conver-
sations. The satisfaction in her voice echoed my own.

"Jan, well done. I wondered when you would let rip. Keep
after them."

"Thanks. There's much more to tell, but I'm in trouble with
Sam and the caucus. He's the only one who's supposed to make
statements. I've given him the lowdown, but he won't use it."

"Oh, your caucus—forget about them. Keep after Oberholzer
and the others."

"Don't worry, I will. There really is going to be trouble, you
know. Today. I'm frightened that today the Management Committee will set the police loose."

"If you need me to go with you anywhere, call, okay?"

"Thanks, I may need you."

My next caller was a surprise, for the state-run radio service
never interviews opposition figures. It was Christopher Dingle
from the early-morning radio news programme. "A live interview on radio today, Mrs. Levine?"

"Sure."

"By how much would the PFP raise white rate payers' taxes to pay for the increase in black municipal wages you are demanding?"

His unnecessary aggression made me angry. He was fudging the issues again, glossing over the genuine worker grievances. They would be heard. Over the air I attacked the Management Committee's mishandling of the strike and dramatically expounded on the living conditions in the hostels. If it had not been a live interview, the state-controlled radio would never have broadcast it.

Shortly after the interview a reporter from the evening *Star* called. Her report, on the front page that evening, was headlined, "Councillor Pinpoints Reasons for Strike," and in it I am quoted as blaming "medieval living conditions, poor wages, and a paternalistic system of labour representation" for the strike. The article detailed the lot of the workers: twelve men at a time sleeping in a doorless cubicle on cement bunks, cooking where they sleep and keeping their food there in cardboard boxes. I also slammed the present system of worker representation and condemned the Management Committee for not talking to the elected representative leaders of the workers.

The other side of the story was being revealed. It was a good feeling to have helped to open the floodgates.

All morning I continued to receive calls of support. Among them were several anonymous calls from white English-speaking staff of the council congratulating me on my stand. Many of them said that they had documented evidence of numbers of unfair dismissals of black staff, that there was mass confusion in the compounds, that many of the black workers could not go to work because of the confusion and because of threats by other black workers and white officials. Some black workers did not even know a strike was on. In response to my request, they said that once "the dust had settled" they would call me with their "documentation." They duly did so.

Four reporters from the Afrikaans press called, as did the deputy editor of the black daily *Post*. The *Post* report was run on the following day with a banner headline: "Jo'burg Strike Blamed on 'Medieval Hostels.' "

Somewhere in between these calls, Jeremy Keenan called, delighted with his ruse to allow me to speak to the press. But he was not so delighted with the morning's developments. The police had cordoned off all the compounds where workers were housed so that crowds could not congregate at Selby as they had on the previous day. Council officials were touring the compounds with representatives of "homeland" governments, telling the workers to return to work. One "homeland" leader had been overheard saying, "The workers are unlikely to respond to 'homeland' representatives." The workers refused to return to work without more pay.

The afternoon was less frantic, and I began to worry about the reaction of Sam and the caucus. To phone him would be unduly defensive, I decided. But the silence was beginning to deafen me, especially because I knew that his phone would be ringing off the hook as my irate "colleagues" tried to harangue him when they really wanted to be attacking me.

Jeremy called again that evening, sounding pleased. "Tomorrow's the day. They've all stood firm. They've agreed that if some are to be fired tomorrow, they'll all be fired."

The strike was broken on Thursday, July 31st. Under police guard at all the compounds, groups of workers were asked if they wanted to return to work. Most replied that they did but that they wanted more money, and they were taken back to their compounds. As the day wore on, the men were not given a choice but had their pass books stamped with a "Strike Dismissal" notice. Thousands of workers were kept overnight in the abandoned City Deep Hostels, prior to being forced to board buses to the "homelands" in the morning. "Next time," one worker who had spent ten years with the council said, "the police will just shoot us straight."

On Thursday morning I received a phone call from an unidentified person who said he was an executive member of the BMWU, was on the run, and wanted to meet with me urgently. My first response was one of distrust and suspicion. It was a trap. Then, responding to the urgency in his voice, I agreed to a meeting. My heart was racing. "On the run"—if ever I was in the mood to grapple with the Security Police, it was then. I think I would even have welcomed a confrontation.

"Where?"

"SACC offices in Braamfontein?"

"Okay, fine. I'll be there in twenty minutes."

Outside Diakonia House, where the South African Council of Churches had its offices, my adrenaline racing, I paused and looked around for men who could be from the Security Police. Any number of men walking by would fit the bill. Stop being ridiculous, I chided myself; you're not breaking the law. You're doing your duty as you see it as a public representative of this city at a time of crisis.

Although I did not know him well, I felt relief when I spotted Bishop Desmond Tutu, looking his usual dapper and unruffled self, waiting for his car on the steps of Diakonia House. I went to greet him. We had met several times before at various functions and sat together on protest platforms over the years. We chatted for a moment about the strike. Then he blessed me, raising his hands to my shoulders, his eyes calm behind his glasses. His matter-of-fact manner helped to quiet my nerves.

Martin Sere and Gatsby Mazwi, two young BMWU office bearers, were waiting for me in the office of a German priest who had been doing fieldwork in South Africa. He left us alone. Both men looked dishevelled and edgy. It was the first time I was seeing either of them. Now that I was actually with them, face to face, I was extremely curious as to what they wanted from me.

"They've called the police in today. They're rounding up the workers, putting them on buses for the homelands." Sere spoke first, impatiently.

"We've told them to come back to Jo'burg as soon as they can." Mazwi was calmer, quieter. "We want to thank you for what you've done for the workers." Their gratitude felt good: it had been difficult for me to stick my neck out as I had.

"We haven't much time; we must keep moving. The Security Police are at our office, at our homes. It's about Mavi we want to talk to you."

"Mavi," said Sere, "they want Mavi. They want us to get at Mavi. If they get him, they'll keep him in solitary, torture him. Can you get Oberholzer to speak to Mavi?"

There it was. A simple request, much the same as Jeremy had made only days earlier. The head of management to speak "off the record" to the head of the trade union representing the majority of his workers. As a member of the board of directors, so to speak, I should have access to the chairman.

Sadly I shook my head, the chasm of all that racism meant inside apartheid yawning before me. "There is no way Oberholzer or any of the Management Committee will meet with Mavi or any of you. And especially not if the request comes from me. All I can suggest is that you get Mavi to go to a lawyer to advise him. I'll phone Ernie Wentzel if you like; he'll talk to Mavi. He's a friend and the best civil rights lawyer in South Africa."

Sere and Mazwi looked beaten. They had been pinning their hopes on me. It embittered me that I could not be the miracle worker they had wanted me to be.

To them I was a voice of reason and understanding from the other side of the divide, the "white" side, despite the fact that in theory anyway we all worked for the same body. To them I was representative of authority in the Council, executive office on an elected basis. The white electorate in my constituency had for the past twenty-five years been a voice of reason and hope for moderation in our country. The matrix of their expectations of me included a faith in that reasonable voice. But I could do nothing practical for them in their moment of greatest crisis. I could not bring Mavi and Oberholzer together. Perhaps the political exigencies that dictated that reality were what embittered me. Perhaps, because the gulfs between us were so enormous that a miracle was truly what was needed to bridge them, I felt as beaten as they looked.

"No, it's all right. Mavi has a lawyer who's been working with the union. He's met with him already. He says he should give himself up." Sere looked at Mazwi. "Well, Mrs. Levine, we must go. Thank you for your trouble to meet us."

We shook hands, and they left the office. The German priest returned, and we spoke briefly about the strike. I felt dispirited and empty.

Late on Thursday night Mavi came out of hiding. He was seized while he was waiting with other BMWU executives and the union's attorneys at the Supreme Court. They were there to bring an urgent application against the Johannesburg City Council and the South African Police Force, restraining them from taking unlawful actions against the workers.

Jaap de Villiers, the chairman of the staff board and the head of the council delegation seeking to discuss the restraint order with the union's lawyers, greeted Mavi.

"Yes, Mavi."

"Yes, Mr. de Villiers," Mavi replied.

De Villiers, knowingly, was being followed by plainclothes policemen who were waiting for Mavi to return the greeting so that they could identify him. Mavi was taken into detention.

On Friday, a cold, misty morning at around six o'clock, I stood in the still quiet street outside of the forbidding brick hostels in Selby compound on the outskirts of downtown Johannesburg and watched the men being forced onto buses that would take them to their "homelands." Many heavily armed policemen, most of them black, stood by, pulling and restraining snarling police dogs. The dismissed workers were sullen and subdued. There was an eerie silence as they shuffled in long lines to the buses. Then the police, some still with their dogs, boarded the buses, too. I watched the convoys drive off. A cluster of white council officials monitoring the departure of the workers looked suspiciously at me. I could see they were talking about me. Several reporters came to speak to me, but I had nothing to say. So I stood alone and watched, dejected yet with a deep anger eating away inside me.

Some of the men had been taken to the various compounds first to collect their belongings. Press reports tell of how other council workers, supervised by council officials, loaded hundreds of garbage bags crammed with possessions onto trucks that were driven away. Press photographers recorded many of the workers' belongings spilling onto the roadway.

By noon the buses had left and the eight-day strike was crushed. Those workers who remained behind said they would return to work, but they still demanded more money. As the piles of stinking garbage were being cleared from city and suburban streets, Councillor Oberholzer emphasised in triumph that there would be no negotiations with workers about pay: "Next time we discuss wages will be next year when we draw up the budget."

The weekend was quiet for me—a lull. Sam had called an urgent caucus meeting for Sunday evening to discuss the strike situation. Aleck Jaffe asked for an item to be placed on the agenda censuring me for breaking the caucus ruling on press statements. Before he could begin his argument, Winston Hertzenberg spoke against the item being discussed at all. He argued that my statements had been taken from the speech I was prevented from giving in the council chamber and said that the press had the speech in hand before the meeting. I knew that he knew that I gave out copies of my speeches only after I had delivered them. Obviously, I was grateful for his intervention.

"How can we sit here wasting time discussing a courageous stand by a colleague who has brought great credit to our party? We should be talking about the Management Committee and their Nazi tactics. Let's talk about what we're going to do about them, rather than waste time on Janet."

Aleck looked like a limp sail that had suddenly lost its wind. As surprised as he, I managed to keep my poise. I had been apprehensive anticipating the bitter acrimony that often surfaced against me in caucus infighting. The caucus chairman looked around the room for consensus with Winston and ruled that there be no further discussion on that item.

Then, after a long debate on the Management Committee's actions, the caucus agreed to ask the town clerk to call a meeting of "urgent public interest," under a provision in the standing orders of the council, to discuss the Management Committee's handling of the strike. The town clerk set the date for August 12, 1980.

Jeremy Keenan's calls all but ceased during the week after the strike. His sources of information had dried up. Most of the BMWU executives were in detention on various charges of industrial sabotage or finding their way back to Johannesburg after the enforced journey to the "homelands."

On Thursday, August 6th, Graham Brown, a *Rand Daily Mail* reporter, called me.

"Have you been to see the men at Priscilla Jana's office yet?"

"No . . ."

"Meet me there then, later this afternoon? I think you should see what's going on. Hundreds of sacked workers back from the 'homelands.' They're giving affidavits claiming unfair dismissal, loss of possessions, so on."

"Sure. Thanks for the tip-off."

"You know where her offices are?"

"Yes, Abbey House. I know the building well. Ma-Afrika, our taxi cooperative's offices, are a floor above hers."

Again, I was incredulous at what was happening and that I had no knowledge of it. It struck home to me again what a deeply divided society we were. Priscilla Jana, an Indian woman, was an attorney, and her legal practise acted as counsel to the BMWU. A lifelong opponent of apartheid, at the time of the strike she was herself operating under a five-year banning order that had been imposed on her in 1977. One of the constraints of her banning order was that she could not be in a room with more than one person at a time.

"So pleased you've come to see for yourself." She took my hand warmly between both of hers. She was a plump woman of about my height, ten or so years older than I. Her black-grey hair was pulled into a dishevelled bun at the back of her head. Her expressive dark brown eyes looked quizzically at me. She wore a brightly coloured sari.

"You're doing a great job," she said to me.

People like Priscilla humble me. She was a frontline activist in the struggle who had spent most of her adult life under punitive state control, and yet she displayed no bitterness toward someone like me who, by her standards anyway, was a voyeur of the struggle.

"What's going on here?" I asked her. We looked at the mass of people in her rooms.

"Many stories of police brutality. We expected that—" she shrugged her shoulders—"but city council collusion, no. We are working on an argument that because the strike was never called, all the dismissals are unfair. Walk around, take notes for yourself. It'll be good material for you."

She winked and motioned me out of her cubicle, allowing another young clerk to enter. Priscilla had told me that she knew of a Security Police informer in her practise. It suited her, she said, to have him there, because it stopped the Security Police from wasting her time either in court or in detention. The informer knew she kept to the letter of her banning order and was never with more than one person at a time.

The corridor and all the office space of her rooms were jammed with men. They were black municipal employees who had been forcibly bused to the "homelands." Now, only days later, they were returning to Johannesburg determined to be reengaged in the council's employ and to seek redress for the loss of their personal possessions. Young legal clerks—black, white, Indian—were moving from group to group writing busily.

As in the aftermath of the clashes in Soweto in 1976, when the taking of affidavits proved effective in gaining compensation for victims of "unnecessary police action," so now, in the aftermath of the smashing of the strike, affidavits would prove effective in gaining compensation for personal losses due to "unnecessary" police action.

Graham Brown was squatting on his haunches across the reception area, talking to some of the workers. He waved his notebook at me.

"Mrs. Levine," a young woman drew my attention, "just listen to some of these stories!"

As I listened and took notes, moving from group to group, I became more and more incensed. Graham's report in the *Rand Daily Mail* on the dismissed strikers' plight the next day was slight, having been edited away to make space for other news. My anger was growing. Somehow those affidavits had to be made public knowledge. Suddenly a thought snapped into my head: use them in your speech for the special meeting. Of course. The speech I wrote for that meeting was inspired, written for me by whatever it was that was driving me at the time—outrage, a sense of justice, an urgent need to be up and doing at this time of crisis. I have never since experienced the feeling I had preparing that speech. And I burned to deliver it.

Tuesday night came. For once, the public gallery was packed. Sheena Duncan and other observers from the Black Sash were there. Ina Perlman and other Institute of Race Relations members were there. Some PFP parliamentarians were there, and many PFP members were there, including most of my Houghton colleagues. The press gallery was full. Members of the diplomatic corps sat in a specially assigned area. Sandy made a rare appearance at a public meeting where

I was speaking. Irene could not be there, which saddened me—
I knew that the night belonged to the strikers and to me.

Waiting to speak was agonising. I asked the whips to let me
speak early, but we were following a strict order of seniority.
As I was still in my "rookie" term, I had to wait until five other
people on my side had spoken.

Most of them spoke in platitudes. They all refrained from
attacking the Management Committee too vehemently. "After
all," I had overheard one of them saying, "what would we have
done if we had been in management?" The six members of the
Management Committee, who had looked grim at the beginning of the meeting, were relaxing, sitting back in their chairs.
Oberholzer was beginning to exchange jokes with Gerrit Bornman, head of the Transport Department, and Venter.

Finally I was on my feet, the first of the newer councillors to
speak. Never before or since have I felt as I did when I began
that speech. The blood seemed to be pounding in my head. I
wondered if I would be able to speak to the end. In a low,
intense voice, turning around in order to face the Management
Committee, I began. Minutes into my speech you could have
heard a pin drop in the cavernous council chamber. None of the
members of the Management Committee lifted their eyes off
their desktop for the thirty-five minutes that I spoke:

> I condemn and censure the Management Committee for its
> arrogance, its shortsighted insensitivity, its disregard for peo-
> ple, and the suffering its strong-arm tactics have brought to
> thousands of our workers and their families. . . .
> . . . Let me give you a few examples of individual cases of
> workers I spoke to last week. And what I tell you is contained in
> sworn affidavits. And if you bluster once again and deny what I
> say, I challenge you all to come with me in the morning to see the
> affidavits and speak to the workers. . . .
> . . . Mr. B is a bricklayer. He is a skilled artisan. He has
> worked for the council for twenty-two years. He did not go on
> strike. He slept at his job in Lenasia because he is a family man
> and did not want to risk losing his gratuities and pension. On
> Thursday, July 31st, he went to Selby compound because he had
> heard "that things were being sorted out there." They certainly
> were! He was herded into a queue, given a number, called into an

office, and told he was being a "cheeky kaffir" when he protested that he had been at work. He went back to the depot at Klipspruit on Monday morning, but despite his supervisor's efforts he has not been reinstated. This is a blatant case of unfair dismissal.

Also at Klipspruit I know of four labourers with long service awards who have been dismissed. Does their loyalty count for nothing? They have been dismissed with no prospect of employment. By your crass insensitivity, you have condemned them to an old age of starvation in the "homelands."

A senior official in the city Engineers' Department, who, with a number of his colleagues, strongly disapproves of what you are doing and has asked me to say so, told me that your attitude is "rather to fire ten who did not want to strike than employ one who did." Refute that if you can, Mr. Oberholzer.

... Mr. E is a thirty-year-old Transkeian. He joined the council in 1970 as a R9.64-a-week garbage collector. He now earns R33 a week. Mr. E is married and has two children. At Orlando on July 24th, he and many others were told by Mr. Barnard that they had been fired. Despite returning to Orlando every day subsequent to that, he and all the others were barred from the hostel and their belongings.

At Selby, where he was taken by bus on Thursday, July 31, he was paid off and given a "72-hour" stamp by WRAB officials in his pass book. Since when is the council an agency for WRAB? But there is another question. Mr. E attests to "rough handling by the police with rifle butts and batons." He says he was "very frightened."

He was then put on a bus and taken back to Orlando, where six people were sent into the hostel in order to verify that there were no possessions there. They returned to tell the others that their lockers' locks had been cut through with bolt cutters. They were told that all their belongings were at City Deep compound.

The bus proceeded to City Deep, where Mr. E was put into a room for 80 people with 120 others. There was little ventilation and no room to lie down. They were not given their belongings. In the early morning Mr. E asked if he could go to the toilet. He was told by a white traffic officer of this city, on guard duty, "Kak sommer daar langs jou kaffir broers." (Crap there next to your kaffir brothers.) What of these acts of inhumanity, Mr. Bornman?

In the morning Mr. E was given a plastic garbage bag with his belongings. He then underwent an uncomfortable twenty-two-hour journey to the Transkei under police escort. Stops were infrequent, and no food or drink was provided.

Mr. E returned to Johannesburg immediately to look for work and "to find the missing money and clothes that were not in the plastic bag."

I accuse this Management Committee of acting malevolently and in panic in dealing with the dismissed workers. I abhor the way in which people have been affronted and humiliated. These cases tell their own story.

I call for the unconditional reinstatement of all workers and ask that no retrenchment be carried out in this ad hoc and blatantly unjust manner. . . .

. . . If it were not so sad, it would be laughable. Do you think you are dealing with innocent children? The men know whom they want to represent them. Your black works committees and your "sweetheart" trade union have come to a dead end. . . .

By your actions over the last weeks, you, the Management Committee, have written a shameful chapter in the history of this city. You have much to do to restore our good name. I hope you have the courage and goodwill to begin now, for, if you fail in this, you fail all the people of Johannesburg.

A burst of applause from the public gallery greeted the end of my speech, quickly hushed by the chairman of the council—the mayor. But my PFP colleagues continued to applaud. It was a rare moment of unanimous support from them. I was exhausted as I sat down, as if I had run a long race, but I exulted in the applause.

In their reply to the debate, not one member of the Management Committee referred to my speech—the surest sign of a victory scored on behalf of the workers. For even if the Management Committee took no remedial action (which it would not), the case for the strikers had been made, and the committee had no answer. A somewhat hollow victory perhaps, but without my speech the truth may never have been known at all.

Roger and Tony, our sons, had a half-term holiday the weekend after the special meeting, and we went to Sunnyside for three days. It was only when I was lying on a sun-warmed rock alongside a gushing mountain stream, with the mountain peaks soaring around me and the valleys and plains laid out below, that I realised how tense and emotionally spent I was.

Sandy was concerned about me. But we agreed that I had to continue with the roller coaster ride the strike had become for me. I could not climb off while it was rushing relentlessly along its way.

CHAPTER 13
When the Migrants Awake

There was no letup when I returned from holiday. While I was away the *Rand Daily Mail* ran on the editorial pages a major report by Jeremy Keenan tabulating the inequities of the council's black wage structure. Jeremy quoted me as a primary source of his documentation.

The publicity brought me a slew of speaking invitations on the strike, mainly from the business and financial sectors of the community. Interestingly, I was invited to speak to a number of young Afrikaner professional organisations, one of them PEIL '80 (Arrow '80), a group of professional managers mainly in their thirties. Even when it was young urban professionals, anyone in the Afrikaner community wanting to listen to a "left-wing radical" point of view surprised me.

Together with the Black Sash I put out a report on the strike, concentrating on conditions of service in the council. The Sash was particularly struck by the fact that most of the workers— even if they had been in the council's service for many years— each year had their contract renewed at the basic wage. The Sash's report also contained these findings:

. . . we have learned that the migrant labour system and the pass laws make it impossible for workers to organise successfully and to press their demands. Once striking workers have been dismissed, endorsed out, and returned under police escort to the bantustans whence they came union organisation is broken into hundreds of pieces and calls for reinstatement become meaningless. . . .

We pointed out that conditions were no better in the public sector anywhere in the country. In fact, appalling as it was, the Johannesburg City Council was among the best employers in the public sector. I worked on a similar report with researchers at the Institute of Race Relations.

But we did not have the field all to ourselves. Here are some statements made by Chairman Oberholzer:

"The root cause of the strike is not wages. Power is what they want. What they will do with it when they get it is another question. I think they will use it as a political instrument."

Oberholzer denied that "those who refuse to work have been deported to the homelands. The workers themselves have asked to go home."

"They all returned to work willingly, and those who wanted to go home were paid off."

"A noticeable aspect of the strike which became evident was that the stoppage was not based on any important grievance or set of grievances. It was, however, associated with such strong and well-organised intimidation that the public could conclude some powerful organisation was behind the strike. . . ."

"Suddenly and without warning the council was faced with a strike. No prior demands had been submitted to the Management Committee for its consideration. It must be the first time in the history of labour disputes that a union negotiated with its employers through the medium of certain newspapers, with their inevitable slanted and sensational reports. . . ."

"Everything possible has been done to make the workers comfortable. The council is a model employer."

In the aftermath of the strike, I suppose because in their eyes I had been a central figure in the drama, I was asked by the people I had worked with before—Priscilla Jana, the Black Sash, the Institute of Race Relations, and the BMWU itself—to continue to monitor events and work on the cases of the return-ing "dismissed" workers. Perhaps because of my undeniable involvement, my council colleagues, with a resigned equanim-ity, allowed me to be cast as their "spokesperson" on the strike—Oberholzer's obvious disagreement with me notwithstanding.

Although it was a major demand on my time, I felt more comfortable dealing with this sort of administrative process than I had with the exigencies of the strike crisis itself. And I really cared about the workers who returned being reinstated in their jobs. Based on my own figures and figures from the council, I estimate that over three thousand workers were reinstated out of about seven thousand who were dismissed. I was as anxious as ever to bring to the public's attention any unjust dealings by the Management Committee with council workers. Sometimes, though, I had negative feelings about the overwhelming responsibility and my own inadequacy for the task. The livelihood of so many workers, and thus the lives of their dependents, rested on my approach to the authorities.

The lack of communication between employer and employee appalled me. It seemed that I was the only "trusted" conduit to the bureaucracy.

It was an issue I returned to again and again in council debates, urging the Management Committee to set up a negoti-ating process with the "legitimate" elected representatives of the workers. But the Management Committee persisted in recognizing only its "sweetheart" union, whose membership numbered a couple of hundred compared with the ten thou-sand of the BMWU. In casting around for models of negotiating practises to present to the Management Committee, I turned to other sectors of the economy and was dismayed to find that few existed. The only models I could find were in some of the more progressive mining houses, and even those were ad hoc, in the process of being formulated and put into practise through trial and error.

Having, almost inadvertently, gained the reputation of liai-son, at least with the BMWU, not a week went by in the next four years, from September 1980 to January 1984, and even in the months after I had resigned from the council, when I did not have at least one visit from a black city council worker with a work-related grievance.

The men would be ushered into my study by Annah Kelefetswe, my housekeeper. Sitting uncomfortably opposite me, they would tell me their tales in halting English.

Many of them could not speak English, and Aaron Dube, my gardener, would interpret for them. Aaron, a Zimbabwean by birth, spoke, besides English, seven southern African languages—his native Nguni, plus Shangaan, Zulu, Xhosa, SeSotho, Southern Sotho, and Ndebele.

"Only the Venda language escapes me, Mrs. Levine," he would say. "It is the language of the wizards and the mountains."

I think Aaron enjoyed his pivotal role in my communication with the workers. He never commented directly on what I was doing, but he was always cooperative and willing to help, even during those times of the day when workers would come to see me and he was off-duty.

If we had a non-English-speaking Venda worker in my office, Simon Modiba, another African linguist who did speak Venda and was in the employ of Gita Dyzenhaus, a Black Sash stalwart living down the road, was summoned to assist.

Annah's reaction, from the perspective that she was a black worker herself, interested me. When she could see that I was exhausted, she would encourage me by saying, "These people have no one else to speak to, Miss Jan. Even if you can only listen, you are doing good for them."

The men themselves never offered direct comment and observations on their interactions with me. They seemed passively accepting of their lot.

In the beginning there was a deluge. The hard-pressed office staff at the BMWU offices, legal workers at Priscilla Jana's office, workers at the Black Sash Advice Offices, and other labour organisations sent the names of "dismissed" workers, or the workers themselves, seeking reengagement, to me.

As I was a councillor, city council officials were obliged to follow up and reply to my correspondence. After establishing lines of communication with Jaap de Villiers, the chairman of the staff board, and Eric Hall, the chief city engineer, I worked for hours every day, writing individual letters to the relevant department heads on behalf of every worker who approached me.

My list of hundreds of names, with notes next to each one, grew: "not on strike, but dismissed," "lost all pensions," "dismissed, pension due next year."

The following exchange of letters is typical of the correspondence I undertook on behalf of the workers.

21st August, 1980
Mr. Hall—City Engineer,
Johannesburg City Council

Dear Sir,

Herewith an additional list of names of men seeking reinstatement. They were all previously employed at Orlando. Could you please let me know the outcome of your investigations.

Yours sincerely,
Janet Levine (CLR)

[Attached was a list of forty-four names and information relating to the workers.]

The reply:

Employee Reengagement

Dear Councillor Levine,

I refer to your letters of 11, 12, 21 (two letters) and 26th August, 1980, connected with the above matter and have to advise as follows:

[Pages of lists of names were attached, with the notes "Not reengaged," "Engaged," "Being investigated," "Referred to Electricity Department," and so on.]

The outcome of investigations not yet finalised, in respect of employees of this department, will be advised to you in due course.

It was the best I could do. I would contact the people at the various offices that had contacted me and ask them to contact, if they could, the worker and pass on the outcome of my petition to the council.

It often seemed a frustrating experience in futility, and as usual, the strike was not all I was involved with at the time. As an interesting record of what else was happening in my life on the periphery of this racing whirlwind, I have a scrap of telephone memo paper with the names of people who called me during one of those days. Looking back, I find it wryly amusing.

- Mrs. T. Graham (a friend and also the coconvenor of a number of programmes involving children in Soweto)
- Granny Levine
- Robin (Robin Harvey, another friend and a Black Sash stalwart)
- Mrs. Suzman from Cape Town (Helen in Parliament)
- Roof Modernizers (Our roof was leaking, and I was collecting quotes to have it repaired.)
- Granny Berman
- Mr. Adler, Fosatu (Taffy Adler, the secretary of the black Federated Union of South African Trade Unions. I had called him for labour law advice.)
- Bongani, Abbey House, Ma-Afrika
- Mr. Zwane, Ma-Afrika garage, Soweto
- Mr. Lukojolo, Standard Bank, Jabulani (Obviously, something was happening with Ma-Afrika that day.)
- Mr. Groenewald, city council (an official returning my call in connection with a rate payer's complaint)
- Irene, PFP, Ivy Road

A month later, in September, I sent my annual report-back letter to my constituents. On the strike I wrote:

... we are in the aftermath of the strike by ten thousand of the City Council's black workers. I believe that nothing constructive can be achieved until the Management Committee of this city is prepared to sit down and talk to representatives the workers have elected to articulate their point of view. Repressive action leads only to bitterness, resentment, and a hardening of attitudes. . . .

The letter echoed some of the despair I was feeling: a double-edged sword of despair. On the one hand I felt overwhelmed and unable to really cope with the sheer weight of numbers of black workers who needed to have their cases processed. On the other hand I felt almost desperate, certainly frustrated that the Management Committee was letting go by a unique opportunity to develop pioneering public-sector labour practises. It disturbed me deeply that in the aftermath of the strike the committee clung so obdurately to its previous stances. I used every avenue to make my views known.

One ward resident wrote in response to my letter:

> . . . Thank you for your report-back letter, which I received last week. It is given only to the very few to wear the mantle of a Socrates, and I think you have done wonders through your courage and integrity in standing up to the wealth and power of the Establishment. . . .

It was a welcome indication that there were other whites out there who felt as I did.

Also in September, I delivered a letter to the town clerk with nine affidavits from men who had been dismissed unfairly. I called on him to appoint a commission of inquiry into the Management Committee's handling of the strike. I knew, however, that the town clerk would have nothing to do with a commission of inquiry, so making the affidavits public was the only way I could air the genuine claims of unfair dismissal of the workers. I released the letter to the press, which splashed these headlines across the papers:

"Call to Investigate the Plight of Fired Workers"

"Willing Workers Fired—Councillor"

"Dismissed Workers Protest"

Then, in October, the Management Committee, using taxpayers' funds, brought out a scurrilous newsletter defaming the BMWU and praising its own handling of the strike. Once again, I seemed to be the only one prepared to oppose the committee. More headlines:

"Official Newsletter Comes Under Fire from Levine"

"Call for Probe into Council Newsletter"

" 'Our City' Letter May Be Probed by Council"

"Council Sends Out Disputed Newsletter"

"Row Threatens over Council Newsletter"

The articles under these headlines conveyed my intention to challenge assertions made in the newsletter, even though I knew I might be prevented from doing so in view of Joseph Mavi's impending trial, affixing a sub judice label to all matters pertaining to the strike.

That month I introduced a motion in the council calling for an investigation into the council's black wage structure and hostel accommodation. I also urged the Management Committee to look at its whole labour relations structure. Councillor Oberholzer's response, reported by the press, was surprising:

> . . . Mr. Oberholzer said that providing the BMWU became registered . . . the management committee would be prepared to negotiate with it.
>
> . . . Mrs. Levine said after last night's meeting that she believed Mr. Oberholzer's statements were a significant breakthrough and also a welcome departure from the Management Committee's previous viewpoint. . . .

We were making progress, if only from a public relations viewpoint, and even that slight advance pleased me and made me feel less beleaguered. For I did not have time then to sit back and reflect on what I was doing and where I was going. It took all my energy and resolution simply to keep my head down and plod on from task to task, demand to demand.

Also that month, a reporter from *The Citizen*, the government's English-language mouthpiece in Johannesburg, came to do an interview with me. Her approach from the "enemy" camp was a surprise to me. I regarded her newspaper so negatively that at first I was reluctant to speak to her. But colleagues persuaded me to make use of the platform to reach a segment of the public that dismissed people such as me as raving radicals. When the article appeared, I had another surprise, this time a pleasant one.

"The Progfed Who Is a Political Fireball" was the banner headline, and the article ran across an entire page. The caption under my photograph read "Janet Levine—concerned about people."

> Janet Levine from newspaper clippings appears to be a political fireball who pursues causes relentlessly.
>
> . . . Those who don't like her politics say she sounds "hysterical." She is a thorn in the flesh of her political enemies, or those who don't see things her way.
>
> . . . "I suppose you could call me 'a fighter.' I know that wherever I see injustice I feel compelled to try to implement changes."
>
> A devoted wife and mother, she nevertheless has the politician's immutable inner core and cast-iron will. A ruthless hounder of the root causes of misery, she is a woman who enjoys demonstrating her concern for others . . . and has campaigned tirelessly to have the dismissed black municipal strikers reinstated in their old jobs. . . .

The article in some measure made me feel good about myself. It vindicated my frenetic political activity: I was not working in a vacuum. I was breaking through to the public consciousness. And the higher my public profile, the higher the profile of the causes for which I worked.

In October too, after anticipating it for a long time, I finally met Joseph Mavi. Mavi had been released from detention on bail. After initially charging him under the Sabotage Act, which carries a minimum five-year jail term and a maximum penalty of death, the state dropped the charges and replaced them with charges under the Black Labour Relations Regulation Act. The case was set for February 1981.

Joseph Mavi was introduced to me at my house by another BMWU executive member, Gatsby Mazwi. Gatsby and I had come to know each other well during the weeks since the strike as he worked with me in our efforts on behalf of the workers.

Gatsby was a slight, short whippet of a man. In contrast, Joseph Mavi was a tall, straight-backed, handsome man in his mid-fifties. His long, ebony face seemed sculpted, and his bearing was dignified. It was the warmth of his smile and handshake and the gentle humour in his eyes that first drew me to him. He sat relaxed in my study, and after thanking me for the work I was doing for his union members he spoke of many things in his life: his childhood and education in the Transkei, his early career in the city council, his later experiences in civic and labour organisations, his job in 1964 as one of the council's first black bus drivers.

The Management Committee's reaction to him is perhaps the surest sign of the quality of Joseph Mavi's leadership. The reactionary ideologues found in all reaches of South Africa's vast state-controlled bodies and bureaucracies regard any black person who displays leadership ability and initiative with deep suspicion and open hostility and label him a "cheeky kaffir." Mavi was one such leader who from early in his employment at the city council felt the ire of his white superiors. His career record shows a steady and growing involvement in organising workers as an articulate leader. In 1977 he was elected to the Transport Department's black works committee. From there it was a logical step to begin organising the Black Municipal Workers' Union with his Transport Department co-workers, Mazwi and Dhlamini, when in 1979 it became legal to do so.

Joseph and I became friends, and he came often to visit in the ensuing months. "There is only one thing wrong with our country," he would say. "This apartheid government. Without this government we could be a great nation, a Christian nation. For this is God's country. God wanted to be here once, that's why He made it such a beautiful place."

Joseph was deaf in one ear and had an endearing way of turning the right side of his head toward me. He had been beaten and tortured during his recent detention, and the deafness in his left ear and the partial lameness of his left arm were the outer marks of his torture. Yet he was not bitter. He said of the government: "It is a dog that knows it is going to lose the fight in the end, so it fights like a mad dog."

At the BMWU trial in February 1981, Joseph Mavi and the others were not convicted of any charges. The judgment read in part that the state has failed to prove that the stoppage of work in which the accused took part was an unlawful act.

Jeremy Keenan wrote a summary of the trial for a labour journal. He concluded:

> The trial as a whole is interesting from the point of view of the state's blind determination to have the municipal worker leaders convicted, despite the fact that it could only muster up witnesses whose evidence was so contradictory and unreliable as to be thrown out of court. This nevertheless reflects the serious light in which the strike was held by the state. That it was unable to resolve the situation within the framework of its industrial relations system is a telling comment on the contradictory position in which the state finds itself when the migrants awake.

That contradictory position has been highlighted over and over again in South Africa in the 1980s, as the state—and management across the board—prefer to use brute police force against black strikers rather than the negotiation system they themselves designed. The rounding up of thousands of black trade unionists in the Draconian states of emergency since June 1986 has destroyed any hopes of negotiation between the awakened black labour force prepared to use its muscle in the political struggle and the obdurate white authorities.

During the year that followed the calamitous events of July 1980, I kept in close contact with Joseph Mavi, Gatsby Mazwi, the BMWU, and the council workers. Trade unionism intrigued me. In answer to that teaser, "If you had your life to do over . . . ," I can say, yes, one of my options would probably have been a career in the labour movement. Through the BMWU I met a range of black unionists. Some were avowedly political and sought political rights through workers' rights; others were genuine organisers of labour. There was such a spirit of enthusiasm and dedication, such a vibrancy about the black trade union movement in the country that I began to predict— both privately and on public platforms—that the black trade union movement would spearhead monumental political and social change in South Africa. More than ever I am convinced of the truth of that prediction.

As of 1988, ten years after they were first allowed to exist, the black trade unions number well over two million workers. In many of the private sectors of the economy, union action has wrung significant wage increases and other employment benefits from employers. The Council of South African Trade Unions (COSATU), with over six hundred thousand members, is the largest trade union body ever in South African trade union history. It is an umbrella body, its largest member being the National Union of Mine Workers (NUM) with over four hundred thousand members. In a three-week strike in 1987, and through a tough bargaining process, NUM gained acrossthe-board wage increases for all of its mine worker members. This was a historic strike, the first successful black trade union strike in South African labour history.

However, the state continues to harass black trade union leaders, and in February 1988, in its clampdown on seventeen black organisations, it restricted COSATU's activities to "trade unionism only" (whatever that broad term means).

Some changes in South Africa will come from internal pressure. And those changes will be gained mainly by the economic muscle of the black trade union movement.

Back in 1981, until I left the council in 1984, in my capacity as an unofficial spokesperson on labour relations, I continued to grapple with worker grievances. The following are extracts from many, many letters from the BMWU to me, carried by hand by the workers to my home.

These letters are different from those I processed in the aftermath of the strike. They reflect the growing confidence of the BMWU, especially since it had been vindicated in court. As an example, whereas previously I had received information on scraps of paper, the BMWU now sent me notes on a boldly designed letterhead, a double-sided logo of a black face with the face, in profile, looking proudly to right and left.

Re: Badge No. Skuenkwe Mdlalose
Former B/N 82712 NIN 4717274 was not given call-in forms when he went on contract discharge in July 1981, but told that he must come back on August 1981, but unfortunately he thought it will be sent and waited for it at home. He came back only to be told that he is no longer needed in the city council as he had

previously laid a charge of assault against the police and their compound manager at Orlando Power Station. Can you please help him.

After an investigation Mr. Mdlalose was reengaged and his yearly contract renewed.

Our friend Xaba seems to have enraged his seniors by coming to you. Judging from some of the things that his supt. said to him, this second suspension is just to get him to come back to you so that they may deal with him properly? According to Xaba, he has been suspended, not for failing to produce a medical certificate, but for allegedly failing to sleep in the compound during his illness. Could you please help.

Jaap de Villiers was efficient in his dealing with Nicodemis Xaba. Xaba, an ambulance driver, was reinstated and his sick leave without pay changed to sick leave with full pay.

Bearer is the man who was punished twice for one offence. The latest is that he has now been thrown out of the police compound at the Electricity Department in President Street. He is quite satisfied or rather resigned to the five-day suspension, and the fact that he was made to run around until he collapsed, but he refuses to take a demotion on top of that.

When he failed to get the clerks of Selby compound to give him more time in which to move his things from the compound, he absconded duty and to date he is still on fed up leave. Please see what you can do.

Thank you.

In reply I was told that "the relevant staff decided to punish him for being late. The so-called punishment 'pack-drill' is of course completely unauthorised, and instructions were given for this practise to stop immediately. Mr. Siyotula was transferred to another depot. He did not turn up for work and was discharged in his absence as having deserted."

At Joseph Mavi's behest I asked the Management Committee to investigate the methods of pension fund payments to ex-council employees living in the "homelands." I also asked for investigations into a medical benefit scheme for the council's black employees, among other employee benefits.

Whenever I could, I spoke in council on the lack of meaningful communication between the Management Committee and the council's black workers. And I continually called for improvements to the council's huge single-sex hostels.

Slowly over the next three years, resolutions were put before the council by the Management Committee that partially redressed some of the previous ills of the council's black workers. The minimum starting wage was raised to 43 rand a week (still a hopelessly inadequate wage), hundreds of thousands of rands were allocated for improvements to the hostels, and a uniform salary scale was introduced for black and white monthly paid workers, who were now entitled to the same benefits. But little was done to evolve a system of communication between management and the workers.

Joseph Mavi never met with Councillor Oberholzer.

In May 1982, two years after the strike he did not call, Mavi died in a car accident on a lonely road in the Orange Free State. In the early morning, with Gatsby Mazwi at the wheel, on a return journey from Port Elizabeth where they had gone to organise municipal workers, their car collided with a truck. Joseph, who was asleep in the passenger seat, was thrown through the windscreen and died instantly. Gatsby was uninjured.

At dusk that evening as I returned from a meeting, I received the telephone call. It was Gatsby, his voice scratchy and odd. "Joseph's late" (a euphemism for someone who has recently died), he said. "We'll let you know when is the funeral." I was stunned by the news. I remember going quite cold and not being able to feel warm again for many hours. I felt desperately sorry for Gatsby too, as he had loved Joseph as a son would love a respected father.

Joseph Mavi's death left me bereft. He was a close friend, a warm political ally. In the past few months I had come to know him really well. The BMWU had expanded out of Johannesburg onto the national labour scene, and Joseph often felt the unwelcome attention of the Security Police. Frequently he was on the run from them. My family became used to Joseph arriving at seven in the morning or eleven at night. He was always welcome and often stayed with us, slipping away in the early morning.

Irene knew of how I felt about Joseph. When I told her of his death and the plans for his funeral, where I, among many others, was due to speak, she offered to accompany me. I was grateful to her for understanding my need to be supported at that moment.

The planned funeral never took place. Joseph's family in the Transkei wanted to bury him there, but the woman he had lived with in Soweto claimed his body first. In the domestic dispute that followed, a full-blooded "political" funeral was put aside.

But during the next month, in the budget debate of June 1982, I had an opportunity to pay a public tribute to Joseph Mavi.

"History Will Mark Mavi's Leadership" was one newspaper headline. "Describing him as the first leader of a major black trade union in Johannesburg, Mrs. Janet Levine, PFP, Norwood, said the city should place on record some acknowledgement of the role he played in the city's and the country's history."

In my speech I said I believed that when the history of black trade unionism in this country was written Joseph Mavi's reasoned, responsible, committed approach would shine like a beacon in a sea of swirling confrontation.

Sorrowfully I believe too that, as the radicalisation of the struggle continues in South Africa, there will be no room for the moderate leadership of the Mavis of the country.

The BMWU is now part of the increasingly powerful Municipal and General Workers' Union of South Africa. Gatsby Mazwi is an activist leader. Along with almost two thousand other black trade unionists, he was taken into custody in June 1986.

CHAPTER 14

Bantu Beware:
This Constitution Holds
No Rights for You

It was an agonising decision for me to stand again in 1982.

I had not wanted to. I had wanted to concentrate on writing, and committing myself to another five exhausting and demanding years in futile opposition seemed like a jail sentence. The challenge had gone out of the game—I had achieved all I could from the platform of public office. Inside I knew I wanted time to myself. I wanted to let my mind sift over the meaning of what I had experienced. The liberal role of protest politics was dying anyway, the time at hand for revolutionary action.

Helen could not understand my not wanting to stand again. "You're throwing away a wonderful career," she said. "Look at what you've already achieved, at what you've learnt, the contacts you've made, the time and energy you've spent—you're on the brink of much bigger things. Don't give up now, don't throw it away."

Irene was sympathetic on a personal level. "I understand your frustration and your need for time alone to write," she'd tell me. "But if we win in Johannesburg, you'll be needed. I don't know if you can let the party down." (She was regional deputy chairperson that year.)

Sam Moss, also working on the theory that the party had an outside chance of taking control of the city council, did not try to coerce me but simply said, "If we win, I'll need you on management."

Sandy helped me weigh the pros and cons: "If the PFP wins and you have a seat on management, that's a five-year commitment. But it'll be different from being in opposition: you'll have a wonderful opportunity to really try to implement some of what you believe in—especially in labour relations. What a challenge to change the working environment of all twenty thousand employees. And what a platform for you. But, if the PFP loses, can you stand another five years of frustration?"

Mylie Richards, a friend and so-called "coloured" leader, came to dinner and demanded, "What is this nonsense about you not standing, Janet?" He flatly stated, "You must stand, especially if the PFP wins Jo'burg. Someone with your credibility is vital for the resolution of race issues in the city. And if the PFP doesn't win, it's even more important for you to be there. Who else will open doors for us, speak in the council for us?"

Striking a compromise with Sam, Helen, and Irene, I agreed that if the PFP won I would shelve my writing plans and devote myself to building PFP credibility in the first forum of power we would have in South Africa. But if we lost, I would be permitted to resign after a year. It was Sam's need for my support and Mylie's appeal that swayed me.

Neil Ross, the party director and an ace election organiser, came up from Cape Town to head the campaign. But he misread this one, probably the most important campaign the PFP had ever fought. While he and Irene and the other campaign executives were claiming twenty-eight or more seats, a clear victory margin, on the weekend before the election Sam and I could find only twenty-two—two short of outright victory.

In any event, we were all wrong. The PFP won twenty-three seats, including mine, one short of an absolute majority, and among those we lost were a couple no one thought we could lose, one of them being in Helen's "safe" Houghton constituency. It

was an invidious position for us. The PFP was the largest bloc
in the council but had to give control of the city to a coalition of
National Party and independent councillors who together could
muster the vital one more seat than we and make up a
majority.

"Defeat Snatched from the Jaws of Victory" was how one
newspaper saw it.

The party leadership was devastated. Irene, particularly,
expressed her deep sadness and disappointment to me. I too
was disappointed and saddened by the opportunity missed, but
on a personal level I was pleased that my commitment was for
only a year after all.

On the council itself I felt uninspired and dispirited, the
challenge and excitement of my first term having dissipated
for me. It did not help that there was a great deal of bickering
and playing of petty caucus politics among my colleagues. We
were like frustrated rats in a maze, turning on one another,
because as the opposition we were making no impact at all. The
Management Committee, hanging on to power by the tenuous
threads of a shaky coalition of National Party (seventeen) and
independent (seven) members, had become more and more
autocratic, exercising its executive power so that the full council itself was simply a rubber stamp, passively and without
debate approving decisions that had already been made by the
Management Committee. There was no longer even the media
platform, for the English-language press, which had been such
a potent weapon for liberals like me, was having difficulties of
its own, and no reporters of any competence were around
anymore.

To add to my gloom, the government was bracing the country
for constitutional changes, which, if one read between the lines
of the proposals, meant the further entrenchment of white
racial superiority—apartheid. Yet I had to admit I was still
deeply engaged at a gut level in the political process, for the
regime's vast social engineering programmes—the uprooting
and resettlement of three million people into barren "homelands," evidence of which was now being made more visible
through the documentation efforts of the Black Sash—began to
obsess me. The ramifications of this Nazilike "final solution" of

long-term genocide, the indisputable evidence of what the regime was doing inside apartheid, made me burn with as much outrage as it ever had.

I was introduced to Len Apfel at gatherings to discuss the vast problems of rural starvation and was immediately drawn to him and the work he was doing. I became determined to be taken by him into the "homelands" to see for myself what was happening there. But that odyssey was still a few months away.

In the meantime, Sandy and I were in London on a working holiday in August 1983, staying at the Basil Street Hotel. It was a heavy, humid, late summer day. Expected at a dinner party later that evening, we were relaxing with a drink and watching an early evening news broadcast on the BBC.

Earlier that day the white minority National Party government of South Africa had unveiled the anticipated draft constitutional bill for the country, supposedly the first major constitutional change in South Africa since the formation of the Union in 1910. The draft bill made provision for granting a limited form of parliamentary representation to the "coloured" and Indian people of South Africa. Racially separate "coloured" and Indian parliamentary chambers were to be created alongside the existing white chamber. But, said the commentator, there was no provision for the political aspirations of the majority of the population of the country, the black people, in the new political dispensation.

As I watched the news item a wave of dismay came over me. Walking to the window, I noted that there was not much to see outside, only the usual dingy London street scene, which seemed to waft in the heat haze coming off the tarmac. Visions of the dry and dusty Transvaal highveld, the tawny browns and light greys of my homeland, came into my mind. Swartkrans now, a windy valley near Krugersdorp, where the first man-ape, *Australopithecus*, had roamed, millions of years ago: the plains of wild grasses rippling like swells in a restless sea, then and now. Then and now, the tawny orange rocky krantzes (cliffs) where the suikerbosch (protea) clung to precipitous life in the cracks of rocks, sturdy roots searching tendrils to grip survival from the earth. The mourning doves calling in a lonely African tone. Sitting at the cave mouth, primeval hearth, I can

look with three-million-year-old eyes and see the blue-ena-
melled sky blown clear, trailing wisps of white cloud.

I belonged there on the high African plateau, far from this
alien northern humidity and the cloying greenery of civilised
parks beyond the steamy streets.

"That document . . ."

Sandy drew his attention away from a cricket game to listen
to me.

". . . that new constitution will polarize race relations in
South Africa as nothing else has ever done before."

Sandy often quotes back to me and to others what he sees as
my prescient prophecy that day, as month by month, year by
year, we impotently watch the racial conflict in South Africa
escalate, worsen, degenerate.

Although I was dismayed by the news on that day, I was not
surprised, nor was my assessment of its impact on South
Africa surprisingly prescient. For almost a year before, political circles in the country had been feeding on rumours as to
which direction the government's constitutional changes would
take.

During this year of political ferment I knew, from sources
within the National Party and from confidential papers I had
read on local government proposals in my capacity as a city
councillor, that nothing about apartheid rule was going to
change. Apartheid was going to be reformulated, streamlined.
But I had no idea then with what cynicism the document was to
be put together or how cleverly the government would dupe the
white population of South Africa and most of the international
community into believing that its further entrenchment of
apartheid, of white Nationalist minority rule, was actually part
of a process of reform. The government's inability to accommodate in any way the demands of black people seemed to me to
be stupefyingly shortsighted. In hindsight, I see it to have been
even more so.

Allan Boesak, Bishop Desmond Tutu, Nthato Motlana, black
trade union leaders, and other black leaders, including Chief
Gatsha Buthelezi of the Inkatha organisation, were virulently
opposed to the new constitutional proposals. In the press, from
the pulpit, and whenever they were allowed to do so from

public platforms, they proclaimed their opposition.

White South Africa was aware of these voices, of this presence, of black demands.

White South Africa chose to ignore them.

There was one positive political manifestation of the new constitutional proposals: they united black opposition in the country on a scale not seen even in the heyday of the African National Congress and the resistance campaign of the fifties. This manifestation enabled the fledgling United Democratic Front (UDF) to grow into a massive grass-roots political movement.

The UDF was an umbrella body embracing black, "coloured," Indian, and some activist white members, people from all walks of life. It melded community club members with highly politicised trade unionists, humble township church groups with militant activist church ministers. It was a genuine people's movement, launched nationally in August 1983 in Cape Town, before more than a thousand cheering delegates.

Its patrons included Nelson Mandela, the internationally renowned jailed leader of the African National Congress, the symbol of black resistance in South Africa, and Helen Joseph, the revered elderly white human rights activist. Another patron was Beyers Naude, a crusading, zealous Afrikaner churchman, a fearless and outspoken opponent of the apartheid government.

The UDF was the brainchild of Dr. Allan Boesak, a frontline militant antiapartheid activist and "coloured" church leader who in 1983 was elected president of the World Alliance of Reformed Churches in Vancouver, Canada. In January 1983 in South Africa he had called for "progressive forces to unite in resistance to the government's constitutional plans."

At the August launch of the UDF in Cape Town a declaration was adopted stating that the aims of the UDF were the creation "of a united, democratic South Africa, based on the will of the people." It pledged to organise community, women's, students', religious, sporting, and other organisations "to unite in action against the constitution, the 'Koornhof Bills,' and other day-to-day problems of the people."

(The so-called "Koornhof Bills," before Parliament in 1983,

were intended to stop the inflow of rural people to the cities by imposing large fines on legitimate urban township dwellers who were found "harbouring" such "illegals." It proposed enormous fines of five thousand rand on employers who were found to be employing "illegals." The bills were seen by opponents of apartheid as a further move to divide black people, this time essentially into the urban "haves" and the rural "have-nots".)

When Sandy and I returned from London, a period of intense political activity began for me. My party decided that we would run a campaign urging our supporters to reject the new contitutional proposals. Although the campaign was planned nationally, each constituency was responsible for organising its own effort. Helen Suzman, as a figure of national prominence, was asked to be available to speak around the country, so she asked me to run Houghton's "no" campaign. (The format of the referendum among white voters had been simplified to a yes/no answer on a ballot form.) As I could never say no to Helen, and because I felt so strongly about the proposals myself, I threw myself into the PFP's campaign to persuade the white electorate to vote against the new constitutional proposals in the referendum of November 1983.

During the campaign, when at one point I addressed twelve meetings in as many days—meetings of rooms filled with fearful, bewildered, reluctant white voters, meetings that left me exhausted, frustrated, and jaded—I was invited to speak at a UDF rally in Coronationville, a "coloured" area about six miles from the centre of Johannesburg.

South African law forbade a politican of one racial group to address either a "mixed" audience or an audience of another racial group during a political campaign. It was an unusual invitation to receive, and it pleased me, for it was a positive comment on my political credibility among black people.

The meeting was arranged for a Friday night at seven o'clock, in the hall of St. Teresa's School in Coronationville. I knew the area well, having been associated for many years with a brave workshop for the "coloured" blind situated around the corner from the school.

On my way to Coronationville I drove through the white, mainly Afrikaans-speaking, lower-middle-class suburb of Triomf (Triumph), with its towering J. G. Strijdom Hospital (named for a former National Party prime minister) on my left, with its neat gardens, streetlights, and sidewalks. Crossing over Ontdekkersweg, a main highway leading to the satellite towns to the west of Johannesburg, I suddenly found myself on another planet: for to cross over Ontdekkers is to cross over to the "coloured" townships of Johannesburg.

On my right were the squalid hovels of Western Township, with no electricity, no running water, no paved streets, and few permanent dwellings. There was a hopelessly inadequate, run-down low-rise city council housing project. Streetlights were few and far between. Groups of children loitered beneath straggly trees. Women called to each other across washing lines strung between the buildings.

I turned left at Coronationville Hospital. In South Africa, state hospitals are run on lines of strict racial separation, and Coronationville is the only hospital for "coloured" people in the greater Johannesburg area. Although it was early evening, there was plenty of activity: ambulances, a few taxis, many people milling around. A man with a gaping wound at the back of his head was being helped to the casualty section.

Friday night at Coronationville will turn even the strongest stomach. Victims of robberies, rapes, streetfights, and domestic abuse make their bloodied way to its doors.

I turned into a side street. There were no streetlights, the road was narrow, and figures weaved mysteriously in the dark around me. The lights of St. Teresa's were a welcoming beacon. Sister Sally, a young Catholic nun and a teacher, waited to greet me.

Hundreds of people were seated inside. There were black, "coloured," and Indian faces before me, with a sprinkling of whites—Catholic clergy, I concluded from their cassocks and habits. UDF posters adorned the hall. We all knew we were breaking the law by being at a "mixed" political gathering. Police agents would be present.

I was conscious of being a singular presence in the hall, for to my knowledge I was the only public representative of my party speaking on a UDF platform during this campaign. I hoped that the press was not present, for if this meeting were re-

ported, Helen would be implicated in some way, she being my
senior party colleague and in a sense responsible for me and my
being there constituting an "illegal" action. I did not want to
give her enemies any ammunition. As for the rest of the PFP,
their discomfort did not concern me too much.

I was aware that being there was also a personal risk for me,
an all too real risk of incurring right-wing reactionary violence. Recently, many like-minded activists I knew had been
the victims of that sort of violence. Gunshots and firebombs had
been aimed at their homes at night, letter bombs had been sent
to them, their car tyres had been slashed, and their pets had
been found dead and skinned on their doorsteps. After all this
time I had learned to live with that threat: my telephone had
been tapped for years, and I had received telephone calls and
letters threatening my life. But my sort of South African
politics involved taking some risks, risks I felt were justified.
An acceptance of the risk, however, did not mitigate my worry.

After intense weeks of operating in the rarefied atmosphere
of the whites-only constitutional campaign, I found it a pleasure to be in touch with a greater political reality. I was
grateful for the opportunity to play even a tiny part in the
growth of this embryonic peoples' movement, which I felt sure
would sweep South Africa in the ensuing years.

The two other speakers were introduced to me. One was Popo
Molefe, the national secretary of the UDF, and the other a thin,
almost cadaverous, man of about my height, a black priest
from the Ciskei. In chatting with him I learned that earlier in
the week he had been released from an East London prison
after months of solitary confinement for his "political
activities."

While we three and Sister Sally spoke together, waiting for
latecomers, an earnest-looking young man of about eighteen
came up to me.

"Will you sign our campaign?"

The UDF had launched a campaign to present to the Nationalist government a million signatures of opposition to the
constitution. The form was on plain yellow paper, with the
UDF logo on the top left side and a black hand holding a pen on
the right side. "1 million!!" the script ran as if written by the

black hand. Underneath those words was the heading "Signature Campaign."

- WE, the freedom-loving South Africans, declare for the whole world to know that:
- WE reject apartheid.
- WE support the struggle and unity of our people against the evils of apartheid.
- WE stand for the creation of a nonracial democratic South Africa free of oppression, economic exploitation, and racism.
- WE say:
  NO to the new constitution because it will further entrench apartheid and white domination.
  NO to the Koornhof Bills, which will deprive more and more African people of their birthright.
  YES to the United Democratic Front (UDF), and give it our full support in its efforts to unite our people in their fight against the constitution and the Koornhof Bills.

MAKE YOUR MARK AGAINST APARTHEID!

Then followed space for twenty names, addresses, and signatures. On the other side of the form was the same declaration printed in SeSotho, Zulu, and Afrikaans.

I willingly signed the form and took a couple of others from the young man with a promise to try to fill them with signatories. He told me that his local UDF group operated in nearby Riverlea, working in a house-to-house canvass of the township to gather signatures and to explain the implications of the new constitutional proposals. It was an impressive achievement. If the UDF already had small cadres around the country, working the townships on a street-by-street basis, it had the potential for enormous political growth.

The meeting opened with a prayer and a hymn, the voices soaring around me in splendid unison. Speaking first, the priest dispassionately recounted his days in prison, his torture sessions, his long hours of solitary confinement. He reaffirmed the justness of his cause and rededicated himself to the struggle, ending his speech with a prayer for his jailors and torturers. There was silence in the hall while he spoke and then a

euphoric eruption of applause. Women were ululating in
triumph.

The spirit of this communion (for that is what it had become,
a communion between the priest and the people) moved me so
that I could not start my own speech for several moments.
Every time I started to speak I felt choked with emotion. The
faces of the audience stared back at me in expectation and
sympathy.

Sister Sally had introduced me as a sister in the struggle, a
fighter for the people, proved by my efforts on behalf of the
Black Municipal Workers' Union. Humbled by this introduction, I felt inadequate, unable to live up to the promise it held
for the audience. My topic had been the details of the new
constitution and the Koornhof Bills. The title of my speech was
"The Implementation of Permanent Apartheid."

But while the priest was speaking, I glanced over it, and the
neat schematic renderings of the inequities of the bills seemed
cold and remote. I placed it on the table. And when I rose to
speak, I spoke only the words that were in my heart at that
moment, sentiments of reaching out to one another, of coming
together in democratic unity, of being human, and of human
rights as birthrights. I told them of the groups of whites I had
addressed these past days and of their fears of black people
swamping them, of their being drowned in a black wave. I
spoke of the government as evil and selfish, of seeking desperately to grasp at power with whatever means it could devise. I
spoke further of the constitutional proposals as a document that
would make war between the races in South Africa. I ended by
saying that I knew I could not be free as long as they were
denied their rights. South Africa could not be free until all
South Africans acknowledged themselves as equal.

The audience roared its approval, but I sat down with cold
fingers chilling my heart. I had met their expectations. They
had taken from me the promise I had held for them, but it was
as chaff in the wind, dreamlike insubstantiality. I had told
them of a dream that could not come true. And I knew that they
knew it was a flimsy dream. We sat smiling and crying together in that hall, knowing the truth, knowing that the future
reality would not be my humanitarian dream, but the nightmare of racial war in South Africa.

Popo Molefe paid tribute to the priest and me, then began to outline the decisions made by the executive body of the UDF concerning the further organisation of the anticonstitution campaign. Members of UDF cells from all around the greater Johannesburg area were present. The UDF, in the Transvaal at least, was well organised.

We sang a closing prayer that began "Come sing a song of joy, for peace shall come, my brother. Sing, sing a song of joy, for men shall love each other." The meeting closed with a fervent and emotional rendering of "N'kosi Sikele Afrika" (God Bless Africa), the national anthem of black South Africa. The words stuck in my throat.

Driving home, I was confused and troubled. The meeting had been a rite of passage for me. In the priest, Molefe, and the young man from the UDF I had seen the faces of the new South Africa, irrevocably committed to changing the country. For the first time in twenty-two years of political involvement I felt the sap rising. It was a different feeling from that I had experienced in 1976. Now their moment—a faint, distant vision coming closer—was at hand. It was not my dream of a shared South Africa, but it was a vision of black nationalism triumphant.

Some weeks later the results of the whites-only referendum were announced. It was an overwhelming three-to-one victory for the government. The whites had been duped into buying sham reform. I hung my head in shame.

Helen Suzman, several other key referendum workers, and I sat on that shameful night in the hall of the Norwood Primary School in the heart of the Houghton constituency while the officials sorted the ballots.

By now Helen was in her mid-sixties. She had become a small grey-haired woman, but her face retained the imprint of her earlier magnetic attractiveness, and her magnificent blue eyes flashed with the vitality and energy that infused the core of her being. One never thought of Helen as tiny, such was the vital force of her personality. As always, even on this fateful night, after a long, exhausting day, Helen was dressed with the impeccable style and grace that had become a hallmark of her more than thirty years in the limelight. Her intellectual integrity, her sharp, cutting wit, and her attractive appearance had made her into a formidable political foe and a household name in South Africa. Even to us in Houghton, her closest political allies, her sharp, abrasive tongue was a weapon of which to be wary.

Helen's Houghton constituency had returned her to Parliament for thirty years. It was a constituency that for thirteen of those years, 1961 to 1974, had kept her in Parliament as the only voice defending human rights and civil liberties in the highest legislative body in the land. It was a constituency castigated by the Nationalist press as the symbol of liberalism and pink-tinged humanism, a hotbed of unpatriotic activities. Nonetheless, the count in the Houghton poll that evening was in keeping with the final national outcome. Three out of four Houghton voters had voted for the government.

At the count after the balloting, Helen and I kept looking at one another as the piles of "yes" ballots rose three times as high as the "no" votes. She looked tired, drawn, and resigned. She sat huddled in her chair, appearing smaller than she was, vulnerable and defeated. She had fought an exhausting campaign, slogging around the country, speaking three times a day in as many different places.

"Don't tell the press," she said softly to me. I nodded. White South Africa had signed away any hope for a peaceful future, and Helen did not want Houghton's part in that to be known just then. It hurt too much. The wounds of a bruising campaign were too raw.

Helen and I had privately discussed the outcome earlier. We had agreed that the PFP was going to be routed. The resistance had been palpable among voters in Houghton on whose support we had previously relied, election after election. The government had to be given a chance to prove itself on reform, they said.

Representative of the international liberal reaction was an editorial in *The New York Times*:

The legal core of apartheid is untouched, and it [the new constitution] perpetuates a system that assures 4,500,000 whites the benefits of black labour without the inconvenience of black votes. The "reform" would only harden South Africa's racial divisions.

It [the new constitution] is prepared to defend, and even toughen, all the hateful pass laws that restrict the movement of urban blacks. It aims to sustain South Africa as a perpetual stockade, whatever the world thinks.

Don't be misled, the argument is about the best strategy for perpetuating—not modifying—the system known as apartheid.

The editorial said that to call the reform "tokenism" was to flatter it.

I held Helen closely at the end of that draining day, a day made all the more trying for her by constituents who greeted her with good wishes on their lips and lies in their eyes. I tried to comfort her.

"We did our best, Helen, we did our best. They must get what they deserve now—the whites—with this new constitution."

Helen did not reply; she just nodded numbly. We were subdued when we gathered in the early hours of the morning at 38 Ivy Road, Norwood. Sitting around in the postmortem gloom, talking desultorily to colleagues, I resignedly acknowledged to myself that it had been the last heartfelt campaign I would fight in South Africa. At 38 Ivy Road, my political home, I finally accepted the ultimate truth: I could no longer breathe in this white man's Eden. The inequities of the race system were finally stifling me.

As I looked around that gathering at Ivy Road, at my colleagues and friends, political comrades, I felt deep sorrow. What would become of us all, the liberals, we who were caught in the Kerensky trap, wedged tightly between the conflicting forces of reactionary white desperation and militant waves of black activism surging toward political domination? Where would we all be, three, five, seven years from now? Claire, Houghton stalwart; Laura, friend and ally; admirable, articulate Irene, whose friendship I treasured so dearly; Adele, who had worked so hard; Brian and Alex; so many others. But mostly I looked at Helen. She was haggard and pensive. Her "peasant" constitution would soon revive her spirits, and her indomitable will would take her to the thickest part of the political battle again. For the moment, though, she embodied the spiritless disappointment we all felt. It was a desperately sad night for us.

Later I tried to work out how I had arrived at that final

truth. After the UDF meeting I had addressed, I knew myself to be on the brink of rash action, of irrational political frenzy. I had deliberately made myself cold, removed, remote. Almost detachedly I had done what remained for me to do in the referendum campaign. Political recklessness then would have given me the martyr's role, but that was an indulgence I had never allowed myself. I did not want to languish in a political prisoner's cell, to prove my father wrong, to prove that Robben Island was a place for me after all.

For twenty years, ever since I had been a young adolescent, I had been passionately involved in politics in South Africa. For all of those years I had burned with anger at the injustice, the immorality, and the inequities of the implementation of Nationalist apartheid ideology. But somehow at this point my moral outrage was no longer enough to keep me involved. I needed something else to convince me of the validity of continuing to pour my energy into the struggle.

Nothing came to mind. During that constitutional referendum campaign of 1983, Steve Biko's words had thundered in my ears again and again: unless you were black in South Africa and living the life of daily humiliation and oppression under the apartheid system, you could not be part of the black struggle. Being white, ultimately, you were free to choose, as I did, whether or not you wanted to fight for your principles. But there was no such choice for blacks. If you were black, you were oppressed, and therefore you were an integral part of the liberation struggle.

Twenty years ago I chose to be involved. The motivation for white activism is not easily understood by other South Africans—mostly it is never understood. And I do not understand it clearly myself. Personally I know it to be a complex matrix of motivations, a fusion of my personality and my outrage at the immorality of the life the government forced us to live. For me it was a random patterning of the conjunction of events, circumstances, personality, and moral values.

And unquestionably the ground had shifted in South African politics during the constitution debate of 1983. It had moved massively toward the nationalistic black liberation struggle, away from liberal human rights issues. Knowing that is perhaps the reason I no longer felt convinced that my moral motivation for an involvement in the struggle was relevant. The government had thrown down the gauntlet to black resistance; the new constitution screamed at black activists that their only option was to overthrow the government and write their rights into a constitution of their own.

Once I came to this realisation, I knew with great conviction that I was reading the situation correctly. The days of the white liberal were over. But I knew that my thinking was now far out of step with all of my PFP colleagues, including Helen and Irene. Helen, certainly, would (and continues to) defy any attempt to define the death of white liberalism in South Africa. After one bitter argument, we never discussed this topic again.

Understandably, she has rationalised her need to stay involved after thirty-five years—and a meritorious contribution—of parliamentary representation. How much easier for me to withdraw myself, one who had never absolutely committed myself to the white electoral arena, who was constantly plagued by qualms and uneasiness at having done so at all. Helen was resolute. And I admired her for that, too. For her, the arguments that had persuaded me in the early seventies— to gain political credibility for the party, to make use of a national and international platform, to put the government "on the record" whenever possible—still held good. For me, the apartheid regime in the eighties had become a vicious de facto police state, and continuing to serve on its "forums" of "government" helped to perpetuate its lies about itself. Yet Helen has told me again and again, even on her most recent visit to Boston in April 1988, that she is the only white antiapartheid politician with an international reputation and that that reputation places an inordinate responsibility on her shoulders to use opportunities for presenting facts about South Africa. But Helen is seventy now, and she will retire soon, unbowed and still fired by her liberal conviction and her great love of South Africa.

Irene says it's boring "to justify one's position" and will not talk about it. Both she and Helen remain in South Africa determinedly working on a range of projects as they always have.

Appearing on the UDF platform that night in Coronation-ville had been pivotal for me in another way. It stripped the veil away from a truth I had been hiding from myself for years, a truth I did not risk sharing with Helen, Irene, and the others after their reaction to other conclusions I had made. But surely they too were aware of it. My white skin had not only ensured a life of privilege for me in South Africa; it had also protected me from the frighteningly repressive machinery of the state security system. The regime tolerated me solely for my white skin and the elected public representation it had enabled me to win. It suited the government to have a small number of out-spoken white liberals shouting the odds. Vocal opposition gave some legitimacy to the farcical parliamentary system of gov-ernment. I had berated, accused, condemned, and vilified the government on public platforms and in the city council chamber for years. If the Ciskeian priest with whom I had shared the UDF platform, or any other black person, or even a white activist without the protection of public office, had spoken the words I had, he would have been incarcerated indefinitely.

It was then, in late 1983, that I saw that if I was part of a game the regime allowed white opposition politicians to play, then I could not be part of the struggle. I had been deluding myself. I could not change places with that black priest how-ever much I might want to do so. The colour of my skin was white. The struggle in South Africa was a black liberation struggle. The game being played by white liberal opposition politicians, whether holding elected office or not, was almost over.

This realisation crystallised for me in a startling way a few weeks after the referendum campaign. I had a visit from two members of the Security Police.

The state security officers did not say outright that they had me under surveillance and knew that I was involved with the UDF. One asked me if my car had been stolen recently. I replied in the negative. The other asked if I knew that a white car with my number plates had been parked outside of various addresses. He enumerated these from a list in a notebook that he laboriously pulled from a pocket of his jacket.

"Yes."

"Where were you then at those times?"

"With my car, at meetings, various UDF meetings."

(Helen had always told me: "Tell the truth.")

"Oh, you don't deny then that it was your car and you yourself at those meetings?"

"No. Anything wrong with my being there?"

"Not yet, but there probably will be sooner or later."

The state security officer, young, dark-haired, and pleasant-looking, smiled at me. "I'd be careful where I parked my car if I were you—you never know where parking your car in certain places can get you."

Smiling back at him, but with a cold sense of dread suffusing me, I asked him, "Are you threatening me?"

"No," he shook his head emphatically, "just trying to be helpful."

Around the dinner table, shortly before the visit from the Security Police, Roger, ten years old then, recounting his daily activities, told of a conversation he had had with some of his classmates.

"They were talking of joining the army when we leave school—it's only in seven years' time—of killing 'terrs' and fighting in the bush, killing blacks." His blue-green eyes sparked with indignation, and he spoke with more conviction than was usual for him. "I can tell you right now, I'm not going into the army to kill black South Africans—so what are you going to do about it?"

Sandy and I looked meaningfully at one another. The shadow of conscription was so close—ten years old and faced with the knowledge of being turned into a murderer because you were white and male and living in South Africa. Roger's challenge to us was another spur to the complex decision-making process of leaving South Africa.

I had rejected the role of becoming a martyr to apartheid since I was a student and it was an option for me. My way did not lie in a political prison, in banishment, under house arrest, or under a banning order. I could see my way lay ahead to bear witness to what I had seen, to what I was still seeing. Like so many others before me, the way of self-exile—of self-banishment from the country I loved, from my people—beckoned in the darkness South Africa had become for me.

Sandy went ahead to organise the return of his family to the country where he had been born. My first step was to resign from the City Council.

Anticipating the opposition I had previously encountered, I simply called Helen, Irene, and Sam and told them that I was resigning the next day. Helen was noncommittal—I think she knew it was coming. Sam sounded sad. "You're right to do it," he said, "for yourself, your children." Irene took the news as almost a personal affront. "You said you wouldn't resign until all your ward canvass cards were in order," she said stiffly. I had hardened myself to stay with my resolve, so I bit off a sarcastic retort. I did not want to become involved in a dead-end argument.

Later, long before I left, we spoke about our inability to communicate at that time. Irene said that she found the thought of my resigning opening a great void for her. It was as if I were denigrating all we had worked for together over so many years. I told her that I had never felt that I was giving up, bailing out on the struggle, but that I wanted to be free to explore other areas and strategies for working against the apartheid regime. We agreed to disagree, for she, like Helen, still found a validity in working with the whites-only electorate. I no longer could.

Awakening at six o'clock in the morning on the next day, I felt my heart thumping. Realisation flooded my consciousness: today was the day I was going to do it. Rehearsing the sequence of events often in my mind did not make the doing any easier.

It was the height of summer, January. Being careful not to arouse the sleeping members of my household, I let myself out of the house and into the garden. The swimming pool glistened, but the lawn was brown, parched from the drought. The water in the pool was refreshingly cool in the early morning. I swam many lengths.

After a cursory breakfast I drove through the heavy morning traffic to the Civic Centre in Braamfontein. It was barely eight o'clock when I walked into the opulent offices of the town clerk, Mr. Alwyn Burger. He had just left for a Management Committee meeting in the Management Committee's suite of offices, his secretary said. Was it important? I allowed myself a little grin. Not to him, I didn't think, but to me. I handed her my letter of resignation. "There's no hurry," I said. "You can give it to him when he comes out of the meeting." I saw her looking sceptically at the envelope. In the past, missives from me to the town clerk had almost always meant controversy and confrontation. I knew she would take it to him in the meeting and that the Management Committee would know of its contents before I was home again.

As I turned away from her, I felt a flash of panic—what the hell was I doing? Nostalgia washed over me as I walked back to my car. Some of the best moments of my life had been spent in this building, as well as some of the worst. It was here that I had proven myself in the public arena of white politics and while doing so had learnt a great deal—about myself, about other people.

Among the memories of the council chamber that came into my mind then were those of the many battles I had fought on behalf of my rate payers. The plan to put a road through a suburban park had been thwarted there, the plan to build a huge bus depot in a suburban enclave had been shelved there; garage developments in a suburban street, veterinarian practises, sidewalks in disrepair, bus services for black commuters, saving the local post office and library from being closed down . . . the list went on. These issues had roused my rate payers. I had worked conscientiously on their behalf and led many fierce campaigns—petition drives, mass protest meetings—and they had forgiven me for what they called my excesses on behalf of those South Africans who did not have the right to vote.

On the day of my reelection in March 1982, I had trebled my majority. Time and again voters had emerged from the polling booth, shaken my hand, and told me that they had voted for me—despite my politics—because I worked so hard for them.

Throughout that week in January 1984, the newspapers speculated on my departure:

"Top PFP City Councillor Quits in Surprise Move"
"Janet Levine Resigns Her Seat as PFP City Councillor"
"Bowing out . . . Janet Levine Says PFP Is Hamstrung"
"Jo'burg's Fiery Councillor Calls It a Day"
"Councillor Out of Politics, to Write Books"

When the press decided that there was indeed no more to my resignation than frustration with my role of perpetual opposition and a desire to devote time to my writing, the weeklong media attention to my resignation came to an end.

Thankfully, there is little as easily forgotten by the public as last week's politician.

CHAPTER 15
"It's the Apartheid, Missus"

White liberalism as an agent for change in South Africa was no longer viable for me. But protagonists like Helen and Irene disagreed, and our debate mirrored the one in the antiapartheid white community as a whole. Many thousands of people continued to work for and support the Progressive Federal Party, while many thousands of others worked in organisations such as the Black Sash, the UDF, the End Conscription Campaign (EEC), the Johannesburg Democratic Association (JODAC), and Jews for Justice.

This sort of divisiveness in strategies to oppose apartheid was evident among all racial groups in the eighties. The regime had succeeded too well in ruling and dividing, and dividing and ruling, and ruling and dividing again.

Among blacks, dissident groups such as Inkatha, the UDF, COSAS, AZAPO, and so on formed, splintered, re-formed, and fought bitterly with one another. But nowhere did the government succeed quite as well in dividing and ruling as it did in splitting the Indian and "coloured" communities by persuading some hitherto bona fide leading antiapartheid political figures to be co-opted into the system. Leader after leader agreed to stand for election to racially separate houses under the unilaterally devised new constitution of 1984. "Coloured" leader Mylie Richards, a friend of mine, agreed to go "in." When I confronted him about it, he became angry.

"Janet, man, you in the PFP have done it for years—fought them from within. Why can't we do the same now?"

"But Mylie, I've resigned because I don't think it's a viable option. I agree with your previous strategy. Why go in? Do you want a ministerial post in their government? Do you want to prop them up some more?"

Mylie shook his head. "I'm tired, man; thirty years in opposition is bloody frustrating. Perhaps we can do something this way."

Both of us frustrated, we seemed to be switching roles, Mylie becoming a "liberal" and I a "radical."

In Mylie's electoral area was a township I knew well, Riverlea Extension. I had a good friend, Mr. Ali (he introduced himself that way, and I never learned his first name), who lived there with his family. In June 1984, a month before we left South Africa, I went to the Alis' home to bid them farewell. I invited a U.S. diplomat, Betsy Spiro, to accompany me.

Betsy was the political officer at the U.S. Consulate General headquarters in Johannesburg, and I had taken advantage of our political acquaintance to become friends with her. She was one of the most effective U.S. diplomats in South Africa, perhaps because she seemed tireless, with a driving need to find out firsthand as much about the confused South African political dynamic as a stranger possibly could.

In any one week she would be present at a meeting of a black removals protest group in the Transvaal rural hinterland, at a black residents' protest meeting against rent increases in the townships, at a rally for detainees in solitary confinement, and at a meeting of the Johannesburg City Council. She also shepherded U.S. congressmen and business leaders around the country and brought together leading South African politicians and journalists of all colours and political persuasions to argue an issue.

We often used to play tennis together. During the rest periods in our fiercely contested games, we would discuss the political happenings of the passing days. I valued her ability to place a perspective on events in which I was personally involved.

"Janet," she would drawl laconically in reply to some glib comment I had made on the events of the past week, her warm brown eyes in her round face flashing amusement, "do you really believe that the Nationalists are sooo stoooopid?" She made me think through my conclusions.

Many months earlier I had promised Betsy I would show her Riverlea. It was unlikely that, in the normal course of her duties, Betsy would ever come to Riverlea Extension. For a number of reasons, I wanted her to see the township. At a deeply subconscious level, I suppose, I wanted her to bear witness to the subliminal evidence of apartheid divisiveness I knew we would find there.

Six miles to the south of Johannesburg in a small valley lies the "coloured" township of Riverlea; on the other side of a railway line is Riverlea Extension. Riverlea has electricity, hot and cold running water, and tarred streets. It has shops, a high school, and a health clinic. The houses are occupied by "coloured" artisans and younger people moving into supervisory and even managerial positions in the white economy. "Coloured" people may own houses in Riverlea, and many do, making improvements on the basic structures. Riverlea Extension, in sharp contrast, is an anomaly, a forgotten, deprived community of about five thousand people.

I wanted Betsy to meet some residents of the township, and I knew that a conversation with the elderly, portly, good-humoured Mr. Ali and his family would be illuminating. Mr. Ali was a community spokesman whom I first met in 1978 when I began to work with him in Riverlea Extension under the auspices of a self-help group, Isongo, of which I was a founding member. We had tried initiating community awareness programmes in Extension, as the residents call their township. (Other "coloured" township dwellers referred to Riverlea Extension, for reasons I do not know, as Zombietown.)

We arranged to meet outside the office building where Betsy worked. Her son, Peter, a brown-haired, well-built, capable young man, was to accompany us. A recent Harvard graduate, he was spending a few months in South Africa before he entered law school, visiting his mother and writing for Johannesburg's *Financial Mail* and Washington's *New Republic*.

It was a cold afternoon in June, a typical highveld winter day, when I fetched the Spiros from Kine Centre, the Commissioner Street office building opposite the well-known downtown shopping mall, the Carlton Centre. The sky was the colour of an aquamarine stone, the air so clear that the city skyline was outlined in stark detail. The temperature was within the winter average for Johannesburg, approximately sixty degrees Fahrenheit at midday and about forty degrees at night.

We drove through the busy city streets, the sidewalks crowded with shoppers and office workers, a pastiche of black and white faces. We drove through the light industrial belt that rings the west of Johannesburg and across old mine dumps, their golden sand now fashioned into motorways and office parks. Beyond this matrix of major highways, small factories, and offices, we entered a blue gum plantation growing on undeveloped old mining land that forms a buffer between the "coloured" townships and white Johannesburg. Then we drove under the railway bridge that carries the line separating Riverlea from Riverlea Extension. A sharp right turn and we were in Riverlea Extension.

The tiny houses on either side of the road were painted either pale blue, dimming pink, or drab brown. The first six fading painted houses on either side of the road were a testament to the initial positive energy generated by the community "committee" in 1979. Together with community helpers from Extension, members of Jean Graham's Isongo had painted those houses on two weekends in the winter of 1979. But in the face of negative official action by the Department of Housing of the Johannesburg City Council, which administers the "coloured" townships, none of the residents had availed themselves of the paint donated to the project by an Isongo member. Stopping the car, I told Betsy and Peter the story of the painted houses.

We drove deeper into the township. The main road, a large loop around the township, was tarred. All the sidestreets were dusty and scoured by miniature canyons where the rain had eroded the surface. Groups of schoolchildren watched us, many carrying toddlers in their arms. The houses were in cheek-by-jowl proximity. There was no grass and few stunted trees. A cleared area to the south of the township, the playground, was a dustbowl with soccer goalposts at either end.

Peter noticed that there were no streetlights. Betsy commented on outdoor pit latrines that stood close together at regular intervals in the township, two facing one way, backed by two facing in the opposite direction. I pointed to the one faucet in the middle of the four latrines—one faucet for four households. Peter said that the houses did not look as bad as some he had seen in the American South and certainly not as bad as in Soweto.

In this community of five thousand people, we saw no shops, no schools, no clinics, no places of entertainment.

Soon we were outside a blue-painted house, the home of Mr. Ali and his family.

We pushed open the broken but neatly repaired wire-mesh gate, took the six steps up the cracked but swept paved pathway, and climbed the five cement steps to the house. Riverlea Extension was built over thirty-five years ago and is situated a mere three miles from the centre of the most expansive industrial metropolis on the African continent, yet there is no electricity, so there was no doorbell to ring.

When I knocked on the door, Mr. Ali's daughter, Fatima, called from inside the house. The Alis were not expecting us. There was only one public telephone in Riverlea Extension, and having a message relayed to the Alis had proved impossible in the past. I had not seen the family in over a year.

After I had identified myself I heard bolts being drawn back and a key being turned in the lock. By now a group of curious children and a few women, shouting garrulously to one another, had gathered to watch this strange trio of white visitors at the Ali home.

Fatima embraced me warmly and shook hands with the Spiros. The room was gloomy in contrast with the glaring sunshine outside, but, explained Fatima, it was too early to light the paraffin lamps. The front room, about six by eight feet, contained a wooden dining room table and chairs, a threadbare carpet, a high sofa, and two armchairs. Starched white lace doilies rested on the backs and armrests of the chairs and sofa. Plaques of garish ducks in flight and a wooden print after Dürer's *Praying Hands* brightened the walls. A small glass cabinet held assorted pieces of household china.

With four of us and the furniture, the room was suffocating. Old Mrs. Ali shuffled in and smiled shyly at us, scarcely moving her lips. She had no teeth. With Fatima translating for the Spiros, Mrs. Ali scolded me in Afrikaans for having stayed away for so long.

As we spoke, Peter's eyes kept returning to the swinging bead curtain that covered two doorways leading off the front room. I asked Fatima if we could show my friends the house.

To the right of the living room was a bedroom with a double bed and a narrow cot behind a curtain. This was where Mr. Ali and his wife slept, with two of their grandchildren. The other door led to the two back rooms of the house. One was the kitchen, with a large coal stove. A smaller space had been created within it, partitioned by boards that were about five-and-a-half feet high. Behind this partition was a bath with taps. Fatima and I laughed when the Spiros expressed puzzlement about the fact that the bath had been made into a bed and another bed had been created on a shelf above the bath.

"How many people sleep in your house?" Peter asked Fatima.

"Eight," she replied, "and when my sister comes with her family from Boksburg we are fourteen."

"And in the other houses?" Peter gestured with his arm.

"Mainly twelve, sometimes a few less, sometimes a few more." Fatima looked at me for confirmation. Nodding in agreement, I explained that the baths had been built by the city council three years earlier, but nothing had been done to supply running water to the houses. Getting the so-called "improvements" to Riverlea Extension was among the bitterest battles I had fought in the city council.

Beyond the bathroom was another tiny room, Fatima's bedroom, which was also the sleeping area of her older children.

At my insistence, the Spiros took note of the rough brick, the unplastered walls held together with powdery cement, and the lack of ceilings. There were gaps between the top of the wall and the asbestos roof. On a winter day it was impossible to keep the drafts out, and in summer the asbestos roof transformed the rooms into a hothouse.

Returning to the living room, we were offered a "cold" drink because it is a major chore to boil the water for tea or coffee. Upon enquiring after the family members, I was told that Mr. Ali was in town, but the children were out in the "Sevens."

The thousand or so houses in Extension are numbered in blocks of a hundred, so instead of being known by its street names, each area is known by its block number. The Alis lived in the "Nines."

"Divide and rule," Betsy muttered to me, "taken to absurdity."

The door opened and a slim girl wearing thick glasses sidled into the room. It was sixteen-year-old Nareen, one of Fatima's daughters. I was surprised to see her, for I thought she was at the School for the Coloured Visually Impaired in Worcester in the Cape, the only high school for visually impaired "coloured" children in the country. An optician I knew who was a Lions Club member had arranged for his club to sponsor Nareen in attending the school.

Fatima explained that Nareen's eyesight in one eye had improved so much at the school that she had been taught to type and was working part-time at a Johannesburg office. The Lions Club was still sponsoring her school studies, which she was continuing by correspondence with the high school in Worcester. Quietly, I tried to speak to Nareen, but her shyness overcame us both.

We were about to leave when Mr. Ali entered.

"Jennet," he said, shaking my hand warmly in both of his, his dark eyes shining happily as he looked up at me, "we were just talking about you the other night. I was going to phone you to come speak to a small meeting, man. It's this UDF and this anticonstitution business. Elections, boycotts. Man, they're driving us mad."

Betsy leaned forward expectantly, her political antennae aquiver—this is what she had come to hear. Peter took out his reporter's notebooks.

"In what way, Mr. Ali, are who driving you mad?" Betsy asked quietly.

"These youngsters from the UDF, they come here every week: 'You must not vote, you must not vote for the constitution, you must boycott all elections.' Then people come from the Labour Party. 'You must vote,' they say. 'You must vote for the constitution and the new chamber.' They say that the Labour Party is going to change things from inside the government. But I can't see that, can you, Jennet?"

"No, I agree with you. I can't see it either."

"But why then did people like Ralph Pfeiffer and Mylie Richards go in? Why did they collaborate?"

I shared his sadness and bewilderment. Though I could understand the disillusionment of the two "coloured" leaders with permanent, perpetual opposition, I was not able to accept Mylie's rationalisations of his co-option. The Labour Party's decision to allow themselves to be co-opted had been a decided victory for the government, a decisive blow at the broad front of opposition in South Africa. The government's easy victory angered me.

Old Mrs. Ali spoke up for the first time (in Afrikaans). "What's going on, Mrs. Levine? It's such a mess." She shook her head. "The Zulus will murder us all." She crossed her hands over her chest and nodded. Mr. Ali looked at her and lowered his voice. "Sometimes I don't think she's wrong, man."

Then Fatima spoke: "These UDF people, they say that we must work with the blacks now; we must overthrow the whites together. And then what, Jennet? What then? The country will be run by savages. I don't want to live like the rest of Africa. Here, read these things!" She drew out some pamphlets from under a cushion on the sofa and flung them onto the table. It was the familiar yellow paper used by the UDF with the logo of the unfurled flag held by marching people in the corner. Quickly I read through the propaganda sheet: unite to gain our rights, stand together, boycott all white elections, all white institutions, for a free, democratic South Africa. I passed the pages to the Spiros.

"I think the UDF is right," Nareen said softly. "It's the only way we are going to be free."

It was the first time I had ever heard Nareen express her own opinion. Mr. Ali rounded on her.

"Free! Free! Nonsense—all nonsense! All this congress nonsense again. In the fifties I was in the congress, and I went to jail with the others. Did that make me free? We are freer with the Nationalists than we would be with the UDF!"

Nareen crumpled into silence again, and Mr. Ali composed himself.

"I didn't know you were an old politician, Mr. Ali," I said. "Congress—"

Fatima interrupted: "Tell me, Jennet, do we have to vote?"

"No, there is no law that you have to vote."

"Well, that's it then, finished and klaar. I'm not listening to that nonsense anymore. I'm not going to vote!"

"But Jennet," interjected Mr. Ali, "the UDF kids in the 'Sixes' say they'll beat up anyone who goes to vote, and the Labour Party is strong in the 'Twos,' and they say they'll beat up anyone who *doesn't* go to vote." Mr. Ali shook his head. "It's a bad business."

"I'll come and speak at a meeting if you want me to, Mr. Ali, but you must know that I side with the UDF on this one. I think it is right to boycott the elections." Nareen smiled at me, and Mr. Ali turned to Betsy.

"What do you think, Missus? You're a visitor from America—what do you think?" Betsy was taken aback by the directness of the question. She managed to avoid a direct answer by asking old Mrs. Ali why she feared the Zulus. But Mrs. Ali had had her say and muttered quietly to herself. Mr. Ali leaned across the table. "They killed some of her family in Durban in the riots."

"Mrs. Spiro is interested in how you came to Extension, Mr. Ali, and why you stay here."

"It's the apartheid, Missus. They dump you here and forget about you. They don't build enough houses. Most of us in Extension could afford the rents in Riverlea, Bosmont, other places, but there aren't enough houses. They won't let us buy this rubbish, so we're afraid to make improvements in case they kick us out. But they won't fix anything, and they give us no electricity, no water, no heating. I have to read the newspaper

by candlelight. It's unhealthy: the lavatories are always broken.
It stinks here. It's apartheid, Missus. That put me here, that
keeps me here."

"But why, then, are you so against the UDF? The UDF
leaders are fighting for your rights, your freedom."

"It's not that I'm against the UDF—I'm against making
trouble. We can never be rid of apartheid, Missus. If the 'Twos'
can't trust, say, us in the 'Nines,' and I must lock my door
against my neighbour in the daytime, how can we be rid of
apartheid?"

By the time we were ready to leave, Betsy looked grim.
Handing Mr. Ali her consular card, she said she was available
to talk to anyone in his community at any time. I promised to
bring my children to visit, to show the Alis how they had grown
since that time four years earlier when they had helped in the
abortive house-painting project.

We were subdued on the drive back to Commissioner Street.
Betsy kept on muttering of apartheid between the "Sixes" and
the "Sevens." Peter was bemused by the fact that families like
the Alis were trapped in places like Riverlea Extension not
because they could not afford better but because the full
weight of the apartheid machine kept them there. He had
known this to be true of black people living in Soweto, but for
some reason he had not thought it held true for "coloured" and
Indian South Africans.

"And some of them are going in with the government, collab-
orating." He shook his head. "That is going to mean one massive
explosion in those communities."

After dropping them off, I drove home in a pensive and
somewhat desperate mood. For some reason, even though I had
told my other black allies and friends, I had avoided telling the
Alis that I was leaving South Africa. Perhaps in the context of
our conversation and its tensions I had been overcome by guilt
about abandoning them to the new constitution, to the UDF, to
apartheid.

My family left South Africa in August 1984. The new constitution became law in the country in September. It was born in
a mood of resentment and bitter infighting in the white, "col-

oured," and Indian communities over questions of co-option and collaboration.

Leaders of the black community stood back a little for a short time. Then came the first clashes between the police and black protesters. They occurred in townships south of Johannesburg. The issue supposedly was rent increases.

Since September 1984, violent protest and state reaction have brutalized South Africa.

Epilogue

As for me, much of the rest is already known—that we came to live in Boston, that after a few months I wrote an article titled "Looking Back in Sorrow, Anger" that was published in the *Boston Globe*:

> . . . There is a muddle of images, memories, questions about South Africa in my mind. Perhaps, in time I can try to formulate some sense from this muddle of perceptions, for now I feel a deep sadness, a nostalgia, a sense of loss. . . .

The article marked the beginning of my public profile in the United States. One thing led to another, and soon, besides my writing on South Africa, I was being interviewed about South Africa on local and national television programs, travelling around the Boston area and further afield, mainly in the New York area, generally spending much attention and time on the body politic of my country.

The major preoccupation of the American public debate on South Africa—and hence a preoccupation that had to become mine—is the "economic sanctions" argument. I hold to my view that the debate has much to do with the realities of American politics and little to do with the realities of South African politics. Economic sanctions will certainly affect in some measure the lifestyle of white South Africans, but the apartheid regime for decades has been preparing white South Africa for international opprobrium—"total onslaught"—and it will thrive in a siege economy. Black people in South Africa and the southern African subcontinent will be affected negatively by a backlash from white South Africa. In a rapidly deteriorating situation it is a prescription for economic chaos and political anarchy.

If Americans really want to push for the human and civil rights of South African blacks, then what is needed is more investment, more involvement, more pressure from within the country, not less. South Africa's apartheid needs to be smothered in a great American bear hug, not made more resolute by a prudish moral standoff.

But of vital importance to America and its future relations with the inevitable black-ruled South Africa is engagement with the spectrum of black leadership in and out of the country, from the radicals to the "stooges." Under the Reagan administration America was only "engaged" to the white regime. This blind spot in American policy to South Africa has disturbed me more than whether or not applying sanctions is the correct thing to do. Apartheid will die anyway, and its death throes are already causing anarchy.

What began as a faint but persistent notion of dread within me, and became part of me for the last seven years of my life in South Africa, has exploded into blood-letting anarchy, the inevitable outcome of the white regime's obdurate racism. An unavoidable fact. It is only a question of putting numbers to the masses caught in the violent racial conflict as it escalates, names to the leaders and the places where the violence occurs, dates to the passage of time for which anarchy reigns.

I was one of the innocents, one who believed in the ceremonies of innocence, who believed that innocence could survive in the turgid waters of white racism and black nationalism, who believed in the libertarian value of a human life, in human rights and goodwill among people and the sanctity of individual worth and love and hope and freedom and humanity. I am still a believer, and my fellow believers and I fought a good fight in South Africa. But the tide overwhelmed us, and we drowned in our own innocence.

Liberals and liberal causes in South Africa were in disarray by August 1984—in distress, ineffectual, unable to structure a role for themselves in the exigencies of a conflict that had taken the middle ground out from under them. They had nowhere to stand, they could find nothing to do. Perhaps because I had—at least intellectually and emotionally—moved to the forces of revolution, to the causes of the United Democratic Front, perhaps because I could reconcile the UDF's cry for freedom with my own cry of liberalism, perhaps because I was leaving, I found myself still filled with conviction, passionate and committed and determined to work for the death of apartheid, but now from outside South Africa. And there were others with me in this conviction, this passion—many thousands of other white liberal South Africans in exile—who were watching the inexorable end of apartheid from afar, saddened that even in its lingering death throes it was tearing apart the country its champions claimed so dearly to love.

"South Africa is a moving target," said one of the chiefs at the South African desk at the State Department in Washington, "but apartheid's dead." He agreed with me that there will be a black majority government in South Africa in the mid-1990s.

"Probably a coalition of radical black interest groups," he added. Another point of agreement.

"Anarchy and violence will be around for a long time." We were in agreement again. "And the country will be ruined—I mean economically, the land too." Yet again we agreed.

"If we agree on all of that," I asked, "how can you justify the administration's stand on remaining engaged with those racists and their brutal goon squads? How can you refuse the hands of the Tutus, the Boesaks, the Motlanas, the others?"

He bristled and countered with his own question:

"How can you support the UDF? You know it encourages an anti-American bias among blacks, and it won't condemn the black-on-black violence."

I could have responded, "What about white-on-white violence in Ireland?" End of discussion.

"Will you go back to South Africa after the revolution?" That question was put to a prominent African National Congress man I knew in Boston by a third person present at our conversation.

My acquaintance laughed. "Of course, but I'm angling for the ambassadorship to the U.S., you know." He added more seriously, "Those positions will go to the soldiers in the field, those who've earned them, but of course I'll go home. It's been so long."

He turned earnestly to me and said quietly, "That is, if there's anything left to go home to. Our greatest fear in the ANC—my greatest fear—is that there'll be nothing left when we gain the freedom of our people."

His words twisted themselves into me. My magnificent, wild, seductive motherland—devastated.

What did you do if you were a white liberal living in South Africa? You were part of the privileged minority in power. You felt guilty because you were white, because you were privileged. You felt impotent because what you believed in was of little value to those around you—black and white—whose narrow nationalism superseded your liberal value system. You felt yourself in revolt against the system of racial oppression, of which by being white you were a part.

How then did you oppose apartheid? How did you oppose the virulent form of black nationalism apartheid had spawned?

My life in South Africa was my answer.

But my choices, my compromises, my complicity, my capacity for brave acts, for defiance, for risk taking were not the answers for other whites.

For many, the outward circumstances of their daily lives tended to obscure the currents of conflict and change moving beneath the surface of the society. For many, these circumstances induced a paralysis of inaction.

In early 1983 I addressed a branch of the Progressive Federal Party in the southern suburbs of Johannesburg as part of its annual general meeting. Most of the audience were English-speaking working-class members with a long history of staunch support for the party. The meeting was held prior to the new constitutional reforms referendum, but the topic was already hot in the white political infrastructure. I was asked to comment on what I thought the new constitution would do for South Africa.

Earnestly I told them of my deepest fears. I told them it would polarise race relations as never before in the country, set the stage for ongoing black resistance—violence in the townships, acts of urban terrorism in the cities. A positive consequence would be to unite black activism across the country on a scale not seen before and to give to black trade unions a central role in the process of change. It would pave the way for more government oppression, make the de jure oligarchic rule of the National Party hierarchy de facto, and usher in the era of the self-fulfilling prophecy of "total onslaught" against the regime. It would prepare the way for ongoing crisis and a permanent state of emergency, which in fact would be martial law, thus mitigating the need to call elections or rendering them even more irrelevant than they already were. The rule by the increasingly militaristic white oligarchy, after a long, bitter struggle that would devastate the land, would be replaced by that of a militaristic black oligarchy.

My white liberal audience was appalled. I was almost hounded out of the house, called a communist, a traitor, a doomsday prophet. Such a scenario could never happen in South Africa—the economy was too strong, the armed forces were too strong, the blacks could never organise themselves, the international community would never let those sort of blacks take over. I was a political masochist, a sadist who took pleasure in gloom and doom. If everyone in the PFP believed as I did, then we might as well all slit our throats.

I never again made public the extent of my anguish over the

new constitutional proposals and what they would mean for
South Africa. In the many meetings I addressed on the new
constitution I ameliorated my apocalyptic vision to that of dire
warnings of a race war.

And I take no comfort in how correct my assessment has
proven to be. Subsequent diary entries, those written in both
South Africa and the United States, show me that over the
intervening years my apprehension has not changed. If anything, I have become more certain of my reading of the
situation.

I believe that I truly know the apartheid beast and the minds
that created it.

But inevitably, considering the demands of the confrontation
of the past few years, white liberal attitudes have changed.

Some white liberals have thrown in their lot with the United
Democratic Front, the black trade union movement, or church-
and community-based activist agencies. Some of them have
been taken into detention along with thousands of black activists during police raids in successive states of emergency.
Many other white liberals, along with other whites, not necces-
sarily liberal, have chosen to uproot themselves and emigrate
from South Africa.

Yet others have stayed in the country and watched the historical shift of power with wary eyes and tension-filled guts. In the
fear and panic that have built in the country, they have looked
to the "strength" of the apartheid government as their lifeline.
This panic is reflected in the sweeping victory of the ruling
National Party in the whites-only general election of May 1987,
when the PFP was devastated at the polls and the far-right,
racist Herstigte Nasionale Party (HNP) replaced it as the
official opposition in Parliament.

Recently I received a letter from an elderly cousin, a lifelong
liberal until she recently began moving to the right. She was a
gracious, well-spoken woman who used her wealthy, privileged
life to further a number of worthy causes. She began, "This is a
painful letter to write to you and possibly a painful letter for
you to receive. However, it is essential for my self-respect that I
write it." She then castigated me for being "an enemy of South
Africa who is cashing in relentlessly through her past position

as a city councillor in Johannesburg" and said she had heard I was justifying my "appalling vendetta," my alleged divestment campaign, "on the grounds that South African blacks favour disinvestment."

She continued:

> People here are saying that you would be made a welcome member of the ANC, which is undoubtedly Moscow controlled and motivated. When South Africa raids are successful, arms caches of Russian-made weapons of destruction are clearly evident. Mandela refuses to renounce violence and is therefore kept imprisoned—quite rightly. Bishop Tutu has been photographed by the press, at a funeral, preaching under a Russian flag (I can show it to whoever may be interested), the hammer and sickle clearly shown. This 'gentleman' has not donated one single cent of his enormous 'PEACE' prize to any black fund. His money, and children, are out of South Africa in the USA, and at least half of the Anglican congregation have abandoned their former affiliation to their church. . . .
>
> . . . can you afford to lose your loyalty to your country and still live with your conscience? Can you now accept with equanimity the loss of your moral integrity? You despise the present government—OK, so do many others, but governments change, and in years to come, if anyone in this country (or, for that matter, in your newly adopted country) ever does remember you, they will remember the self-aggrandisement, plus the monetary gain, you derived by pandering to the largely ignorant (of South Africa) masses of Americans, whose hysterical and totally misguided belief was that apartheid could be abolished only by the ANC's promulgated revolution. Thank God President Reagan does not share this view. . . .

It was a painful letter to receive, but less on an emotional level than as a reflection of the paranoia and desperation of many South Africans whom I once considered to be in political agreement with me. And my awareness of this sad state of mind had been reinforced by communications I have had with other white South Africans.

A contrast to this attitude is that of Motlalepula Chabaku, who had spoken a week before me at a college in March 1986. Several members of the audience asked me if I knew her, for we had said more or less the same things about South Africa, although from different perspectives. I did—and liked her— and I wrote to her to renew our acquaintance.

In South Africa I had known her as June, and in her response to my letter she explained why in the United States she went by her birth name instead:

> I affirm my African heritage and identity, hence I use my own true name given to me by my parents. The name is truly South African, and it means 'one who comes with the rain.' I truly identify with its life-giving essence. Thus I prefer to be called Motlalepula—never mind how unusual it may be. . . .
>
> . . . I love my motherland. I have given thirty-seven years of my life in the struggle for justice and freedom. For me, the time is past to expect or struggle for a change of heart by South African whites without a drastic shake-up in their lifestyles that are rooted largely in selfishness, greed, prejudice, exploitation, and the misuse of religion. These evils are propped up through pressure and violence. I am tired of talking about disinvestment, divestiture, or peaceful change when the system is still so insolvent!

Like Motlalepula, I too felt committed to seeing freedom and justice in South Africa. I would fight against the entrenchment of black racism and a black oligarchy as strongly as I have fought against white racism.

Someday South Africa will be free, and I will be free to return.

In the meantime, my life in self-imposed exile in Boston goes on.

It is really no longer exile at all and is slowly becoming home. I value the freedom of human rights and liberties that the U.S. Constitution and Bill of Rights protect. These freedoms may seem abstract to many Americans, but to me, who was so aware of their absence in South Africa, they are real and comforting.

I feel good about having left South Africa: the action of a survivor, surely? I am able to move on, to live my life as I want to now, not as the state dictates I should. But I miss my old haunts and the physical beauty of my motherland with a great, tearing sense of loss. How often have I lain awake at night and retraced every step of the paths in the Drakensberg, on Robbeberg, and on the cliffs above the Soutrivier at Nature's Valley? I have the pansy shells in my bones, the mystical seascapes of the Indian Ocean in my mind, and the colours of the Knysna loerie in my soul.

And I miss my friends.

Helen visits the U.S. often, lecturing and garnering more and more awards. We saw each other when she gave two major addresses at Milton Academy, where I teach English, in April 1988, and we keep in touch by mail and telephone. Because her husband has business here, and they have three children living here, Irene is often in the U.S. and we see each other. Of my other Houghton allies, Laura visited me in October 1987, and Claire writes every month from the Johannesburg City Council chamber, where Alderman Oberholzer still presides.

Bongani writes, Len Apfel writes. My mailbox holds letters from many other friends and colleagues. Many have visited. But it is not the same, and I miss them all.

The people in my new home are warm and friendly. The wooded environment of the suburbs is most pleasing. My children are well ensconced in the nurturing educational institution Milton Academy, and I teach there among supportive and like-minded colleagues, some of whom have become good friends. Sandy has integrated his business life into the high-tech business world of Boston. Even our much beloved labrador, Thamba (South Sotho for "the faithful one"), has settled down to the life of a New England dog, as if he had been born here. As part of the general movement of young professionals out of South Africa, my brother and his family settled in Toronto in 1976, and my mother followed in 1980, and now we are able to see them regularly, so Roger and Tony have come to know their cousins.

Other landscapes of striking natural beauty have curled themselves around me—in Maine, Vermont, on Cape Cod. They do not have the soaring grandeur of the cliffs and forests of my beloved Eastern Cape haunts but are gentle, with rolling hills and meadows covered in fields of wildflowers.

The initial trauma of leaving my motherland is hopefully

behind me, and I now concentrate on exchanging a life of frenetic activity and responsibility for one of interactive instruction and the lonely contemplation and discipline of writing. My mourning, my feeling of loss has been lived through— that rite of passage is behind me.

My environment has changed, my lifestyle has changed, I've changed. The writing of this book has left me surer of my identity as a South African than I have ever been before. At a distance I can understand more.

The way has been marked by many milestones. It has been a rewarding journey, although the road ahead is not too clear from here.

I have looked in wonder into the past and seen my ten-year-old self boarding the bus that would take me to witness the Alexandra bus boycotters trudging their way home along Louis Botha Avenue. I have heard myself holding forth in my high school classroom in support of equal opportunities for all the people of South Africa, the old catch phrase of the Progressive Party. I have seen myself as a teenager interacting with reactionary Marie Langley and as an earnest university student marching in protest against the detention without trial of my student leader, Ian Robertson. And not flinching when someone's spittle landed on my head. I have seen myself fighting my inclination to embrace the party political system and then successfully using the platform it gave to me. I have seen my Ma-Afrika colleagues, my friendship with Len Apfel, Joseph Mavi, Sam Moss. I have seen Helen, political mentor whose principled loyalty to the liberal cause and tireless commitment still astonish me. I have felt my love for Irene, my friendship with Robin, Claire, Laura, Teresa, so many others.

I still do not know why I felt compelled to live the life of political activism that I did in South Africa. But at least I know that part of that compulsion was to become a witness bearer.

When I was about eight years old, my parents went away and left my brother and me with an aunt and her family for a week.

Elizabeth, my aunt's maid, had gone home the month before to have her baby. We were served by a temporary maid, a cousin of Elizabeth's.

During that week, I was sitting with my aunt on the verandah of her house one afternoon when I heard her exclaim in surprise. Elizabeth had walked into view along the wall at the end of the garden, and she was approaching my aunt, who was now standing in the driveway waiting to meet her. She was a beautiful woman, her smooth ebony colour adding distinction to her striking profile. Her eyes were heavily lidded, and her whole body seemed to sag under some great weight.

"Elizabeth, you're back so soon. Where's the baby? How can you leave the baby so soon?"

Elizabeth sighed and shifted her weight from one foot to the other. Her shoes were scuffed and worn.

"The baby, he died, ma'am."

"Oh, Elizabeth, I'm so sorry. What happened?"

"He died after the birth . . . he couldn't breathe."

My aunt was at a loss for words. Elizabeth helped her out.

"The funeral was yesterday. I came back today, ma'am, to my job."

"But you should've stayed at home, Elizabeth, had a rest—you look exhausted. You know I'm keeping your job for you."

"Yes, ma'am, but I need the extra money for the school fees for the other children, now that the money is used for the coffin, the burial."

"Okay, I'm pleased you're back. Mary doesn't know the way I like things done; she's not as clean as you, as good as you."

My aunt came back to her chair on the verandah and poured herself another cup of tea. She shook her head and spoke more to herself than to me and my seven-year-old cousin.

"Those blacks. Things don't mean the same to them as they do to us. Imagine coming back to work the day after the funeral, leaving those other children . . . they just don't feel the way we do."

There was nothing for me to say. I knew, I simply knew deep inside myself that she was wrong, that Elizabeth was torn apart by the death of her baby. Anyone really looking at her face could have seen so, too.

It was that which made me see the truth about Elizabeth's feelings that has also led me along the way I have taken.